SPECULATION AND REVELATION
IN MODERN PHILOSOPHY

Westminster Press books by Richard Kroner
on
SPECULATION AND REVELATION
IN THE HISTORY OF PHILOSOPHY

~

Speculation in Pre-Christian Philosophy

Speculation and Revelation
in the Age of Christian Philosophy

Speculation and Revelation
in Modern Philosophy

SPECULATION AND REVELATION
IN THE HISTORY OF PHILOSOPHY

Speculation and Revelation in Modern Philosophy

RICHARD KRONER

Philadelphia
THE WESTMINSTER PRESS

LIBRARY OF CONGRESS CATALOG CARD No. 61–5222

PRINTED IN THE UNITED STATES OF AMERICA

To My Wife

who in perfect loyalty stood by my side for more than fifty years blessed with that love which combines Eros and Agape

CONTENTS

FOREWORD

THIS is the third and the final volume of the trilogy on Speculation and Revelation in the History of Philosophy; it deals with modern times. Whereas the selection of thinkers and thoughts in the first two volumes was facilitated because the historical tradition itself had already singled out the most eminent figures and movements, modern philosophy is so rich in names and works that it was much more difficult to make the right choice. I had to confine my discussion to the most powerful and influential philosophical systems. I regret that I could not treat the views of many writers whose thoughts were relevant to my theme; the Cambridge Platonists, Malebranche, Rousseau, Butler, Shaftesbury, and many others should have been taken into consideration. Educated as I was in the German tradition I regret especially that I could not exhibit the relation between speculation and revelation in those poet-thinkers who show how central this relation in modern thought has been, in men like Lessing and Mendelssohn, F. H. Jacobi and Hamann, Herder and Schiller, Friedrich Schlegel and Solger, and many others. But such an extension would have unduly increased the number of pages in this volume.

The reader will perhaps most seriously miss a statement about Schleiermacher, who interfered in a momentous way in the development of German thought. However, I have discussed elsewhere the " *Reden über die Religion* "; from the perspective of speculation, moreover, his contribution was less original than the contributions of Fichte, Schelling, and Hegel; the lectures on dialectic were published only posthumously and had no effect upon the development of philosophy. The student of Christian theology can easily famil-

9

iarize himself with the views of Schleiermacher in this field. I had, therefore, to resist the temptation of including his position in this work.

The representation of Kant and his successors is supplemented by my two-volume work *Von Kant bis Hegel* (1921 and 1924), furthermore by the short account *Kant's Weltanschauung* (now translated into English under the same title, by John E. Smith, University of Chicago Press, 1956), by my English books *The Primacy of Faith* (dealing with Kant in Chapters II and III), the *Introduction* to the translation of *Hegel's Early Theological Writings* (now available in the collection of Torchbooks at Harper & Brothers), and finally by my article on " The Year 1800 in the Development of German Idealism " (*The Review of Metaphysics,* Vol. I, 1948).

In modern times speculation and revelation were no longer related to each other in the way they had been related in the Middle Ages when religion dominated and united all realms of culture as art had done in antiquity. Science and politics were now placed in the forefront and took the lead. The unity of ancient and of medieval culture has no equivalent in modern times; instead, a plurality of more or less unconnected realms grew and threatened to involve mankind in chaos. In such an age speculation and revelation also parted; philosophy and theology were even more fatefully divorced than they were at the end of medieval culture. The philosophers imitating the pattern of modern science no longer felt obliged and inclined to conform their thoughts to the faith and doctrine of the organized church.

However, this change does not imply that the bond between speculation and revelation was completely and irrevocably torn. Rather, the modern thinker remained more or less inwardly tinged by the religion that had determined Western civilization for so many centuries and was interwoven with all its institutions, its habits, its morals, and its entire way of life. His speculation sprang from this very same civilization as Greek speculation had sprung from the mythological background of Greek life and culture. The age-old tension between speculation and revelation therefore came again to the fore and engaged the builder of a philosophical system. The dynamic force of the antagonism between thought and faith again irritated and coerced the metaphysicians to settle it in a new fashion and on a new level. This desire increased to the same degree to which the systems developed a metaphysical ambition and denounced the epistemological resignation which the English school, but also the critical attitude of Kant's idealism, had demanded and practiced. Since this metaphysical tendency culminated in Schelling and Hegel, it was in their systems that the reconciliation of speculation and revelation was most vividly carried through as it had been in the Middle Ages.

But this time speculation, no longer fettered by the strings of Greek conceptual ideas nor by the ecclesiastical orthodoxy of the Roman Church, was bolder than it ever had been in aiming at the highest crown of thought. It claimed to have overcome all obstacles that the earlier attempts had encountered, and it arrogated an ability to penetrate into the innermost core of the religious mysteries. It pretended to establish a full and perfect harmony between philosophic and religious theology. This was the end toward which modern thought moved; and this movement is the theme that the present volume undertakes to treat.

As in the previous volumes I was kindly supported by colleagues who improved the English of my manuscript. Often they found a word that was nearer the meaning I wished to express than my own words. I am greatly indebted for this service to Prof. David H. Freeman and Prof. Ronald Jager, both at the University of Rhode Island, to Prof. Gloria Livermore at Wellesley College, and to Prof. John E. Skinner at the Divinity School of the Protestant Episcopal Church in Philadelphia.

RICHARD KRONER

Philadelphia

INTRODUCTION

MODERN philosophy is mainly characterized by its separation from sacred theology, i.e., by its secular trend. It is "scientific" and not religious. Whereas in antiquity speculation fought polytheistic religion, philosophy in the Christian age relied upon revelation and united natural and sacred theology in one all-embracing *Summa*. This bond was already rent asunder at the end of the Middle Ages, and it was more radically broken by the Renaissance and the Reformation. Modern philosophy was predominantly influenced by the Renaissance and therefore resembled ancient more than medieval thought. Of course, modern speculation is not entirely divorced from Christianity, yet it is no longer Christian in the sense of patristic and Scholastic philosophy. The Christian faith was although not overtly, yet indirectly guiding the modern thinker. It is true that some systems were more or less hostile toward organized religion and some were even outright anti-Christian. Nevertheless a Christian atmosphere surrounded modern speculation, especially in the great systems. Ancient paganism could not be restored any more than the faith in the mythological gods could be revived.

The chief difference between pre-Christian and Christian philosophy was brought about by the high moral and metaphysical rank of the Christian religion. The Greek thinker was justified in criticizing the low moral standard of his national religion, and he gained the courage and the energy for speculative thinking precisely from his opposition to the mythological gods. This motive no longer spurred the medieval thinker. The holiness and majesty of the Biblical God could not be surpassed by speculation. When the modern philosopher attacked the Christian faith, he did so because Biblical revelation is pictorial and metaphorical, while metaphysics is logical and conceptual, rational and theoretical. Greek ideas and notions were therefore used by modern speculation as they had been used by the Christian thinkers, but the modern philosopher felt freer in this respect than the medieval theologian, because he was no longer a theologian in the same sense. Figures like Giordano Bruno, Spinoza, the French materialists, the positivists of the nineteenth century, Nietzsche or the atheists of today were the outcome of this independence. But all these attempts at emancipation from the Christian revelation were even less able to produce a substitute for the rejected religion than Greek metaphysics had been able to supersede the national religion and to replace it by means of speculation. Modern thought did succeed in weakening the ascendancy of Christianity as the regimes of fascism, Bolshevism, and nazism demonstrate. But the philosophy underlying those political systems is obviously inferior to that of the classical systems; its religious significance as compared with the gospel is null and void.

The Christian tradition may be compelled to alter its strategy and perhaps even its doctrine in some way in order to stand against the aggressive irreligiousness of modern times, but it cannot be destroyed or injured as Greek mythology was destroyed by Greek speculation. Thought cannot surpass the sublimity of the Christian revelation. It is, in the last analysis, this sublimity which gives modern speculation in its most profound ideas a religious power superior to that of Platonism and Aristotelianism. Although the modern thinker does not feel obliged to agree with the prophetic revelation, he also cannot ignore its existence. The Biblical background is perceptible even when the Biblical creed is rejected. The very word " God " cannot be uttered in modern thought without evoking the picture of the Lord who is the commanding figure in Biblical revelation; even atheism refers to this figure. The religious or pseudoreligious enthusiasm of Giordano Bruno would have been impossible in ancient times, as we will see later. Spinoza's God, although utterly distorted by his geometrical method, and his physical prejudice, nevertheless shows distinctly enough the traces of his Biblical origin. And even the extreme aestheticism of Nietzsche, his attempt to revive Dionysos and the ancient belief in a cyclical return of all things, could not prevent him from retaining a certain delicacy of feeling which was evidently an inheritance of the Christian religion.

The separation of speculation from revelation and the rise of a secular philosophy were promoted by three historical events. The first was the Renaissance. It made the original texts of Greek thought available; the study of these originals disclosed that medieval Scholasticism had not been loyal to these texts and thus not only engendered interest in ancient speculation but also encouraged thinkers to imitate the Greeks and to philosophize as they had done. The second was the Reformation, which generated a completely new conception of the Christian faith, the Christian creed, the Christian doctrine, and even the Christian institutions and the Christian life, so that the relation between speculation and revelation also had to be revised. The third event was the establishment of modern science, which revolutionized the methods, as well as the results, of the investigation of the visible world. All these innovations contributed to the downfall of that synthesis which was the basis of philosophy in the age of Christian thought.

Renaissance and Reformation were the most obvious symptoms of that breakdown: the elements that had been united in medieval thought fell asunder. Each returned to the state in which they had not yet been elements within a synthesis. They separated radically. As Greek speculation was rediscovered in its original meaning, so the Christian faith was led back to the gospel unadulterated by the subsequent interpretation and codification of the centuries of Catholic supremacy. In both cases it was a process of purification that developed. The Renaissance promoted the rediscovery of an unchristian cosmology; the Reformation, that of an unphilosophical, purely religious Christian faith. In such a manner both movements worked closely together for the same end: the disengagement of the two constituents bound together in the medieval synthesis. Both movements had the same effect; they went as it were hand in hand in spite of their opposite motives and aims.

However, neither fulfilled its purpose. Paganism could not be restored and therefore pagan speculation could not be renewed. The Reformation could not bring back the conditions of the original Christian community; it could not ignore the fact that in the meantime Christianity had assimilated ancient civilization and that in state and art, in life and thought, the consequences of this merger were still alive. Therefore new intellectual, cultural, political, and spiritual activities arose out of the two movements. As the classical art of the Italian Renaissance was not identical with that of the ancient artists, so modern speculation could not simply return to that of the ancient thinkers. Nietzsche praised the pagan tendencies of the popes in the cinquecento, and complained that the barbaric German monk Luther frustrated this hopeful revival of the ancient heroic temper and the ancient love of beauty, but even if we recognized that the Christian spirit was indeed grossly offended in those days, still the chasm between the Athens of Phidias and Polyclitus and the Rome of Bramante and Michelangelo remains considerable. In a similar vein the speculation of Heraclitus or Parmenides, of Plato and Aristotle, was not recovered by the Italian cosmologists. If nothing else could distinguish the time of the Renaissance from the ancient period, the fact that the Renaissance was accompanied by the Reformation would by itself prove that the modern revival of antiquity was not undisputed and did not control the entire scene of modern life and thought.

The Reformation was instrumental in the survival of Christian standards; in Germany even philosophic speculation turned " evangelical " in some Lutheran mystics and especially in Jacob Boehme. And even in Italy, where the Renaissance reaped its greatest triumph, philosophy was not absolutely paganized. Marsilio Ficino, who was an enthusiastic Platonist and who tried to create an academy modeled after that of Plato, nevertheless was much more of a Neoplatonist than a Platonist; that is to say, he was as much influenced by the Christian spirit as Plotinus had been and perhaps even more. The Renaissance had indeed a tremendous influence upon modern speculation, but from the beginning this influence was tempered by the remnants of Scholastic thought which can be observed in Descartes, Spinoza, and Leibniz, and through them in Kant, Fichte, Schelling, and Hegel.

The restoration of pre-Christian art and poetry had another effect. Instead of reviving the ancient religion, it generated a humanistic trend. The idea of a human culture, instead of a national one, has many sources. The cosmopolitism of the Roman Empire, and especially of Stoicism, and the supernational character of the Old Testament prophets contributed to the feeling that the highest values are not confined to the peculiar tradition of particular peoples. They have a validity for all mankind. The Greeks thought of their own culture as privileged in comparison with all other peoples of the earth. All other nations were " barbaric," while they alone were human in the noble sense of the word. When the Romans inherited the Greek civilization, they did not think of themselves as being Hellenized, but rather as equally " human." Thus the term *human-itas,* as Jaeger has pointed out, became an exalted idea embracing the highest standards of culture and moral virtues. Only in the Renaissance was the word " humanity " identified with the ancient grandeur and glory in contrast to the medieval lack of aesthetic taste and beauty. The ancient classics were admired and revered as the true models of artistic perfection. This tendency was strengthened and fostered by the fact that medieval Latin was indeed an artificial language, spoken only by the scholars and utterly impoverished as compared with the style of Cicero, who was now regarded as the paragon of classical writing. The term " humanities " assumed the meaning of the studies of the Latin and Greek classics and of polite-ness and aesthetic qualities in general.

The humanism of the Renaissance has still another significance. The second volume of this work has shown that together with the theocentric and theological trend of Christian philosophy the con-ception of man was also deepened because of the inseparable con-nection of God and man in the Biblical sense. Man was regarded solely as a part of the world in pre-Christian thought, although a special part, endowed with reason and thereby enabled to know the truth and to acquire wisdom. In the Christian era, however, man no longer belonged merely to the world. He was now regarded as being created in the image of God and thereby exalted above the con-fines of space and time. Christ had come to man in order to recon-cile him to the Creator and to found a kingdom of love, in which " the old Adam " no longer existed. Man was now a new creature purged from sinfulness and permitted to participate in the grace of God. Speculation was therefore faced with a new task in under-standing man, his knowledge and moral standards, state and society, history and all cultural realms. This new understanding resulted in man's gaining a position between God and the world. Man, although he did not occupy the center of thought, became a special problem of a special magnitude not known in antiquity.

Modern times inherited this new valuation of man. Modern philosophy, released from the authority of the Christian religion, of the church, of the dogmas and doctrines of medieval theology, enhanced the dignity and excellence of man to the point where man was placed at the center of thought. Modern speculation was thoroughly humanistic in this sense. While pre-Christian philosophy was cosmocentric and Christian philosophy was theocentric, modern philosophy was anthropocentric: man was the main problem of its speculative interest and endeavor. The world and God took a secondary position with respect to their speculative rank. Inquiry into everything human prevailed in modern times. Therefore the sciences dealing with man were tremendously enlarged; new sciences were devised such as sociology, economics, statistics, psychoanalysis, psychobiology, psychogenesis, and many medical sciences. Psychology gained an authority and significance it had never enjoyed before. A special science dealing with the comparison of the human races, often called anthropology, was developed. Cosmology and rational theology, on the other hand, were neglected and pushed into the background. They were, in fact, already dying when Kant gave them the deathblow. Within philosophy those branches were favored and flourished which were concerned with human activities like the theory of knowledge, logic, methodology, linguistics and semantics, the philosophy of language, of history, of culture, of religion, of mythology. Theories about state and classes multiplied. Ethics and aesthetics, the philosophy of human conduct and of artistic creativity, were privileged. The history of philosophy was raised to the rank of a new philosophical discipline. The historical perspective as such was made a philosophic principle in so-called historicism. Even the world and God were seen from the point of view of human knowledge and human needs. Modern thought seeks an answer to the question, What is man? It is characteristic of modern times that even a theological work could have the title *The Nature and Destiny of Man*.

Man could acquire such a dominant role in thought because the authorities that had guided man and to which he had been subject, whether the authority of the cosmos or that of God, no longer dictated the direction and the standard of investigation and speculation. Man found himself, as it were, alone. He was left to his own judgment and conscience. He was the only arbiter in the competition of world views. Since the Christian faith continued to impress man's heart, it still exercised a certain power over his thought, a power checked, however, by the revival of the ancient systems. In this situation man felt himself to be the only source of certainty and truth. The dictum of Descartes: *Cogito ergo sum,* which made man's own existence the Archimedean point for all knowledge, expressed pointedly and accurately the speculative center of modern philosophy. Man was caught between the antagonistic classical and Christian values and thrown back to his own resources. He became the only undisputed authority, the only judge in the contest of views. Fichte, who dared to think of the human ego as producing the world content and the maxims of his moral action, represented in that respect the apex of modern speculation. Kant's thesis that man's practical reason postulates the existence of God epitomized the predominance of humanistic thought. This predominance was also manifested when David Hume called philosophy "the science of human nature."

In poignant contrast to the stress laid upon the sciences of man was the emergence of the third factor inspiring modern speculation, the growth of the natural sciences. The relationship between the humanistic and the naturalistic trends in modern philosophy belongs to those problematic points which obscure and render difficult the understanding of the main features of modern speculation. The natural sciences represent the modern version of cosmology. They differ from ancient physics, which was never completely dissolved from metaphysics, in that this separation took place in the modern era. The natural sciences are "empirical," that is to say, deliberately unspeculative. They rest upon experimental observation and investigation, while physics in the Platonic, Aristotelian, and Stoic or Epicurean sense was permeated by philosophic theories or presuppositions. Aristotle's physics dealt with questions that we would reckon as being metaphysical, questions like the nature of space and time, of corporeality and movement. Stoic and Epicurean physics was at the same time their metaphysics. In modern times a complete break not only between philosophy and theology but also between philosophy and the natural sciences occurred (although a certain ambition on the part of the natural sciences to solve the problems of metaphysics does exist, in the eighteenth century physics was still called "natural philosophy "). Philosophy in the strict sense was treated, not as a natural science, but as somehow transcending the horizon of the natural sciences.

The natural sciences in the modern sense also deviate from scientific studies in the Middle Ages, because then the Hellenic tradition was upheld which tied physics and metaphysics, metaphysics and theology. However, as the second volume of this work has shown, empirical observation and even experiment already began to take hold in the thirteenth century and was expanded in the fourteenth and fifteenth centuries. There is a continuous development in this respect from the Middle Ages to modern times. But the interest in nature and the methods of investigation also increased continuously and brought about the independence and the peculiar sway of the natural sciences characteristic of modern times. Nature superseded step by step the conception of the cosmos. As the age of Christian philosophy had degraded the ancient cosmos by understanding it as no longer sovereign and all-embracing, but as created and governed by the transcendent God, so the ancient cosmos was degraded for a second time when modern times replaced it with nature.

Nature, in contrast to both the cosmos of the Greeks and the creation by God in Christian philosophy, no longer has any cosmological or theological connotation. The term " cosmology " in modern times was itself degraded to mean the empirical science of the constitution of worlds composed of stars and their constellations. Kepler still had a kind of religious reverence for the cosmos. He believed in the " harmony of the spheres," and this belief led him to discover the laws regulating the motion of the planets around the sun. Even Newton preserved a certain remnant of such cosmological faith; space was to him the " sensorium of God." But the ever-growing tendency of modern science was to eliminate all metaphysical and religious significance and to study the heavens as the chemist studies the affinities of substances. Astrophysics and astrochemistry have developed in modern times into the proper cosmological sciences. The cosmos understood as nature has lost its metaphysical charm; the disenchantment of the visible universe marks the course science has taken in modern times.

The cosmos in ancient times embraced men and gods, the world soul or the world mind, the visible as well as the invisible spheres, so that even the cosmos of the Ideas belonged to this All. And this conception was not entirely abandoned in Christian philosophy although it was transferred to God's Creation, so that men like the Victorines and Bonaventure could interpret the beauty and order of the visible world as symbols of the glory of God. Nature in modern science, however, has lost this divine character completely. Only the poets still feel it and instill a soul into its phenomena. Modern nature has become something at the disposal of man, either of his knowledge or will. It has become the mere object of investigation in the empirical and experimental sense, and the storehouse of forces and materials for technological purposes. Nature is subject to man, man is its overlord. It is true that man today is in danger of becoming the slave of his own inventions and instruments, but nature does not profit from this new development, since the inventions and instruments, the machines and tools, remain man's own products, and nature still serves man's self-destructive investigation and technical transformation.

It is ironical that the natural sciences originated in the superior role man acquired through the Christian message. Man would never have dared to extend the kingship of his understanding and will to nature if the gospel had not so highly exalted his standard and position in the created world. The enormous aggrandizement of man's own consciousness of his significance and power alone encouraged him to undertake the investigation of nature, which in turn led to his technical conquest of the resources of nature and to the establishment of the technical empire that is now his greatest pride. I shall subsequently illustrate this growth of man's pride in the Renaissance.

But it is even more ironical and almost tragic that the rise and power of the natural sciences had another consequence which involved man's own self-degradation. The more the natural sciences advanced in stature, extent, and skill, the more they subjugated the science of man. They forgot that man is the knowing and willing subject, the self, which had made nature the object of its reason and understanding. They treated man merely as an object, as if he were nothing but the product and creation of that very same nature which the sciences succeeded in subjecting to their methods, and which the technical arts used to satisfy the needs and whims of man. The sciences of man themselves became natural sciences. They treated man as a special kind of animal that is quantitatively and qualitatively different from the other members of the animal kingdom. This trend was completed when Darwin discovered the development of the species and when a Darwinistic " philosophy " was composed which took upon itself the special task of interpreting all human affairs, achievements, institutions, and norms according to the principle of " evolution," entirely forgetting that the natural sciences were not permitted to think of evolution in a metaphysical and speculative manner.

This naturalistic speculation had already begun in the epoch of Galileo and Descartes. But in this early age man was not yet thought of as an object of the natural sciences. Descartes was aware of the uniqueness of the thinking ego and even when he was increasingly persuaded that nature was the Absolute, he still distinguished between extended substances and thinking substances. Moreover, Descartes knew that man, as a thinking being, has an inner relation to God. Seen from this angle, his famous and much-criticized " bifurcation " was not a mistake but rather a merit. Descartes followed the general trend of his period toward a naturalistic metaphysics. As were most thinkers of his time and even of the following centuries, he was greatly impressed by the success of the new physics, so that he deemed that its method was the sole guarantee of scientific rectitude and exactitude. It was therefore to be imitated as far as possible by philosophic speculation. Nevertheless, Descartes at least recognized man's peculiar position as the knowing subject. Spinoza was even more tempted to make nature the Absolute, but even he retained the bifurcation of extension and thought and regarded the capacity of thinking as the source of man's nobility and of his opportunity for acquiring virtue and happiness.

The naturalistic prejudice was broken by Kant. This is his unique discovery. Already in his precritical period Kant realized that the method of the natural sciences cannot and must not be transferred to philosophy. In philosophy, he argued, definitions are the result of inquiry, not its beginning, while in mathematics and physics the definition has to precede the proof. Kant saved the human ego from being swallowed up by the objective knowledge of the natural sciences as applied to man by Hume. Kant gave the monadology of Leibniz an ethical interpretation and added in his last *Critique* the most ingenious ideas about nature by conjoining the principles of organic life with those of the beautiful and the sublime. He thus achieved the most " scientific " system of modern philosophy. The term " scientific " stands here, not for a method that imitates the natural sciences, but for a logically and methodically conscientious and meticulous procedure that marks the precise meaning of what Kant himself called " critical."

However, the reconciliation of the old enemies and allies, speculation and revelation, was not satisfactorily discharged by Kant. He was too much a child of the period of the Enlightenment to see the full significance of this task. His great successors undertook to find a solution of the time-honored problem. The most profound and most magnificent speculative systems the world has ever seen were thereby erected. Hegel, in particular, recognized that the time had come to unite the principles of ancient, Christian, and modern philosophy on the level of the new insights achieved by Kant. Cosmology, theology, and epistemology were interwoven in his speculative logic, the boldest and most profound attempt at a metaphysical knowledge of the Absolute, using for this purpose all the materials and categories of the whole history of philosophy. In his philosophy of nature Hegel was dependent on Schelling; but he was in closer touch with the empirical sciences of nature than his predecessor in this field had been. The philosophy of nature was supposed to look at the phenomena of the visible universe with a speculative vision, thereby discovering the meaning of these facts instead of merely finding the mathematical laws governing them.

In spite of the profundity and eminence of the Hegelian system, in spite of its grandiosity, loftiness, and riches, it was too confident that the human mind can tackle the thorny enterprise of rendering the content of revelation in the language and by means of a dialectical method. The latter was all too human to perform such a superhuman work. The history of philosophy ended therefore in failure and frustration. The reconciliation of speculation and revelation was not accomplished, in spite of the most gigantic efforts and the most marvelous designs. It seems that this reconciliation has to be tried again in every epoch. If it were not so, human life would probably turn stale. The task is infinite, and finite thinking can only approach it from the perspective of ever-changing intellectual situations and historical circumstances. The Epilogue will add some more words about this task as we confront it today.

I

AUTONOMY

MODERN philosophy centered in man. The Renaissance and the Reformation, each in its own fashion, emphasized the central position of man, in spite of the fact that the Renaissance went back to the cosmocentric speculation of the Greeks, and the Reformation went back to the theocentric faith of the primitive Christian community. The Renaissance and the Reformation both stressed the decision and the judgment of the individual person who found himself amidst the authorities of the past, and who no longer believed in the primacy of institutions. Whereas the church had swayed the conscience and the thought of the individual in the Middle Ages, the two revolutionary twin movements declared that man is free to choose where he will stand. The Renaissance and the Reformation, each in a different way and in different directions, proclaimed the autonomy of man. The Renaissance understood this autonomy more as the dignity that distinguishes man in contrast to all other beings and entities in the world. And the Reformation turned to the conscience of man in contrast to the church and its sacramental tutelage of the believer. In both cases the autonomy of man was emphasized in opposition to the cosmonomic principle of antiquity and to the theocratic principle of the Roman Church. Man discovered that he was in the center of the world and that he had to seek truth and guidance within himself. No outer authority can assume ultimate responsibility for the individual character of the person or for the faith that a man may accept as the ultimate source of all his decisions and norms of conduct.

All modern philosophy is based upon these presuppositions. Man had never before felt his absolute freedom so strongly. The term

25

" autonomy " was used by Kant only to characterize the principle of morality, but the idea of autonomy was alive and present from the beginning of modern times. Burckhardt, in his famous book on the Italian Renaissance,[1] stresses the development of the individual consciousness shown in expressions like *" uomo singolare "* or *" uomo unico "* ("the singular" or "unique man"). "Man becomes a spiritual individual and recognizes himself as such." Burckhardt mentions a variety of personalities who were conscious of their individual power not as men of rank and consequence, but only because they were these particular men. Dante was one of the first. He "emanated in all his writings an abundance of a forceful personal power, which impresses itself upon the reader even apart from the content." Petrarch was another representative of this new personal power. He is a good example of the man who discovers his individual responsibility for the universal view he has chosen. He faced the choice between Christ and Cicero and was stirred by their antagonism, but he wished to reconcile the one to the other.[2]

Martin Luther left the monastery because he felt that even the most punctilious observance of the religious vows and the monastic rules did not alleviate his conscience. Of his own accord he resolved that not " works " but only faith can bring about the salvation of his soul and assure him of the redemptive grace offered by Christ. He revolted against the institution of the Roman Church, trusting rather his own inner judgment. For the first time in history the " protestant conscience " manifested itself; it led eventually to the divorce of the protestant from the Roman Church and thereby founded the modern religiosity based upon the individual conscience. Of course, " autonomy " in this religious sphere must be restricted because the Biblical word remained the authority to which Luther and the other Reformers referred. Nevertheless, it was a kind of autonomy that encouraged Luther to make his grave and fateful decision.

In philosophic thought the term " autonomy " is also not unequivocal. It can signify the autonomy of the individual person, or of individual reason, or of reason in general. In the Renaissance all

[1] *Die Kultur der Renaissance in Italien. Ein Versuch.* 1st ed. 1860.

[2] Cf. "Francesco Petrarca the Laureate on His Own Ignorance," in *The Renaissance Philosophy of Man,* ed. by Ernst Cassirer, Paul Oskar Kristeller, John Herman Randall, Jr. (University of Chicago Press, 1948), p. 115.

these meanings were seen without distinction as a new discovery. In his famous *Oration on the Dignity of Man* (written about 1486), Pico della Mirandola glorified the autonomy of man in general and of the individual person in particular. In a partly Platonic, partly Christian, spirit he says: " God the Father, the supreme Architect, had already built this cosmic home we behold, the most sacred temple of his Godhead, by the laws of his mysterious wisdom. The region above the heavens he had adorned with Intelligence, the heavenly spheres he had quickened with eternal souls, and the excrementary and filthy parts of the lower world he had filled with a multitude of animals of every kind. But, when the work was finished, the Craftsman kept wishing that there were someone to ponder the plan of so great a work, to love its beauty, and to wonder at its vastness. Therefore . . . he finally took thought concerning the creation of man." But while all the other created things and beings had a prescribed nature, man was of an indeterminate nature so that he " should have joint possession of whatever had been peculiar to each of the different kinds of being." God therefore assigned man a " place in the middle of the world " and addressed him in the following way: " Neither a fixed abode nor a form that is thine alone nor any function peculiar to thyself have we given thee, Adam, to the end that according to thy longing and to thy judgment thou mayest have and possess what abode, what form, and what functions thou thyself shalt desire. The nature of all other beings is limited and constrained within the bounds of laws prescribed by us. Thou, constrained by no limits, in accordance with thine own free will . . . shalt ordain for thyself the limits of thy nature. We have set thee at the world's center that thou mayest from thence more easily observe whatever is in the world. We have made thee neither of heaven nor of earth, neither mortal nor immortal, so that with freedom of choice and with honor, as though the maker and molder of thyself, thou mayest fashion thyself in whatever shape thou shalt prefer. Thou shalt have the power to degenerate into the lower forms of life, which are brutish. Thou shalt have the power, out of thy soul's judgment, to be reborn into the higher forms, which are divine." [3]

This passage is of supreme significance. It shows that the Renaissance philosopher was still dependent upon both the Greek inherit-

[3] Cassirer, Kristeller, Randall, *op. cit.,* pp. 224 f.

ance and his Christian faith, but at the same time an absolutely new self-assurance and self-dependence was emerging in his consciousness of man. Man as such is free to choose his place in the universe according to his individual character or inclination. He can fall as low as the beast, but he can also ascend as high as the deity. He is perfectly autonomous as man and as an individual. His nature is not predetermined; it is his own work. Moral freedom and metaphysical self-determination are fused. Such a statement already anticipates in a half-mythological, half-speculative fashion Kant's principle of moral autonomy and even Fichte's idea of the absolute Ego. Although the cosmological concept of the wonderful universe and the theological concept of man as a responsible moral being are taken over from antiquity and Christian philosophy, a new tone can be heard indicating the centrality and unique selfhood of man. Pico was aware of his double heritage, but also of his new confidence that philosophy can make a man autonomous. " Philosophy herself has taught me to rely on my own conscience rather than on the opinions of others." [4]

In another vein the same new trust of man in his own judgment and in his own creativity was expressed by the Englishman Francis Bacon (1561–1626). Although not a deep thinker, he had a touch of the modern temper. He was the prophet of the conquest of nature by means of investigation and inductive thinking. He was also the prophet of our technical age, its peculiar inventiveness and its rational autonomy. He did not truly see the source of the triumph of modern science because he was still too much ensnared in medieval forms of thought, but he did anticipate the possibility of knowing and using the natural forces for the sake of aggrandizing man's power and self-dependence. He was also the first modern philosopher who dared to repudiate the ancient classical systems and to insist that absolutely new methods should be applied. His well-known words: " *Scientia est potentia* " (" Knowledge is power ") say enough. He makes it more explicit when he adds, " It is my purpose to try out whether the foundation of the power and grandeur of man can be established." In the Renaissance several pictures of an ideal society were given. Bacon offered his own version under the title *New Atlantis,* in which he described the scientific and technical institu-

---

[4] *Ibid.,* p. 238.

tions of that utopian island. Here he predicted the future knowledge and the future achievements of mankind.

In this essay Bacon lets the president of a learned body of scholars say, "The end of our foundation is the knowledge of causes and secret motions of things, and the enlarging of the bounds of human empire, to the effecting of all things possible." It is the technical civilization of our own days which he helped to bring about by his vivid narration. Bacon speaks in his *New Atlantis* of chemical and biological laboratories, factories and machines, natural museums and botanical gardens, artificial tissues, drugs and medicaments, artificially cultivated flowers, and so on. He only omitted the Sputnik and the Lunik which we have seen. Bacon was the first to announce the enterprising spirit of human autonomy and adventure which still dominates our civilization, and which has a part in all modern speculation.

Another thinker who can be mentioned in this context and who greatly extolled individuality was the Frenchman Michel de Montaigne (1533–1592). Like Pico and Bacon he does not belong to the system builders in modern philosophy, but his influence upon the modern mind in general is inestimable. He was one of the most original personalities that ever lived. Montaigne rejected the title of philosopher, but his attitude toward the world and life, and toward God and man, had a philosophic significance. His thinking was highly independent and exclusively determined by his own pronounced individuality. Today one is tempted to call him an existential thinker because he refused to make any objective statements and was deliberately and pointedly subjective in all his utterances. But in a sense he was more "existential" than any of the existentialists of the present, even more than Kierkegaard in the nineteenth century. "I study myself more than any other subject. That is my metaphysics, that is my physics." [5]

Montaigne is often called a skeptic and in a way he certainly was. He did not hold any system to be true. He did not believe in cosmology or theology, nor did he develop a theory of knowledge, a methodology, a psychology, or indeed any other scientific theory. He was disinclined to believe in any speculation. But in this negative

[5] *Essays* (1580), tr. by Donald M. Frame (Published for the Classics Club by Walter Black, Roslyn, N.Y., 1943), Book III, ch. 13.

respect he can be compared with Socrates; there is in fact a definitely Socratic trait in him. But the difference between the two men in other respects could not be greater. Montaigne was interested solely in his own individuality. His peculiar habits and predilections, his strength and his weakness, his intellectual tendencies and his emotional sympathies or antipathies, his opinions about almost all matters of daily life, were the real and the only subject of his inquiry and observations. Never was a man more autonomous. "Authors communicate to the people their thoughts. . . . I am the first to communicate myself by virtue of my universal individuality as Michel de Montaigne, not as a grammarian or a poet or a jurist." [6]

Montaigne was not a skeptic in respect to his own self-knowledge. Proudly but not without a touch of irony he remarks: "No man ever treated a subject he knew and understood better than I do the subject I have undertaken; in this I am the most learned man alive. No man ever penetrated . . . more deeply into his material, nor plucked its limbs and consequences cleaner, nor reached more accurately and fully the goal he had set for his work. . . . I speak the truth, not my fill of it, but as much as I dare speak it. . . . We go hand in hand and at the same pace, my book and I. . . . He who judges it without knowing it will injure himself more than me. . . . I do not teach, I tell." [7]

As Augustine had portrayed himself in his *Confessions,* so did Montaigne in his *Essays.* But this comparison is no sooner made than it becomes evident how far the two authors differ. The contrast illuminates the difference between the two ages of Christian and modern philosophy. Whereas Augustine turned to God in order to confess his sins and shortcomings, Montaigne speaks only to himself and to the reader. Whereas Augustine prays throughout his book, Montaigne has no God to pray to. And yet the book of Montaigne, his whole attitude, his inner freedom, and his intense feeling of autonomy would not have been possible without the age of Christian philosophy, which prepared the way for the self-respect of the Renaissance author and his enhanced consciousness of the peculiar value of every human soul. Duns Scotus had already spoken of an "individual form," and Cusanus had said that individuality is

[6] *Ibid.,* III, 2.   [7] *Ibid.*

" something peculiarly dear " to man.[8] Even so, the chasm between the two ages is amazing. There is not a bit of Scholasticism in Montaigne. It is another intellectual world in which Montaigne lives and writes. The " individual form " of Duns Scotus was incarnate in him; it took on personal actuality and expressed itself with an emphasis unknown in the Middle Ages.

The autonomy of Montaigne's individuality, like that of Petrarch, can be traced back to his position between antiquity and Christianity. Montaigne was educated in the spirit of the Romans. He spoke Latin until he was five years old before learning any other language. Rome made him an honorary citizen because he was so familiar with the city and was perfectly at home there. Nevertheless, he was a loyal and even a patriotic Frenchman. Although he was not an ardent believer in Christ, he was aware of being a member of the church. " As I am a Perigord, I am also a Roman Catholic." But his own individuality and personality stand out pre-eminently precisely because all other ties were only attributes of his peculiar and unique being. Although he was formed by Roman literature and thought, he felt free to adopt or reject it. And the same was true with respect to his religious devotion. Since none of these traditions had an absolute sway over his soul, he was first of all himself. " I have my own laws and court to judge me and I go to them more than anywhere else." [9] Heidegger does not exalt " authenticity " more than Montaigne.

He lived as it were in his own solar system and he was the sun around which the world rotated. He was to himself the measure of right and wrong. A stronger contrast to the Christian conscience and also to that of the ancients can hardly be imagined. Since he felt himself the center of his world, he did not know repentance. " I seldom repent, my conscience is content with itself — not as the conscience of an angel or a horse, but as the conscience of a man." The principle of the autonomy of man could not be pronounced more clearly or succinctly. It is a universal humanism that Montaigne teaches. No wonder that Nietzsche was enthusiastically sympathetic with this audacious preacher of a morality that does not

[8] Richard Kroner, *Speculation and Revelation in the Age of Christian Philosophy* (The Westminster Press, 1959), pp. 224, 250.

[9] Frame, *op. cit.*

acknowledge any judge beyond himself! " I know," Nietzsche exclaims, " only one author whom I would set in the same rank with Schopenhauer as regards honesty, nay, whom I would deem even higher: this is Michel de Montaigne. . . . If the task were put to make the earth a home, I would choose him as a guide."

Montaigne extended this self-sufficiency and self-legislation to every human being. Although Montaigne was preoccupied with his own individuality, he was not an egotist in the usual sense of the word. On the contrary, he allowed everyone to be himself, and like Heidegger, he would even make it a moral demand to be, and to act as, the individual every human being is. " There is no one who, if he listens to himself, does not discover in himself a pattern all his own, a ruling pattern, which struggles against education." [10] He had a kind of aesthetic delight in the vast variety of human characters and souls; therefore he loved to read history and poetry. " History is my chief study, poetry my only joy." He was himself a poet, although not a great one, as he himself knew. And yet his *Essays* can be reckoned among the greatest works of literature ever composed.

One would think that such a man, without any faith in a cosmic order or in a gracious God, should have been melancholy or at least of a gloomy temper. And indeed there is a dark note underneath the hilarity of his style and eloquence. In any case he did not like the world, his family, his estate, his servants, and therefore sought solitude, as one chapter in his *Essays* suggests. " Certainly a man of understanding has lost nothing, if he has himself. . . . We must reserve a chamber all our own, entirely free, in which to establish our real liberty and our principal retreat and solitude. Here our ordinary conversation must be between us and ourselves, and so private that no outside association or communication can find a place. . . . We have a soul that can be turned upon itself, it can keep itself company." [11] There was a Stoic cast in his personality, although he did not have the Stoic belief in the order of the cosmos to which man should adapt himself.

In spite of this dislike of the world (or perhaps because of it?), Montaigne believed that " the surest sign of wisdom is a constant cheerfulness." " Its view," he writes, " is like the air above the moon permanently bright." [12] Montaigne's wisdom was neither that of

[10] *Ibid.*   [11] *Ibid.*, I, 39.   [12] *Ibid.*, I, 25.

ancient philosophy nor that of the Christian faith. It was a distinctly modern wisdom strongly colored by the modern knowledge that neither the earth nor the sun rests in the center of the universe; that there is no resting place at all in the world; that all things constantly move and change and that therefore the human soul also should not worry about its own endless alterations and restlessness. Whereas the Christian thinker thought of an inner calmness and peace as the status of a soul resting in God, Montaigne's was a restless mind and did not even strive for peace. Clement of Alexandria said: "Congenial to the man of falsehood is shifting, and change, and turning away, as to the [Christian] gnostic are calmness, and rest, and peace." [13] In striking contrast are the words of Montaigne: "The world is but a perennial seesaw. All things in it are in constant motion: the earth, the rocks of the Caucasus, the pyramids of Egypt, both with the common motion and with their own. Stability itself is nothing but a more languid motion. I cannot keep my subject still. It goes along befuddled and staggering, with a natural drunkenness. . . . I do not portray being: I portray passing. . . . I may presently change, not only by fortune, but also by intention. . . . So, all in all, I do indeed contradict myself now and then; but truth . . . I never contradict." [14]

If Montaigne was a skeptic, he was quite a modern one. Ancient skepticism was confined to the negation of human knowledge or the capacity of human knowledge in a special sphere. Even the most radical skeptic did not doubt that there was an absolute truth behind man's ignorance or inability to reach that truth. Only because he believed in truth as such was he a skeptic. Not so Montaigne. He did not believe that there is any absolute truth at all; there is truth only for the individual mind, and the individual can attain it if he observes himself accurately enough. Since all things permanently change, truth itself is as ever-changing as man himself is. Montaigne anticipated Bergson and Whitehead. No one could ever be more "modern" than the author of the *Essays*.

The influence of Montaigne was enormous; although great from the beginning, it increased from century to century. It is no exaggeration to say that modernity was to a great extent molded by his spirit. Shakespeare has been called his "best" reader in every sense. One

[13] *Stromata*, II, 11.   [14] Frame, *op. cit.*, III, 2.

can also perceive Montaigne's spell in Descartes, even though the two men were worlds apart. The intellectual power of the *Essays* was so irresistible that even a mathematical and physical scientist and philosopher like Descartes could not escape it. The autonomy of the thinking mind claimed by *Cogito ergo sum* would not have been articulated without the impression of the perfect freedom of thought which is the lifeblood of the *Essays*.

Of course, there is autonomy of thought in Descartes, which, however, varies markedly from that of Montaigne. The ego of the *Cogito* is not that of an individual person, but that of the thinking mind in general or of reason. The term " reason " has so many connotations that it is difficult to enumerate them all. But when we speak of the autonomy of reason in modern philosophy, we do not think of Montaigne, but of Descartes and Kant. We mean that autonomy which does not acknowledge any statement, axiom, or principle not examined by logical reasoning — a reasoning certainly not valid for one individual only but rather for every individual. Reason in that sense is a binding force upon anyone who argues, be it in the realm of philosophy, science, or practical life, especially the life of jurisdiction and legislation.

The term " reason " is typically modern. The Greeks had no corresponding word, at least in classical times. In the age of Christian philosophy *intellectus* came nearest to reason, but its meaning was more intellectualistic than the modern equivalent. Autonomy of reason in philosophy means independence from any nonphilosophical source of thought, whether imagination or faith. Modern philosophy desires to proceed without any presupposition not proved by philosophic methods. Descartes sought such a principle and assumed that thought itself at least guarantees the existence of the thinking self. Kant also thought that reason itself is the ultimate tribunal of truth and that it bears within itself certain supreme principles that guarantee the possibility of knowledge. In the practical field Kant believed that reason is the moral lawgiver and that there is no higher instance for right or wrong. The French Revolution felt the same belief, which was philosophically supported and elucidated by thinkers like Rousseau and Voltaire. This self-assurance of reason is the common basis of all modern speculation. Of course, the more speculative philosophical thought is, the more the term " reason " includes some kind of intuition or faith. Hegel says that thinking implies a supersensuous, inner intuition. "Philosophy," he insists, "has the same content and end as art and religion; but it is the highest manner of comprehending the Absolute Idea, because its manner is the highest — the Notion." [15]

The term " autonomy " has still another connotation or implication. If thought is autonomous, it is sovereign in its own realm. This inner sovereignty, however, was not only maintained in the realm of thought; it was extended to all other realms of culture. The autonomy of the cultural realms, of the arts, economy, politics, science, and morality is one of the signs of modernity. Ancient culture was held together by the common bond of aesthetic imagination. Religion and the state, morality and speculation, all were permeated by this imagination. Therefore religion was mythological, the state was a religious affair, morality was controlled by the aesthetic idea of the right means between the extremes, and speculation was cosmological, i.e., in conformity with the aesthetic imagination of the All. Medieval culture was held together by the supremacy of the Christian faith as interpreted and guided by the Roman Church. All cultural branches were subordinated to this faith. Modern times differ from both the ancient primacy of art and the medieval primacy of religion. Although science in fact has a similar supreme position, it does not control all the realms of culture to the same degree as art and faith had controlled them in the former ages. It is true that the influence of science upon all fields is conspicuous. Nevertheless there is a relative autonomy of each cultural realm as in that of philosophic thought; each realm demands independence from any other realm. Culture is therefore in danger of falling asunder; it is no longer as uniform and united as it had been in antiquity and the Middle Ages.

It is the peculiar character of Protestantism to protest against the synthesis of the Roman Catholic Church. Protestantism refused to merge with Greek philosophy, as well as with the fine arts (this trait is most markedly developed in Puritanism), or with the state or any other realm of culture; it is ironical that Protestantism, just because of this refusal, provoked a self-dependence of culture so that

[15] *Science of Logic*, tr. by W. H. Johnston and L. G. Struthers (George Allen & Unwin, Ltd., London, 1929), Vol. II, p. 466.

"Protestant culture" is a predominantly negative concept implying that culture developed outside of Protestantism and was neither disturbed nor fostered by it. "Protestant philosophy" is therefore less Protestant, and often even less Christian, than Catholic philosophy was Catholic. The cultural realms in the protestant period of history strove for independence not only of faith and religion but also of the other cultural realms. Each desired to be autonomous. As we have seen, philosophy therefore refused any Christian obligation, although some systems were thoroughly Christian and written in a protestant mood, like those of Kant and Fichte, and to a lesser degree those of Hegel and the later Schelling; but even then the autonomy of philosophic reason was primary. Philosophy also declined to be tutored by an intuition that would have the cosmos as its object. Already Bacon says: " I demand the annihilation of these foolish models and counterfeits of the universe which have been fancied in the philosophical systems." He denounced all aesthetic influences in philosophic thought; therefore Plato is to him only a "bombastic poet." But this view was extreme. The very fact that systems were built in modern speculation, indeed, most elaborate and most presumptuous systems like those of Spinoza or Hegel, shows that the idea of the cosmos was not completely dead in modern times.

The autonomy of the cultural realms is evident if we think of modern slogans like that of *" l'art pour l'art"* (" art for art alone ") or that of "free enterprise" in the economic realm, meaning that no political, administrative, police, or juridical surveillance should hamper the development of economic aims and ends, that in particular no religious or ecclesiastical coercion should interfere with the absolutely autonomous evolution of economic expansion and way of action, as had occurred in medieval feudalism. As the artist should follow no goal except that prescribed to him by his own genius, so the industrialist, the merchant, the manager should be free to act according to no other rules except those which are dictated by his economic advantage. Man was more or less divided into departments of autonomous agents. An "economic" man was invented who was nothing but an economic agent following the purposes and motives of his economic task. A religious man was isolated from all the other interests and incentives of life. Man was specialized. Indeed, the idea of the specialist is typically modern. There were craftsmen, of course, in antiquity and the Middle Ages, as there were several professions, but in modern times specialization has increased to an unprecedented degree. Not only in medicine but in every science, the specialist emerged who was at home in some particular, often tiny, field of study, so that a botanist would know accurately the physiological and biological characters of only one particular plant or group of plants; the zoologist, a special branch of his science; and so on. Whereas Aristotle embraced all provinces of learning and similarly Albert the Great tried to know everything knowable, the modern scientist is obliged to specialize on an increasing scale.

The autonomy of the cultural realms also had the consequence that when dealing with them philosophy itself was compartmentalized into a variety of special philosophic disciplines, so that " philosophers" often became merely epistemologists, ethical theorists, aestheticians, philosophers of religion, and nothing more. Such a division into fragmentary philosophic subjects and specialties of course contradicts the idea of a speculative system; it even contradicts the very idea of philosophy which, according to its ancient origin, is a universal science dealing, if not with the universe, at least with the Absolute, in one or the other sense. The separation of epistemology from metaphysics, and also the separation of ethics, aesthetics, politics, etc., from the common ground of speculation often made those philosophic disciplines unphilosophic; it permitted special principles, often borrowed from the science of the day, to penetrate the heart of speculation and to deprive it thereby of its universal and essential significance or to falsify outright the Absolute into some relative entity or feature. Because of this autonomy of the philosophic disciplines modern philosophy was always in danger of losing its true meaning and becoming dissolved into a manifold of single sciences.

Epistemology attained a sovereignty and supremacy it had never assumed before. It was almost regarded as a self-evident principle that a philosopher's first task was to inquire into the conditions, the possibility, and the limitations of knowledge. Particularly the English schools but also Descartes and Kant thought such an inquiry to be the primary duty of a thinker. If you do not know what can be known, how can you dare to start thinking about the Absolute?

The task of the theory of knowledge was not to produce knowledge in the original sense, but only to prepare the way for it and to warn against the transgression of the limits of knowledge. Hegel ridiculed such a preparation. "How can you learn swimming before you go into the water?" he mocks at an epistemologist. And yet Hegel also wrote a kind of epistemology: the *Phenomenology of Mind,* which leads the student from the immediate sense perception to ever higher and higher stages of knowledge and ends in the knowledge of the Absolute or in absolute knowledge.

The separation of ethics from metaphysics was also fateful. If one remembers that Plato's speculation reached its climax in the Idea of the Good and that his whole system was thus made into a kind of universal ethics; or that Augustine, like Plotinus, identified Being and the Good, one can infer that it was a loss of depth and speculative insight when ethics was cut off from universal consideration. Of course, even in modern times the inner bond between metaphysics and ethics is not always broken. Spinoza's main work is entitled *Ethics* (although not by himself, since it was published after his death), and Kant set great store in the primacy of moral reason, in its connection with theoretical reason, when he considered the idea of God. The separation of ethics and politics was also fateful. To the ancients it was a common axiom that the state had an ethical basis and that morality and politics were intimately and intrinsically tied up with each other. In Christian philosophy politics was of course dependent upon theology. Only in modern times was the theory of state and society dissolved from all relation to ethics. The first to proclaim this autonomy of politics was Machiavelli.

Machiavelli wrote his *Discorsi* in order to find out the best way to serve the state in isolation from any other purpose or norm. The *ragione di stato* was the autonomous reason of politics or the principle of political reason divorced from all moral, religious, or metaphysical arguments. He came to the conclusion that "the religion of the Romans was more advantageous to the life of the state than is the Christian because it reckoned fortitude and patriotism among the highest virtues, while Christianity teaches humility and longing for the world to come." [16] He formulated in other places an extremely immoral or at least amoral conclusion of how a statesman

[16] *Discorsi,* II, 2.

should make his decisions and act. The *sacro egoismo* of Gabriele D'Annunzio was already anticipated by him. The "totalitarian" state of fascism and Bolshevism is only the final conclusion of this political autonomy. It is, of course, a conclusion that makes the autonomy of the state all-inclusive, so that the autonomy of all the other cultural realms is thereby destroyed. In such a way the state arrogated to itself pantonomy, i.e., the state was made a surrogate for the totality of all cultural realms; the ancient cosmocentric and the medieval theocentric unity was replaced by a modern unity based upon the omnipotence of the state. Similar attempts at a recovery of an all-inclusive totality of culture were made by other cultural realms.[17]

The most powerful of all the cultural realms in the modern world is science, in that peculiar sense which the word has assumed since the foundation of mathematical physics. Although the Greeks applied mathematics to the physical universe, they did it only in a very restricted area, mainly in that of the celestial bodies and their movements. They never founded a mathematical physics that would methodically investigate all physical phenomena. Neither did medieval science proceed to such a goal. Not even Francis Bacon was aware of the centrality of mathematics in modern science. The method as proposed in his *Novum Organum* was based upon the Scholastic and Aristotelian doctrine of the substantial forms. Although some late medieval minds did approach the principle of mathematical physics, only Galileo succeeded in applying it to the phenomena of mechanics. This was an immortal feat not only in the realm of physics itself but in the wider realm of the conquest of nature by the human mind and thereby in the realm of modern culture in general. Aristotle was definitely defeated not in the sphere of metaphysics, cosmology, and theology, not in psychology, ethics, politics, or aesthetics — in all these spheres he retained a certain authority, and rightly so. But he was absolutely and demonstrably defeated in the physical field. Galileo could victoriously show that the physical principles of Aristotle, especially with respect to falling bodies, were wrong, and that the only reliable and fruitful method of investigating the laws of gravity was the mathematical one.

[17] Cf. Richard Kroner, *Culture and Faith* (University of Chicago Press, 1951).

Galileo radically separated physics from metaphysics. All modern scientists are the disciples of Galileo. "Physics, beware of metaphysics!" Newton exclaimed. *"Hypotheses non fingo"* was his slogan, i.e., I do not set up hypotheses by means of speculation. Galileo made physics perfectly autonomous. He severed radically the tie between speculation and mathematical physics. From now on neither cosmology nor theology was permitted to direct physical theories; mathematics alone was made the queen of all physical investigations. Methodical observation, based upon experiment and mathematically formulated questions, was the pillar of the Nuova Scienza. The effect of this new science was profound. It overthrew Scholasticism in general and for all times. Nothing made the break between the Roman Catholic age and that of modern times as definite and definitive as Galileo's innovation. The ideal of exactitude became predominant not only in the field of physics but in all the natural sciences, and finally even in metaphysics itself. Speculation itself was tempted to yield to that ideal. Mathematics and its application seemed to be the only unerring science. Wherever quantity and number have a part, the mathematical method seemed to be the only one that was not subject to human prejudice or to human superstition. The world of antiquity and of the Middle Ages seemed to go down the moment Galileo succeeded in subjecting the phenomena of the physical universe to mathematical calculus. The autonomy of mathematical physics was the cornerstone and the very foundation of modern times.

For a long period — indeed, until Kant — this new science seemed to be the ideal of reason in every field. Descartes, Spinoza, and Leibniz were completely caught by the spell of the mathematical method. They dreamed of a universal mathesis, which would give the key to all problems of logic, ontology, and metaphysics in general. The Pythagoreans seemed to have gone in the right direction after all; the essence of things seemed to be arithmetical or geometrical. Spinoza undertook to establish a geometry of God and man. The charm which the word "science" assumed held sway even over the later thinkers. Kant was convinced that only mathematics and mathematical physics are true sciences. Hegel, who was certainly not under the spell of mathematics, deliberately named all his works "sciences," e.g., "science of the phenomenology of the mind," "science of logic," "encyclopedia of the philosophic sciences." Fichte called his chief metaphysical work *Wissenschaftslehre* (Doctrine of Science). And Marxism would not have conquered one half the world if it had not claimed to be built upon "scientific" ground. Modern times almost adored the scientific mind; even Christianity was interpreted as a "Christian Science."

II

FROM SPECULATIVE COSMOLOGY
TO MATHEMATICAL PHYSICS

The Italian Renaissance generated some remarkable cosmological systems, which anticipated the interest of modern times in the investigation of nature, but did not yet anticipate the main feature of modern science, its mathematical exactitude. The cosmological speculation of the Italian Renaissance can be compared with that of early Greece although it was no longer as original, naïve, and archaic as ancient speculation. Many diverse elements were now brought together which were often without inner agreement. Most of the Italian system builders were hostile to Aristotelian and Scholastic concepts. They emphasized and overemphasized the contribution made by sense perception to knowledge, sometimes even asserting that all knowledge in the last analysis is sensation, thereby returning, in part, to nominalistic theories of the late Middle Ages, and, in part, anticipating British empiricism of subsequent centuries. But in spite of this predilection for sensation they dared to think out conceptual pictures of the universe. They fused their naturalistic constructions not only with elements taken from Plato or Plotinus but also with medieval magic and astrology. Fantastic imagination, together with penetrating acumen, mathematical studies and discoveries, together with bold and overbold hypotheses and arbitrary speculations, generated a very unequal result. They all felt that the tide of history was turning, but they were not called upon to direct the new course of thought, except by means of very vague and impure conceptions. The greatest of these speculative naturalists were Tommaso Campanella (1568–1639) and Giordano Bruno (1548–1600).

The Italian philosophers of the Renaissance had a tendency toward sensualism and naturalism, but they were by no means atheists.

They all tried to conceive of God in various ways, and most of them pointed to revelation as the deepest source of that knowledge. Therefore they made a distinction between speculation and revelation, or between philosophy and sacred theology, but they did not arrive at a clear notion of the relation between these opposite sources of knowledge. They frequently held it possible to unite Neoplatonic emanation theories with the Biblical idea of Creation, materialistic conceptions with panpsychism, the denial of metaphysical comprehension with very extensive metaphysical theories. It is therefore vain to seek clarity and precision in their works. Nevertheless, they manifested the trend toward innovation, the audacity of " adventures in ideas," to use the title of Whitehead's book. They illustrated both the dichotomy in speculation and revelation, as motives in philosophic thought, and the longing for a synthesis of the two antagonists.

Plato and Neoplatonism enjoyed a kind of resurrection after the primacy which Aristotelianism had gained at the end of the Middle Ages. The most outstanding among the Platonists was Marsilio Ficino (1433–1499), the translator of the dialogues into Latin. He founded a Platonic Academy in Florence under Cosimo Medici and wrote a *Platonic Theology*.[1] Ficino resembled in his own speculation the other Italian philosophers, but his thought was more imbued with idealistic elements and with Christian reminiscences. Like Augustine he interpreted the doctrine of the Ideas as an inner illumination of the human mind by God. But he also adopted elements of Aristotelian philosophy such as the distinction of matter and form. Eventually (1473) he even became a priest of the Roman Church. Kristeller calls Ficino " the first speculative philosopher of the Italian Renaissance." [2] Although he was less original than Bernardino Telesio (1508–1588), Geronimo Cardano (1501–1576), or Francesco Patrizzi (1529–1597), Ficino was more profound and less sensualistic and naturalistic. Ficino's cosmology is a cosmotheology, like that of Plato and Aristotle, but it is also, to a certain degree, Christian. Ficino refers occasionally to the Gospel of John. However, his idea of God was still that of the supreme substance, not

[1] See, on Ficino, the work of Paul Oskar Kristeller, *The Philosophy of Marsilio Ficino* (Columbia University Press, 1943).

[2] Kristeller, *op. cit.*, p. 13.

that of a personal Self. It was the idea of an object not of a subject. God belongs, according to his system, to the cosmos, although he stands at the top of the hierarchy of beings, and in that sense transcends it, as the Aristotelian god who is also separated from the world, and yet is its head. Like Thomas Aquinas, Ficino assumed the existence of angels and of divine star souls. " To the individual souls belong first the souls of the stars, then the souls of men, and last the demons." [3] God was still regarded as " a member of the series " of existing substances, himself an objective, though incorporeal, entity. [4]

GIORDANO BRUNO

The cosmos of the Italian speculative thinkers was not yet " nature " in the modern sense. It was not yet deprived of its aesthetic and religious splendor. It was still a living organism. All things were endowed with life and soul. Therefore, it was not difficult for them to find a bridge between ancient speculation and Christian revelation. This harmony was shaken when the Copernican theory, which was already accepted by some philosophers, notably by Patrizzi, began to unfold its explosive metaphysical consequences. The man who first descried the impact of the heliocentric system upon the entire *Weltanschauung,* and who drew all the consequences with the greatest enthusiasm, was Giordano Bruno. More than any other Italian cosmologist, Bruno was a representative of the spirit of modernity. He realized that this astronomical theory enlarged the whole horizon of faith and thought, if understood in its full significance. As long as the earth kept its central position in the universe, the visual vault of the heavens permitted the view of a closed universe, as Aristotle cherished it. The distinction between an upper, celestial, and a lower, terrestrial, sphere could be upheld as the Aristotelians of the Middle Ages had done. This astronomical distinction could be combined with the rank-difference between the perfect motion of the celestial bodies and the irregular movement of bodies on the earth, and this differentiation could be interpreted as that of the divine and the human. Man could feel at home in such a closed universe. He could at the same time imagine that God lived beyond the celestial sphere in his own abode, which man cannot reach with

[3] *Ibid.,* p. 386.   [4] Cf. *ibid.,* pp. 231 f.

his eyes. Greek cosmology or theocosmology and the Christian faith could be united on this ground.

When the psalm says that " the heavens declare the glory of God; and the firmament showeth his handiwork," this religious admiration of the celestial world and its symbolic understanding could easily be translated into the speculative language of the Aristotelian or the Thomistic metaphysics. Platonism and Neoplatonism too could agree with the spirit and imagery of the psalm. This harmony was destroyed when it was fully acknowledged that the earth is not the center of the universe, and that even the sun is not this center. The whole imaginative and aesthetic intuition of the universe, even the idea of a universe at all, was endangered if not denied. An angelology could no longer be maintained, when the conception of that " upper " sphere was lost, and when the whole notion of space, as the place in which bodies exist, was abandoned. The sensuous, imaginative, and conceptual basis common to both speculation and revelation was suddenly imperiled. Without such a basis a rational and speculative cosmology seemed no longer possible. The balance between the outer and the inner world of the mind, between thought and faith, between philosophy and theology seemed to be in jeopardy.

The geocentric system of Plato and Aristotle, of Plotinus and Christian Neoplatonism, had been infinitely more than a mere scientific theory or an astronomical hypothesis. It had been the very mainstay of cosmological and theological speculation, the firm ground upon which the building was erected, its indispensable coping stone. When the cosmos itself does not exist, how can cosmology be maintained, and if cosmology is given up, how can theology be saved — theology in the sense of Christian speculation? Much, almost everything in past thought, was at stake. The idea of the closed All had united the visible and the invisible sphere, the world of sense and the intelligible world, understanding and perception, intellect and imagination. This union was the presupposition of both pre-Christian and Christian philosophy. What if this presupposition had to be recognized as an illusion? The structure of society, of the church, of the relation between state and church, dogma and doctrine — the foundation of life — was now problematic. One can sympathize with the grievous situation in which medieval mankind was brought when all these consequences were realized. One can understand why the church was frightened and why it used every weapon at its disposal in order to suppress such a dangerous and revolutionary innovation. The very fact that astronomical observation and calculus were able to generate a rift in the imposing and seemingly indestructible house in which the medieval man had lived was truly alarming. Even Luther felt obliged to reject the Copernican theory.

Giordano Bruno was selected by destiny to become the man whom the gathering storm caught. He suffered all effects of the mortal combat that was provoked by the speculative conclusions of that theory. The revolution of the earth around the sun was transposed to the spiritual area within man's mind, imagination, faith, and thought; it was transformed into a revolution of man's entire life. We have seen before how deep was the impression of the Copernican theory upon the individualistic philosophy of Montaigne. But the speculative conclusions of Giordano Bruno were of a more public and social kind. Giordano Bruno was burned alive as punishment for his audacious and inflaming heretical views. Of course, this burning did not change the intellectual and spiritual situation. It did not refute the daring ideas formulated by Bruno.

The astronomical question whether the earth revolves around the sun or not had still another aspect as grave for the Christian faith as those mentioned so far, and an even graver one. If the earth is the center of the universe, it is easily conceivable that the world logos became incarnate in a human being for the salvation of all mankind. Such a dogmatic idea is harder to understand and to accept if the earth is not that center. Nicholas of Cusa had already suggested that other stars might also be populated by beings like us. What about them? Is the work of God's salvation exclusively directed toward the inhabitants of this little star which we call the earth? Demythologizing today is the farthest consequence of the revolution brought about by Bruno's innovation. Indeed, not only the incarnation but revelation, which is addressed exclusively to man on earth, appears in a strange light when the earth is only one star among millions of other stars, in no way privileged by its situation. Bruno was probably led by considerations of this kind to become more and more radical in his anti-Christian attitude.

He rejected not only the dogma of the Catholic Church but also Christianity as such, together with the Christian cosmology and theology of the Middle Ages. He became an ardent pantheist. The universe, he concluded, is not limited at all, it has no center at all; it is the universe just because it is infinite and consists of infinite worlds like that of our solar system. Copernicus himself, and after him Kepler, still clung to the idea of a finite universe. We must not forget that Copernicus was not only an astronomer but also canon of a cathedral in East Prussia and a devout Christian theologian. He was in many respects very conservative, even in the field of astronomy itself.[5] It was Bruno who first proclaimed the boundlessness of the universe. This new idea was, of course, in line with the purely mathematical concept of an absolute space which does not tolerate any limitation or boundaries. Bruno resolutely rejected the Aristotelian definition of space as a place in which limited bodies exist and move. Here one can see the change in the whole world view produced by the mathematically minded modern thinker. According to Aristotle, universal space was determined by the extension of the outermost sphere. It was the boundary line of the visible world. Bruno abstracted from all visible boundaries and taught the boundlessness of the world space. Aristotle had expressly excluded the possibility that this space could be without confines. " The view that there is an infinite body is plainly incompatible with the doctrine that there is necessarily a proper place for each kind of body " [6] — a statement which, of course, begs the question as the word " plainly " shows.

Aristotle's half-sensuous, half-aesthetic view of space, retained by Christian philosophy, was rejected by Bruno and replaced by mathematically infinite space. There was no " place " outside space, and no universe where God could dwell. A " housing problem " resulted for God, as Heinrich Rickert, in his lectures on the history of modern philosophy, used to say when he spoke of Bruno. It was no longer, as with Copernicus, a merely astronomical question; it was a question of cosmology and theology, a question of speculation in

[5] Cf. the chapter "The Conservatism of Copernicus," in Herbert Butterfield's book *The Origins of Modern Science*, 2d ed. (The Macmillan Company, 1957).

[6] *Physics* 205b. Place is defined by Aristotle as " the boundary of the containing body at which it is in contact with the contained body " (*Physics* 212a).

its relation to revelation. The heaven of Biblical faith was demolished, together with the cosmos of the Greeks. The cosmocentric and the theocentric horizon was surmounted in favor of a speculation based upon a mathematical conception of space. " The world is out of joint " — this phrase comes to one's mind. Here was the turning point from Renaissance philosophy to the age of Galileo and Descartes. Bruno was not particularly interested in astronomy or mathematics. At bottom he was a poet, as his beautiful sonnets demonstrate. But he was also a passionate, speculative thinker to whom his new metaphysical outlook had a religious significance.

The position of Bruno, however, was by no means simple. He was still a cosmological thinker in spite of the fact that he destroyed the ancient cosmos and its Christian successor. His cosmology was as central as it had been to the Greeks. This is the paradox of his metaphysical position. How could he uphold the idea of the cosmos while undermining its very presupposition: the closeness and roundness of the visible world? How could he still cling to a cosmocentric metaphysics while demolishing the balance between sensation and thought? While enlarging the universe to the infinite, he was unconsciously guided and inspired by the spirituality of the Christian faith. It was this faith which destroyed the visible vault of the celestial sphere. Only the Christian tradition could enable him to spiritualize the cosmological view to the point where the universe was no longer a finite and closed sphere, but rather unbounded and therefore no longer discernible by the senses. He was the first modern man to feel that the Aristotelian finitude of world space did not harmonize with the spiritual infinity of the God who reveals himself in the gospel. His metaphysics was, therefore, not simply astronomical and cosmological; it was also of religious and theological concern, and this was why the Roman Church was so upset at his great influence and popular appeal.

It is a tragic irony that the same man who was so deeply religious in his own way (this religiosity was the real cause of his fanaticism), and whose mind was so imbued with the spirituality of the Christian message, was nevertheless so attracted by the ancient idea of the beautiful All that he tried to unite what could not be united: the mathematical and abstract infinity of number and space with the speculative and concrete totality of the world. The result was his new cosmology, which reveled in the idea of an infinite and divine cosmos. "From the eternal, immeasurable, and innumerable reality of the visible universe we deduce that eternal beauty and majesty which can never be content with a finite abode, and the holiness of which could never be conceived and worshiped in terms of a finite number of spirits."[7] In this sentence all the different strands of Bruno's speculation appear in their full light. God cannot live "beyond" the spheres because he is an infinite God who has created an infinite world that reflects his majesty. Bruno merges, thus, Greek cosmology with Biblical transcendence, so that a new spiritual and mathematical cosmotheology results. It was a strange blending of speculation and revelation which did not do justice to either. Bruno's metaphysical position corresponded accurately with the historical position in which he found himself — between the Italian naturalistic cosmologists, who wanted to renew a kind of pre-Socratic speculation, and the approaching mathematical physics of his great countryman Galileo Galilei. And both these strains of thought were joined together by a religiosity permeated by Christian spirituality.

Bruno's enthusiasm for the infinity of space and number directly contradicts the Greek idea of form and therefore of beauty. Aristotle would have vehemently rejected Bruno's cosmos because of its formlessness. And even Origen would have refused to accept it, because of its lack of shape. Origen expressly states that the number of spirits created by God is finite, otherwise God could not even know them all. The notion of form was so much in the foreground of his mind; he was still so thoroughly Greek that to him, as to Aristotle, infinity meant merely the deficiency of truth and beauty, of knowledge and contemplation. Bruno, in spite of his being a poet and in spite of his being an ardent worshiper of cosmic beauty, was a modern mind in that to him infinity seemed to surpass in sublimity and truth a finite number of existing things. Christianity in alliance with the new emphasis on mathematical abstraction resulted in the creation of his infinite cosmos.[8]

[7] Giordano Bruno, *On the Infinite Universe and the Worlds.*

[8] Scripture in some places identifies the majesty of God with the quantitative infinite: "I would seek unto God, and unto God would I commit my cause: which doeth great things and unsearchable; marvelous things without number." (Job 5:8–9.) "God is great, and we know him not, neither can the number of his years be searched out." (Job 36:26.) "How precious also are thy thoughts unto me, O God! How great is the sum of them! If I should count them, they are more in number than the sand." (Ps. 139:17–18.)

To Aristotle the conclusion that everything existed " in infinity "
was absurd. The infinite has no actual existence, it has only a potential being like matter and is not yet formed. If we raise the question
whether Aristotle or Bruno was wrong, we must answer that Bruno
was in agreement with the mathematical view of nature as it emerged
in the century after his death, but he was wrong to ascribe beauty
and divinity to such a mathematical universe. Aristotle would have
been right in insisting that such a universe is no longer a cosmos in
the ancient sense, and that such a cosmology therefore cannot be
true metaphysically. Bruno was not yet able to answer the difficult
problems which he encountered and which he solved with a kind
of aesthetic naïveté. He could not yet guess that Kant would prove
both the finitude and the infinity of the physical world and would
conclude from this contradiction the impossibility of any rational
or speculative cosmology.

Bruno's ecstatic and aesthetic contemplation of the infinite universe was Christian in so far as it assumed that the cosmos of the
Greeks had been transformed into God's creation and that the idea
of a finite form was no longer applicable to the Biblical God; but it
was Greek in so far as it tended toward an immanent God who revealed himself in the quantitative greatness and immensity of the
visible world. A subtle illusion marred Bruno's speculative intuition,
an illusion underlying all his writings in Italian, especially that *On
the Immense and the Innumerable Worlds*. On the one hand, the
kind of beauty that Bruno exalted was the " beauty of holiness,"
that inner and divine beauty which the psalms glorify; on the other
hand, he believed that he could contemplate that inner spiritual
beauty in the heavens as interpreted by modern physics. He fell
victim to this ambiguity. He thought that he conceived of a modern
kind of cosmos, but, in fact, he denied any kind of cosmos in the
ancient aesthetic sense. His modern cosmos was on the verge of
disintegrating aesthetically into the nature of mathematical thinking, but while the latter is arranged physically, aesthetics is not
its principle of order. One might say that Bruno's poetic genius surpassed his speculative ingenuity. The thinker was defeated by the
artist.

The All according to Bruno is a work of art and God is its artist
(*artefice interno*) who creates the world from within. Like Averroës

before him and Spinoza after him, Bruno distinguished between the creative nature, which he identified with God, and the created nature, which he identified with the world.[9] At bottom both are one. Matter contains all forms; the potential actualizes itself. Aristotelian categories were thus easily assimilated into his thought. Bruno preceded Leibniz in using the word " monad " for the ultimate single substances composing the world. Nature is mirrored by every monad because its unity is present everywhere. God is the monad of all monads and comprises them all.

The church was right in condemning Bruno's speculation, because it destroyed the Christian faith without creating any tenable new view. But it was tragic irony that the church defended the ancient pre-Christian cosmology, while Bruno's impossible aesthetic infinity was religiously much more cognate to the spiritual beauty of the Christian God. The church wanted to keep an impossible and untenable Christian cosmos, half Greek and half Biblical. Bruno's cosmology was certainly not an acceptable substitute for the Thomistic Aristotelianism, but this Aristotelianism was similarly unchristian. The slow development of speculation in modern times disclosed both errors, partly by making it clear that the mathematical method was not to be integrated with a speculative cosmology but had to produce its own strictly scientific theories independent of any religious inclination; partly by criticizing speculative cosmology and theology in the radical philosophic manner which Kant presented to the world. Bruno's speculative cosmology and theology did not satisfy religious, scientific, or philosophic needs. Therefore, it was doomed and did not find any disciples of great stature.

GALILEO GALILEI

The Italian philosophers were not scientists in the modern sense. But it was an Italian who created mathematical physics, Galileo Galilei (1564–1642). He did not have a speculative, or even a philosophic, mind, in the traditional sense. Nevertheless, his new physics had tremendous philosophical implications, if for no other reason than for its separation of physics from speculation, which was its immediate outcome. Before Galileo physics had been a philosophical discipline, most intimately connected with metaphysics. Now physics

---

[9] *Unità producente* and *unità prodotto*.

ceased to be such a discipline and became instead a science allied with mathematics; indeed, a kind of mathematics applied to the phenomena of the outer world. The whole relation between metaphysics and mathematics was thereby revised, but it was never entirely clarified. Plato, like the Pythagoreans, regarded mathematics as a preparation for philosophy and as a basis of all higher knowledge, although he distinguished carefully and in principle mathematics and dialectic. Aristotle also philosophized about the difference between the forms and mathematical entities, but he was less inclined to appreciate the value of mathematics for knowledge of the phenomenal world. The Middle Ages also wavered in their judgment about the application of mathematics to the investigation of nature, but on the whole, in their understanding of causes and change, they favored the method of logical and ontological analysis more than mathematical calculus.

Galileo inquired into the quantitative relation between certain numerical factors implied in the movement of bodies. In his famous work *Discorsi e Dimostrazioni Matematiche intorno à due nuove scienze attenenti alla mechanica e i movimenti locali,* he gave an exact demonstration of a new geometry, a geometry of motion which was as methodical and conclusive as Euclidean geometry had been, although it did not concern merely geometrical entities, but physical reality. In antiquity only Archimedes' theory of the weight of a body measured in water and in air had approached something of that kind. The book of Archimedes was translated and published in 1543. Galileo resumed this first attempt on a broader basis. Such a new mathematics was much more abstract than Aristotelian and all subsequent physics. As Euclidean geometry abstracts from all physical qualities and relations in order to isolate the merely quantitative properties of geometrical figures, so the mechanics of Galileo abstracted from all physical qualities except those which had a quantitative measure. Galileo isolated these quantitative determinants and made their relations the only object of his investigation. The time-honored problem of philosophic speculation: how thought and reality, logic and being, the conceptual and the sensible, the invisible and the visible, are connected with each other thus gained an entirely new aspect. No longer was it a matter of dialectical theory as in the Platonic and Aristotelian ontology of Ideas and forms, but it now involved exact observation, experimental investigation, and mathematical analysis. Metaphysics seemed to have been surpassed and obliterated. Not only was the ancient and medieval physics completely reformed, but metaphysics also seemed to be replaced by this new method. Since physics and metaphysics had always been intimately tied together, such a conclusion was by no means absurd.

No wonder that the effect of Galileo's achievement was tremendous. He himself was fully aware of the importance of his work. "The true book of philosophy is the book of nature which has always opened before our eyes, but it is written in letters different from those of our alphabet. The letters are triangles, squares, circles, spheres, cones, pyramids, and other mathematical figures," he says confidently and authoritatively. Whereas Aristotle believed that the movement of bodies can be explained in terms of substantial forms and final causes, Galileo proved that such an explanation is childish when compared with mathematical analysis and theory. Aristotle declared that natural causes determine the effect only "for the most part" (*"epi to poly"*); Galileo showed that the true causes, namely, the mathematical laws, determine the movement of bodies with absolute certainty and with the same exactitude as that with which geometrical axioms and propositions determine the relation between figures in space. "Logic," he says, "is an excellent guide in discourse, but it does not, as regards stimulation to discovery, compare with the power of sharp distinctions which belong to geometry. Logic teaches us how to test the conclusiveness of any argument or demonstration already discovered and completed; but I do not believe that it teaches us to discover correct arguments and demonstrations."[10] Logic, in other words, is secondary: it does not help to inaugurate and establish the science; it only helps to test the conclusiveness of the demonstrations already given in the science. Geometrical propositions now take the place of ontological arguments. The eternal debates of the schools are abolished. It was as if light had illuminated the former darkness of speculative metaphysics.

Galileo's physics is abstract not only because it abstracts from all nonquantitative determinants but also because even the quantitative

[10] Galileo, *Dialogue Concerning Two New Sciences* (Dover Publications, Inc., p. 137; National Edition, p. 175).

determinants are abstract themselves as compared with the individual quanta. As there is no point in the correctly geometrical sense since every physical point has some extension, there is also no straight line, no real triangle, no true square in the physical world; nevertheless, the physical world is subject to the laws of geometry inasmuch as all physical points, lines, triangles, etc., approximate geometrical regulation and order. By the same token the laws of mechanics and dynamics can be applied to the physical world, although there does not exist any motion that corresponds exactly to that which the laws define and determine. The bodies which according to Galileo's physics fall or move are not concrete, qualitatively and quantitatively individual bodies like those which " really " fall or move, but " geometrical bodies," [11] bodies which the theory constructs for the sake of mathematical exactitude.

Aristotle taught that different bodies have different " places " which are proper for them. Since the stone has its proper place on the earth, it falls; since the air has its proper place above the earth, it ascends; and so on. According to Aristotle, bodies of different weight fall with different speed; according to Galileo, the weight of a body is indifferent: bodies with different weight fall with the same velocity. Galileo abstracted from the medium through which bodies fall in order to set forth the general mathematical law of their fall. According to Aristotle, the concrete world of individual bodies is absolute but to Galileo the abstract space and the abstract motions of abstract bodies are the " really real." Galileo is therefore more akin to Plato than to Aristotle. His principle of " isolation " allows him to find absolutely valid propositions which, however, do not take into account the individual differences of physical processes. In the world space there is no " high " and " low " in an absolute sense as there is no " here " and " beyond." Galileo was the immediate precursor of Newton in this respect. The law of inertia as formulated by Newton rests upon this abstract mathematical principle of motion. The motion of a body is determined by its resistance against being set in motion when it is at rest and against being changed when it is in motion. Neither rest nor motion is a " natural " state for the body, both are the result of forces that work according to mathematical laws.

[11] Butterfield, *op. cit.,* pp. 13, 84.

The "Platonism" of Galileo however, does not imply that he believed in a realm of Ideas. He did believe in mathematical laws which determine the real processes of nature. But he was not a metaphysician. He did not believe that the newly discovered mechanical laws represented the ultimate reality. It was the error of some Kantians in the nineteenth century to make Galileo a philosopher who had succeeded where Plato and Aristotle had failed, or, in other words, to interpret mathematical physics as a new and better kind of metaphysics which, they thought, Kant also had acknowledged. Galileo himself was perfectly aware of his true position in the history of thought and of the real significance of his work and method. Although he occasionally used the word "philosophic" in a loose sense, as did Newton, Galileo knew that his physics did not replace the metaphysical systems of the past.

"We are satisfied with the knowledge of some empirical characters. The attempt to penetrate into the true inner substance of the world by means of speculation is, I hold, an undertaking as empty and vain with respect to the nearest earthly as well as to the remotest celestial bodies. We know as little the substance of the earth as we know that of the moon, as little the substance of our earthly atmosphere as that of the solar spots." [12] What Galileo calls here "the true inner substance" can also be called the ultimate essence or the metaphysical nature of things. Physics mathematically understood does not tell us about the purpose of the universe or its ultimate end, about the relation between the mathematical order of nature and the mind which finds this order. Ontological and epistemological questions are excluded from the new science which is confined to "some empirical characters," as Galileo modestly says.

Galileo not only separated physics and metaphysics, experience and speculation, but he himself did not believe in the possibility of any theoretical metaphysics. In this respect he was, in fact, a predecessor of Kant, who shared this negative conviction. "Man never, not even in his deepest inquiries, attains to the ability of understanding the structure of the All or even of a single natural effect, be it ever so modest; only some fragments of the truth can be collected on the way of natural knowledge." [13] But a Kant was needed to substantiate this

---

[12] Ernst Cassirer, *Das Erkenntnisproblem*, I, p. 402.
[13] Galileo, *Dialogue About the Two Cardinal World Systems*.

verdict and to display the reasons why the " structure of the All " cannot be understood by the human intellect, although this intellect is able to discover the mathematical laws that govern physical processes.

Galileo contributed to the destruction of speculative cosmology, but he also aided in the creation of an epistemology that was able to understand his own method and the whole relation between physical objects and the knowing subject. In other words he promoted indirectly the shift of philosophic speculation from the objective world to man as the knower of that world. Thus he paved the way for the epistemological emphasis of Descartes, Locke, Leibniz, and Hume, and he prepared the framework on which the Kantian transcendental idealism could be based. But some Kantians, especially the so-called Marburg school, exaggerated by making the mathematical method of Galileo a forerunner of Kant's transcendental method, or even by identifying the two. Galileo was guided by mathematical reason, Kant by philosophic (logical, critical) reason. These two kinds of reason must be accurately distinguished from each other. Galileo's undertaking was definitely not philosophic, although it had momentous philosophic implications; Kant's concern was definitely not mathematical or physical, but transcendental; i.e., epistemological. Kant was the founder of a new approach to the problem of knowledge while Galileo founded a new method of investigating nature.

These two profoundly different approaches and goals should not be confused. Galileo inquired into the objects of knowledge; Kant, into the knowing subject. Galileo was not interested in a knowledge of knowledge; Kant was. Galileo was a mathematical physicist; Kant, a transcendental logician. But it is true that for two reasons Kant could never have done what he did do without the work of Galileo. First, Galileo had to abolish speculative cosmology before Kant could write his *Critique of Pure Reason*. This critique analyzed the method of Galileo (transcendental analytic). It examined and demolished speculative cosmology in its second dialectical part (transcendental dialectic). What had been an unreflected, logically naïve undertaking with Galileo became a careful reflection with Kant. Galileo had denied the possibility of knowing the " true inner substance " of physical substances without demonstrating the impossibility of such a knowledge. Only a philosophic critic and logician could deliver this demonstration.

The second reason why Galileo had to precede Kant lies in the fact that Galileo showed by practicing his method how nature could be known exactly, namely, by " sharp distinctions," i.e., by well-defined concepts that only the thinking mind can produce. Galileo thereby clarified instinctively the way in which sensation must ally with the understanding in order to arrive at exact knowledge. Whereas the speculative Italian philosophers of nature like Telesio, Cardano, Campanella, and others had stressed sensation exclusively and believed that natural knowledge can be attained by the senses alone, Galileo's method refuted such a naïve and false epistemological theory and showed that reason or the understanding is involved in the knowledge of nature, and that false results originate from sense perception not guided by the intellect. Ironically, only Galileo could prove that Aristotle had been wrong, precisely because he had not applied mathematical reason, but had trusted naïve sense perception too much, while Galileo's speculative forerunners, who were anti-Aristotelians, had shared in the prejudice and deficiency of the Aristotelian method. Through the practice of his partly experiential but partly constructive and rational method, Galileo directed Kant's epistemological thought toward the discovery that sense and understanding must collaborate in order to achieve knowledge of the physical substances and processes.

Another historical consequence of Galileo's work should be mentioned. He contributed not only to the demolition of speculative cosmology, but also to that of speculative theology, both of which had been inseparably connected in the age of Christian philosophy. By denying the possibility that we can ever understand the " structure of the All," Galileo also implicitly doubted the possibility of ever understanding the Creation and the Creator by speculative means. Whereas the Italian philosophers of nature in the sixteenth century, in spite of their crude sensualism, had said that God and the All can be known philosophically, Galileo recognized that both surmounted the human intellect. This insight agreed with the thesis of Protestantism that philosophy and human comprehension in general were unable to build up a " natural theology " or a knowledge of God unsupported by revelation. In this way the Roman Catholic Galileo unconsciously helped the cause of the Reformation! Kant, like

Galileo, admired mathematical physics and protested against the medieval synthesis of Greek cosmology and Christian theology. The " Critique of Reason " was the outcome of these historical presuppositions. This famous book would never have been written without the Protestant background of its author.

III

PROTESTANT SPECULATION

I s THERE any Protestant speculation? One should expect that there cannot be any, since Protestant Christianity protested against the synthesis of pre-Christian speculation and Christian revelation, as it protested against any form of paganized Christianity; indeed, it protested against philosophy in general; many pithy and ferocious words of Luther attest this critical attitude. Luther understood the warning of Paul in a literal sense. If it had been up to Luther alone, a Protestant speculation would never have arisen. But some of his close friends, such as Sebastian Franck, were inclined to speculate; later even his closest collaborator, Melanchthon, turned back to Scholastic philosophy. Can we explain this strange historical phenomenon in terms of the nature of Protestantism itself?

The idea of a Christian culture was not entirely abolished with the rise of Protestantism. The primitive Christian community had to grow into the Roman Church and make its peace with ancient philosophy and with many other cultural traits of antiquity. The reader will recall that Clement of Alexandria, a missionary to the Greeks, merged his Christian faith with Greek speculation and poetry. And even before Clement, men like Justinus and others understood Christianity as a new philosophy, blending the speculative Logos of the Stoics with the Logos of the Fourth Gospel. It is, therefore, not surprising that a similar trend set in immediately after the Reformation. As the primitive Christian community had to learn that the Advent of Christ did not mean the disappearance of the temporal world, that the Kingdom of Heaven and the kingdom of this world had to live side by side, so again the early enthusiasm of the Reformers had to give way to the recognition that a certain compromise was necessary in order to survive in the midst of secular political and social conditions. Culture itself had to become Protestant; Protestantism had to become cultural. It is obvious that terrific difficulties stood in the way of these two necessities, and that compromise could assume a great variety of forms and degrees. It is also clear that the new Protestant culture could not resemble the Catholic culture of the Middle Ages, if it was not to lose all its peculiar spirit and aspirations. This new culture had to become much less pagan than its Catholic sister. It had to retain the tension between the message of the gospel and the ambitions of culture. It could not be so harmonious and naïve a reconciliation between the pagan inheritance and Christian piety as the Roman Catholic culture had been.

We can observe this inner tension in many guises. We can see it in a painter such as Rembrandt, who had to invent a special *clair-obscure* (half bright and half dark) to express his religious sentiment. We can hear it in the music of Bach, so much more complicated than that of medieval composers. (Counterpoint!) We can find it negatively in the lack of a Protestant architectural style and in the enmity against artistic decoration and adornment of church buildings. We can also discover it in comparing Milton with Dante, Klopstock with Petrarch. We can learn of it from the separation of state and church, of philosophy and theology, of science and speculation. Protestantism continually protested against any amalgamation with culture, even if it did combine with it. There was a permanent *concordia discors* in the alliance between Protestantism and culture; the dialectic of Kant, Fichte, and Hegel still evinces this inner tension, this precarious harmony between speculation and revelation in systems of thought molded by Protestant Christianity.

On the other hand, Protestantism released a cultural creativity of the greatest dimensions. This extraordinary phenomenon can easily be explained if we remember that Protestantism, precisely because it did not favor the synthesis of antiquity and modernity, of worldly and divine things, allowed culture to develop itself according to its own needs and rules. Paradoxically, secularization of culture was the immediate effect of this Protestant attitude. The refusal of Protestantism to adopt worldly motives and intentions had two aspects; one was the religious purity and integrity of religion, the other was the relatively nonreligious deportment of culture. The term " secularization " is characteristic of the modern trend. Where state and art, science and morality were not formed outright by the Renaissance spirit and thereby more or less paganized, they were in any case estranged from the Christian faith; this faith was not of any great, or indeed of any, consequence in the creation of the natural sciences and of most works of art, in political programs and actions, in moral norms of honesty and dishonesty, and so on. Secularization was not at all paganization. Antiquity did not know secularization except when its decline was approaching. The ancient arts, ancient morality, the ancient state, ancient speculation, were far from that religious indifference which is the mark of modernity. Culture was deeply tinged by religion in Athens as well as in Rome.

Secularization is a by-product of Protestantism. Because the Reformers stressed so much religious purity and holiness of life as the demand of Christ, and because they denied so strongly the paganization of the Roman Church, they permitted culture to turn away from religion. Secularism is thus the negative concomitant of the Protestant movement. Speculation no longer bound up with revelation, philosophy no longer fused with theology in one and the same *summa,* could and did grow in its own " secular " direction. Of all branches of culture, science was the most secular, because mathematics and mathematical physics and all the other natural sciences were not at all directed by any faith, except the faith in scientific reason and the rational order of nature. In so far as it was the ideal of philosophy to become " like science " or as scientific as possible, speculation also was secularized even when it was not under the sway of the Renaissance.

Descartes was still a Scholastic in some respects. Spinoza was a Biblical believer in spite of his extremely naturalistic bias. Leibniz was an outspoken Protestant, although he tried to reconcile revelation and speculation. But all these thinkers were secularized to the degree to which they were tinged by the scientific ideal which they pursued. The British philosophers, especially Berkeley, were loyal to the Christian faith, although both Locke, and Hume even more so, were independent in their half-psychological, half-epistemological methods. Kant has often been called a Protestant thinker, and it is true that he never lost touch with the pietism of his mother. Nevertheless, his thinking was also secularized if we compare it, for instance, with that of Thomas Aquinas, although Kant's idea of the primacy of moral reason is more Christian than the intellectualism of Scholastic Aristotelianism. Fichte, Schelling, and Hegel had been theological students before they began to philosophize and to build their systems. These systems show traces of their theological past, but only traces; they are even more secularized than the critical philosophy of Kant.

There were, however, a group of thinkers who sprang directly from the German Reformation. In order to understand their systems we must turn for a moment to Luther. He was thoroughly antiphilosophic. His thinking was much less systematical than that of Calvin; in fact, he did not believe in systematic theology. Luther had a keen understanding of the Christian paradox. He believed that the God who permitted the free will of man to sin, and who could be as wrathful as he could be gracious and loving, that this God of the Old and the New Testament could never be comprehended by the human mind. He was antiphilosophical not only because he distrusted the pagan thinkers, but also because he was disinclined to speculate about the God to whom he prayed and whom he preached. Luther held that the Christian faith was in the first place a stimulant to the will and the heart. The Christian man cannot comprehend things divine, but he has to fight sin within himself and within the world, and he has to trust that the Lord will help the man who fights. The believer in Christ should therefore not hide behind the fence of the monastery; rather, he should live in the midst of sinful society and should stoop down to the sinner as Jesus did. "All Christians are taking holy orders; no difference is between them except that of the office." "By baptism we all are consecrated as priests as St. Peter says." [1]

Luther regarded Aristotle as the corrupter of the Christian soul. To him Aristotle was "this damned, supercilious, roguish pagan" who taught in his best book, *De anima,* that the soul is mortal together with the body.[2] His book *Ethica* "is more wicked than any other book, outright contrary to the grace of God and the Christian virtues." He called the Scholastic universities therefore "the true

[1] Luther, *An den christlichen Adel deutscher Nation* (To the Christian Nobility of the German Nation), 1520.
[2] *Ibid.*

castles of the devil on earth." [3] But the same Luther was himself a professor at the University of Wittenberg and was most intensely interested in the humanistic studies and later in the establishment of schools. Before he attached his theses to the cathedral, he wrote in a letter to Spalatin, the chaplain to the Elector of Saxony: " If it were possible to reorganize the university (in accordance with the humanistic movement), what an honor would this bring to the prince and to the university! It would occasion the reform of all universities, it would after all eradicate all barbarity, and augment abundantly all the sciences." In a similar vein he uttered ideas for such a reform in the writings in which he passionately defended the cause of the Reformation and made proposals for its educational policy. Luther was by no means the barbarian who is sometimes portrayed. He wanted to conjoin the gospel with humanism and science; he respected the task of culture and planned to build a Protestant culture.

His friend and collaborator Melanchthon closely followed him in the beginning of the Reformation; he too rejected philosophy entirely. " Thou may'st despise all other sciences; to neglect the study of St. Paul is to throw away the hope of beatitude." [4] But later he felt the necessity of restoring a philosophic theology and himself toiled to perform this work, so that he was finally called *praeceptor Germaniae* (the teacher of Germany). He even adopted Aristotle's system in its original version and he " knew how to sift, arrange, and set forth the material in his textbooks with so great a skill that it became the basis for a doctrine which was in the main one in its nature, and as such was taught at the Protestant universities for two centuries." [5]

Although Luther was averse to philosophy in general, he was deeply affected by the mystics of the Middle Ages, especially by John Tauler. He read with enthusiasm the so-called *Theologia deutsch* (*German Theology*) which he believed to have been written by Tauler, the disciple of Eckhart. He edited this book in 1516 under the title: " A spiritual, noble little book, of right discernment and understanding, concerning what the old and new man be, what the

[3] Luther, *An die Ratsherren der deutschen Städte* (To the Councillors of All German Cities), 1524.

[4] Melanchthon, *Exhortation Concerning the Study of the Pauline Doctrine.*

[5] W. Windelband, *A History of Philosophy,* tr. by James H. Tufts (The Macmillan Company, 1893), Part IV, ch. 1, 28.

child of Adam and of God be, and how Adam should die and Christ should rise in us." In the Preface he says: " This noble booklet, poor and unadorned as it is in words and human wisdom, is nevertheless very rich and most delightful in art and divine wisdom. Except the Bible and St. Augustine, I did not learn from any other book better what God, Christ, man, and world be." These words attest the strong impression which German medieval mysticism produced upon Luther's mind.

Like the mystics Luther was convinced that the redemptive atonement of Christ has to be understood as an inner truth that must be experienced by the soul, that God is not an object of doctrine, but the supreme goal of the will and the heart; not a " form " in the Aristotelian sense, but a living power, and that man cannot unite with God by theoretical knowledge, but only by inward regeneration and devout surrender. God is not to be found as the cause of the world, but only within ourselves. When we give up our natural, selfish desire, God will dwell and work in us. Sacrificial love is the only way to approach the divine mystery. God is not a substance, an idea, or any objective energy, as the Aristotelians teach, but rather a will, a self, a thou that we encounter in prayer and meditation alone. In the last analysis, he is the true and perfect self of our human and forever imperfect self. These half-Biblical, half-mystical thoughts struck a cognate chord in Luther's own soul.

A circle of Protestant mystics gathered around the Reformer, men like Kaspar Schwenkfeld, Andreas Osiander, Johannes Denk, Valentin Weigel, Sebastian Franck, and others. Whereas the Italian philosophers of the Renaissance speculated about the outer world, the German philosophers of the Reformation speculated about the inner world of the soul and the self. The most brilliant and audacious among them was Sebastian Franck (1500–1545). He was a man of genius, a thinker and writer of high rank.[6] He had been a Catholic priest, but was inflamed by Luther's famous theses and went heart and hand with him. He became a fervent Lutheran, an " evangelical " minister, and preached the Word with the greatest zeal. But he was ultimately disappointed in the course of the Protestant movement and abandoned his office after a few years; afterward he lived and worked alone in accord with his mystical insight. He was of the

[6] Cf. Wilhelm Dilthey, *Gesammelte Schriften,* II, pp. 80 ff.

opinion that Luther made too many compromises; therefore, he wanted to be free from all ecclesiastical obligations so that he could express his innermost mind without any inhibition. This resolution was pertinent to the history of the relation between revelation and speculation; it was symbolic of the inner tension between these rivals.

Franck was essentially a mystic like Eckhart, Tauler, and the author of the *German Theology,* whoever that may have been. But while those medieval mystics preserved their membership in the Roman Church and accommodated themselves more or less to the official dogma and doctrine, Franck could no longer do this. He did not believe in the possibility of any church at all. Not only dogma and doctrine, but the institution as such, was too external to his view of faith. The church on earth is tinged too much by the world to be the true church of Christ. The opposition between the world and God is insurmountable and inexorable. All outer expressions of faith contradict the inner light. The contrast between the letter and the spirit seemed to him so overwhelming that the truth could be found only in the silence of inward experience. When we try to say what our inner experience tells us, we falsify at once the original meaning, the unfathomable and ineffable truth. " Everything written about God is only an image and a shadow," Franck exclaims, and quotes the word of Isaiah: " ' Verily thou art a God that hidest thyself ' (Isa. 45:15)." [7] " Only God knows himself." [8] " God is the opposite and the opponent of the world." " The only way of life is not to stick to the world." [9] God does not act in time, he is timeless and everything is present to him. In his Preface to the *Paradoxa* he calls Scripture an eternal allegory. God, he insists, has no definition. " How can you define him who is all in all? " " God does not properly love anything, but he himself is Love, Wisdom, and Goodness."

In his book *Gnothi seauton* (Know Thyself, 1615), Valentin Weigel emphasized that the best knowledge is the knowledge by which each man knows himself. Man has a twofold mind, one belonging to this world or to nature, the other to God. Every man has two fathers, the one natural and transitory, the other divine and eternal. But in the same book Weigel also indulged in utterances which betray that he was a child of his period, open to many kinds

[7] *Paradoxa,* I. [8] *Ibid.,* VII. [9] *Ibid.,* XVII.

of superstition or magic. He believed in astrology. Man has obtained his mind from the firmament. There is " no more noble, high, and dear art than astronomy . . . ; it opens what is hidden in the heart of everyone." Although he stresses the incompatibility of faith and knowledge, he defends philosophy; but he adds that there is a philosophy in Holy Scripture itself which is preferable to that of Aristotle.

Another group of Protestant philosophers was more inclined to interpret the Christian revelation by means of ancient thought, in a pantheistic or in a naturalistic fashion, as had the Italian Renaissance philosophers. Like Weigel but in a grosser form they allowed magic, cabala, alchemy, and astrology to creep into their thought. Agrippa von Nettesheim was the leader of this group to which Johann Reuchlin, Paracelsus, Van Helmont, and others also belonged. In reading the writings of these men one feels that they lived in a period of great intellectual and spiritual unrest and excitement. The old standards of knowledge were not yet entirely discarded, and new standards were emerging, so that the minds of many were in a state of tumult and agitation. These men were aware of the revolution going on in the heart of faith and culture, but they were themselves only superficially touched by the new ideas and had not yet attained clarity about the value of past and present elements of thought. None of them was able to anticipate modern philosophy.

The general whirlpool of innovations, discoveries, and inventions in that period, the presentiment of tremendous social, spiritual, cultural, and intellectual upheavals, the sincere wish to help people suffering from this confusion and fears, all this in addition to the basic ignorance in which we humans always live, contributed to the rise of a tremendous ferment, in which ambition and ingenuity were strangely mixed. Paracelsus, physician, chemist, magician, and philosopher, was a prototype of this curious medley. He was the discoverer of new medical insights, but he also wanted to be a speculative thinker without possessing sufficient talent for such a task.[10]

---

[10] Erasmus, speaking about the various kinds of self-praise common in the European nations, says, " The Germans pride themselves in their tallness of structure and skill in magic" (*Praise of Folly*).

JACOB BOEHME

Jacob Boehme (1575–1624) belongs to a new period of Protestant speculation although he was not untouched by the situation just described. Boehme was influenced by Paracelsus; he too blended mystical and speculative ideas with medieval astrology and alchemy, magic and cabala, physics and medicine, but he had much greater spiritual power and productivity. He was also the heir to that type of mysticism which arose with Eckhart and which had its modern friends and adepts in Luther, Franck, and Weigel. He was a godly man, sincerely devout, an ardent professor of his faith. His was also a brooding mind which wanted to solve all problems of cosmology and theology, although knowing and acknowledging at the same time that the way to their solution is barred by the immeasurable mystery of things divine. But the depth of his speculation, the energy of his imagination, the penetrating boldness of his intellect, combined to make him one of the prominent philosophers in modern times; he found many disciples in Germany, England, and elsewhere and he had a considerable sway over the post-Kantian speculative system builders.

Boehme was a Lutheran and although the Protestant Pastor Primarius of his native town ridiculed his writings and the Town Council even forbade him to publish his manuscripts, he never stopped believing himself to be a loyal member of the church and a good Lutheran.[11] No doubt there is a close connection between Luther's faith and views and those of Boehme. One might even say that Boehme's speculation sprang directly from the religious convictions and theological conceptions of the great Reformer.

Of course, this spiritual kinship between Luther and Boehme must not conceal the enormous difference between the aspirations and achievements of the Reformer and the speculative cobbler. Boehme was certainly a disciple of Luther, but there were also many other sources of his thought, influences which were hard to combine with his Lutheran faith, not only medieval mysticism but also Ren-

[11] Cf. Introduction to Jacob Boehme's book *The Way to Christ,* tr. by John Joseph Stoudt (Harper & Brothers, 1947), p. xvii. Also Boehme's *Confessions,* compiled and edited by W. Scott Palmer, with an Introduction by Evelyn Underhill (Harper & Brothers, 1954), pp. 22 ff.

aissance nature philosophy. Although Boehme was by no means a learned man in the sense of university studies, he had read a good deal and he had the amazing instinct of selecting those elements which fitted his personal vision and his religious leanings. Parmenides and Heraclitus, Plato and Plotinus, John Scotus Erigena and Nicholas of Cusa, were indirectly known to him and he made use of their thought on occasion.

This Silesian artisan confronted in the seventeenth century the same ultimate riddles that had occupied the mind of the first great thinkers in pre-Christian times — an illustration of the eternity of the basic problems and of the continuity of Western speculation throughout the centuries. Of course, the concrete form in which those eternal problems stirred the mind of Boehme varied immensely from the appearance of the same problems in early Greek thought. And yet, if one pierces the surface into the kernel, one finds that the same ultimate difficulties bar the way for the ancient, and for the modern, mind, both wrestling with the abysmal mystery of Being and Non-Being.

Reduced to the most fundamental categories this mystery is indeed common to Parmenides and to Boehme. It is the contrast between the One and the Many, between Identity and Change, and other ontological opposites. Learning, in the scholarly sense, is less important for the discovery of these opposites than devotion. The fashions of thinking, the methods of scientific investigation, the number of facts known, the cultural habits and inclinations change, but the stubbornness of those ultimate questions remains forever the same. Boehme belongs to the class of thinkers who are able to discern the roots of speculative thought. It is hardly possible to compare two thinkers more different in outlook and erudition, temper and education, intellectual climate and religious background than Parmenides and Boehme. And yet both met the same problems in their different intellectual worlds. Stripped from the respective temporal situation the basic problem was this: How can we understand that the Absolute and the Relative, the Immutable and the Changeable, the Indestructible and the Transitory, the Eternal Life and the sphere of decay and death belong to the same Being?

In Boehme's case the Absolute was represented by the Creator God of Biblical revelation. His Protestant faith, however, did not permit him to understand this God as he was understood in the age of Christian philosophy; he could not conceive of God any longer in terms of ontological categories like Being and Becoming, Essence and Existence, or Substance and Accident; he was forced to think of him primarily as Will. Origen, Augustine, and Duns Scotus had stressed the thesis that God is Will and that the Creation is an act of his free decision. But in the Scholastic system of the Aristotelians, notably by Thomas Aquinas, the will was more or less identified with the intellect or the essence of God.[12]

The peculiar contribution to Christian speculation made by Boehme was his insight that God is Will first of all and that we must understand the essence of God from his will. But what is will? Does not the will always imply a certain insufficiency, a lack of perfection, a striving after a goal, features that are incompatible with the absolute perfection, self-existence, and self-sufficiency of God? A being that wills something does not possess the object of his will and to that degree he is not yet as absolute as God is supposed to be. It seems difficult, if not completely impossible, to transfer the will from man to God. Man wills because he has needs, desires, impulses, ideals, and obligations. Can we think of God in an analogous way? None of the Christian philosophers had ever raised this fundamental question. They were always content to point to the portrait of God in the Bible where we see him will and act. Origen says that the son is a product of God's will, but he does not expound this statement. Augustine speaks about memory, intellect, and will in God, but he insists that these human features can be ascribed to God only by analogy and that we cannot know them as attributes of God's mind with the same directness as we know them as attributes of our own mind. The divine will was always regarded as a mystery that only revelation discloses. The absolute freedom which characterizes the divine will seemed to forbid any speculative illumination or exposition of this mysterious trait.

Jacob Boehme dared to penetrate into this hidden center of the Biblical Creator. He became thereby the first Christian philosopher to develop theosophic thoughts. There is, he said, something in God which has to be understood as a fathomless abyss. He called this

[12] Cf. Kroner, *Speculation and Revelation in the Age of Christian Philosophy,* pp. 208 f.

abyss by the German word *Ungrund,* which means that it has no basis, but is rather itself the ultimate basis of everything else. This, indeed, is a circumscription of absolute freedom. In so far as the will has no motive, no purpose, no end outside itself; in so far as nothing whatsoever can account for the action of the will except the will itself, it may indeed be conceived as absolutely groundless. It is true that such a fathomless will is also unfathomable, unintelligible, incomprehensible, but such a negative thesis cannot do away with the positive statement that this incomprehensible and unfathomable *Ungrund* can be and has to be understood as free will. After all, we do know what will is by our self-experience. In ourselves too there is this free will, although in us it is never absolutely free because we are not absolutely self-dependent and self-existent, as God is. But by a kind of empathy we can know the unknowable, comprehend the incomprehensible. Boehme relied upon this empathy.

The innermost center of God is his will and this will is not determined by anything else. Precisely because it is impossible to trace back this fathomless abyss to any cause or reason, we meet here the divine essence which is not accessible to the intellect, but only to the will in ourselves. We must philosophize with our will, then we will be able to sense the will in God. Boehme describes here the way in which the believer approaches God. But he is convinced that this approach can lead to a speculative penetration of the divine mystery. Speculation cannot even wish to make the *Ungrund* intelligible in the sense in which we can understand other things. If we could make this groundless abyss intelligible, it would cease to be divine because the peculiar essence of God is distinguished from the essence of all other things in that they are grounded in God. Only thus can the absolutely independent and unconditioned be conceived. Of course, we encounter here a supreme contradiction: God cannot be conceived at all, but even this insight is a kind of conception of him. It is the old contradiction of negative theology which is repeated in Boehme's speculation. But Boehme tried to conceive of this inconceivable essence as Will.

Scripture says more about God than this. It reveals him not merely as a willing being, but as the almighty, all-wise, and all-bountiful Creator of the world. Can we understand this revelation if we conceive of God in the first place as Will? Boehme concedes that there is a *Mysterium Magnum* which cannot be unsealed by the mind of mortal man. Nevertheless, he feels sure that it is possible to articulate this mystery or to make it manifest without harming its mysterious quality. If God is Will, we can conclude that he acts. Acting implies movement, energy, purpose, end, and goal. Boehme, in contrast to Aquinas who is a static thinker, is a dynamic one. In order to grasp what is dynamic, our thoughts must be dynamic too. Boehme endeavors to make the solid fluid, the quiet restless, the definite indefinite. He transcends the boundary between qualities and notions. There is a Bergsonian impetus in his language and thought. His imagination is at work everywhere. One might also say that he is a dialectical thinker, but his dialectic is not logically disciplined; it follows his vision and toils to express this ever-changing object. He sees the truth, which he wants to communicate with the inner eyes of his mind. He gives, therefore, a more or less clear picture of that great mystery which we call God. But this picture is not methodically developed; he would say that a methodical knowledge contradicts the nature of the Supreme Being, and that therefore a methodical treatment of theological speculation would necessarily falsify its object. There is, nevertheless, an inner consistency in all he says. He steers his ship with a skillful and steady hand. He knows his goal very well. He sticks boldly to his intuition. He is much more sagacious and shrewd than a superficial glance at his writings and doctrines would imply.

Boehme feels himself guided by a power higher than that of his own intellect. "Since God in these latter days wanted to reveal himself to the artless, I let him work in me and drive me. I am only a little spark." [13] He admits that he has drawn his knowledge "from the source and gazed upon Infinity by virtue of a divine light within himself." [14] He does not pretend to arrive at his insight or vision by logical and scientific means; on the contrary he admits that he feels inspired and that no one can penetrate the supreme light without being led by this light. He sometimes seems simply to babble, and one is tempted to lose one's patience and to let him alone. But then in the midst of seemingly incoherent and even absurd chatter one suddenly meets beautiful, profound, and sincerely devout sentences, betraying the sensibility, humility, and purity of his soul, the riches

[13] *Aurora,* ch. 2. [14] *Mysterium Magnum,* ch. 5:15.

of his wisdom, the insight into the tragic and embarrassing conflicts and contradictions of life. One of the often-repeated views of
Boehme concerns the mutual permeation of good and evil: " Nothing is intrinsically evil or created for the sake of malice; although in
part it may harbor grimness, in part it also harbors light and good
will . . . ; nothing is so evil as not to have some good in itself so
that it can control evil." [15] " Darkness is the source from which light
arises. Without grief no joy! " [16]

The *Ungrund,* the abysmal arche of all things, is the divine will.
This will is absolutely independent, unmotivated, not impelled by
any desire. The primordial will wills nothing; as compared with all
definite things, it is itself Nothing. Boehme frequently avails himself
of the phrase that God isolated from the world " plays " with himself. He lives in a state of eternal felicity or joy. " God has not begotten the Creation in order to make himself perfect, but in order
to reveal himself for the sake of his great joy and glory; but this
joy did not only originate from the Creation, no, it was from eternity
in the *Mysterium Magnum,* but then only as a spiritual play with
itself. The Creation is this very same play as the model or tool of
the eternal spirit with which it plays; and it is therefore like a great
harmony of many a multifarious lute-playing." [17] In God is no desire.[18]

But if there is no desire in God, if God is so perfect that he does
not need anything and therefore has no purpose or end, how can
he nevertheless be Will? After all, the will must will something in
order to be a will. Boehme knows the solution of this riddle. There
is something indeed for which God longs in spite of his perfection
or rather because he is as perfect as he is. The eternal, ever-joyful
will longs for its own self-revelation, self-manifestation, or self-contemplation. As pure Will, God does not know himself, he does not
confront himself, he is not conscious of himself. In this respect God
is indeed lacking something. Being infinite he is also indefinite. The
abundance of his will is curtailed by the poverty of his knowledge;
the power of his freedom is restricted by the impotency of aware-

[15] *Ibid.,* ch. 29:11.
[16] *Ibid.,* ch. 5:7.
[17] *De signatura rerum* (On the Spiritual Figure of Things), ch. 12:2. Cf. also
Mysterium Magnum, chs. 3:6; 29:5.
[18] Cf. *De electione gratiae* (About Election by Divine Grace), ch. 1:7.

ness. Only by revealing himself to himself, by articulating himself, does the impersonal *Ungrund* become the personal author of the Creation. Although we cannot fully understand this great mystery, we at any rate feel it in our own longing for communication and contemplation. Boehme himself was very familiar with this longing, since it was the main impulse of his writing and thinking. He was so strongly moved by this impulse that he transgressed the verdict imposed upon him by the magistrate not to write and to publish. He could not keep silent, he had to speak out in order to reveal what was in him, to teach and to guide, to lead people to the light which shone so purely and so brightly in himself. Out of this overwhelming desire he expounded the nature of God.

A historic reflection may be permitted here. Aristotle thought of God as the mind which eternally contemplates itself and thereby is permanently joyful. Aristotle probably formed this portrait of God from his own self-experience, since contemplation, as he says, is the sweetest thing and since his own greatest longing was to know the full, pure, and absolute truth. God in his eyes was, as it were, the perfect philosopher who is always contemplating the absolute truth, that is: himself. Such a God was in perfect harmony with the basic Greek attitude. He was the archetype of speculation. The Protestant philosopher thought of God as Will. But as a thinker he had to account for the origin of contemplation. So he thought of the divine will as a will to reveal himself; this self-revelation is, however, impossible without ideas.

At bottom it was the problem of selfhood with which he wrestled. If God is personal, then he is a self; but the human self is finite, so how can we conceive of an infinite self? This question occupied all his thinking. He did not reflect explicitly on this problem as Kant and his successors did, but implicitly it was present in all his utterances. Infinite selfhood was the dynamic force in his thought, the motif of all his speculation. The self as a self is not only will, but will that knows itself. There must be an initial separation of the will from itself, in order to bring about this self-knowledge. " In the beginning the groundless will separated itself and fashioned itself into essence." [19] Since he found the key to the riddle within himself, he could say: " The source of the Creation of this world is much easier

[19] " Of Divine Contemplation," ch. 1:17, in Stoudt, *op. cit.*, p. 165.

to understand in the will of God by the inner man than the visible things by the outer one." " If thou willest to behold God and eternity, turn thy will around into thy inner self, then thou art like God himself, for so thou art created in the beginning and so thou livest in accordance with the inner will of God and in God." [20] Augustine and Luther said the same.

The obvious logical deficiency of Boehme's " system " is a necessary symptom of its contents. His philosophy does not have in the first place a theoretical purpose; it is religious through and through. Not truth in the sense of cosmological or theological speculation, but salvation, is the primary and chief end at which he aims. Therefore revelation, not speculation, is in the foreground of his philosophy. And thus it takes on the character of a theosophy. The redemption of the sinner is his main subject; understanding, knowledge, insight, serve this purpose. Biblical phraseology is his natural language. Knowledge and redemption are inseparable in his thought. But he is not a Gnostic who wants to redeem by means of knowledge, although sometimes he seems to approach such a belief. The redemptive aim is not coupled with knowledge as its necessary condition, but the two are bound up with each other. Boehme believes too much in the Bible ever to fall into Gnosticism. His language points to revelation as its source. Yet he does transcend the Biblical horizon by his speculation; he does " reveal " a secret not revealed by revelation. Speculation as it were sets forth God's revelation within Boehme's own mind: this at least is his own self-understanding. He tries to explain what is not explained in the Bible, but he believes that his explanation only makes explicit what is implicit there.

The book *Mysterium Magnum* is written in the form of a commentary on Genesis. And all his books refer to sayings or proverbs in Scripture. It was his intense faith which drove him into speculation and which made him a visionary. " Though my body and soul should faint and fail, yet thou, O God, art my trust and confidence; also my salvation and the comfort of my heart." [21] " When in my resolved zeal I have so hard an assault, storm, and onset upon God and upon the gates of hell, as if I had more reserves of virtue and power ready

[20] *De triplici vita hominis* (On the Threefold Life of Man), ch. 10:27.
[21] Palmer, *op. cit.*, p. 52.

— suddenly my spirit did break through the gates of hell, even into the innermost moving of the deity, and there I was embraced in love as a bridegroom embraces his dearly beloved bride." " In this light my spirit suddenly saw through all, and in, and by all the creatures. . . . In that light my will was set on by mighty impulse to describe the Being of God." [22] " The true heaven is everywhere, even in that very place where thou standest and goest." [23] " Beloved Reader, out of love to thee I will not conceal from thee what is made known to me." [24] Many similar phrases could be added to these.

What is this self which believes in God and yet feels unable to obey his commands? this self which lives in two spheres, the one of spiritual joy and peace, the other of sensual pleasure and desire? How can I understand this duplicity which tempts me to sin and which generates longing for redemption? How can I understand myself as a creature and child of a loving father and yet given over to the temptations of this world to envy and lust, enmity and strife, destruction and desolation? How can I reconcile God and Satan within myself? These riddles prompt him to speculate about the nature and origin of the human, and ultimately of the divine, self. The origin of his speculation, as well as its end, was religious.

In the self he also found the solution of all problems. A self cannot be simple. It is always twofold. The very nature of selfhood demands that I am conscious of myself. How can I be two in one and one in two? I am a self in so far as I am both the subject and the object of this self-consciousness. Being and knowledge are here inseparable. I cannot be a self without knowing myself to be a self and I cannot know myself without being a self. What a mystery! Boehme dived deeply into this abyss. He was the first thinker to formulate this riddle. Kant, Fichte, Hegel, were his successors. Of course, Boehme did not yet see clearly all the implications of this discovery. He was not an epistemological thinker, he was not even interested in metaphysics as a " science." But it is astounding how much he did see and understand. To be a self God also must know himself. To know himself he must be both subject and object of his knowledge. Therefore he cannot rest, he must work, strive, plan, create. He must go outside himself. How can I think of such a combination of rest and unrest, of sameness and duality? How can identity and dif-

[22] *Ibid.*, p. 56.   [23] *Ibid.*, p. 61.   [24] *Ibid.*, p. 171.

ference be combined in the same being? Boehme tried to penetrate this wonder. He knew that logic alone cannot help to disentangle this knot. But the self finds it in itself, for the self is its own counterpart.

The primordial, fathomless, bottomless will wills nothing — except itself![25] But to will itself, the will must be set apart from itself and contemplate itself as an object. This separation in spite of the sameness of the self opens the door that eventually leads to the duality of God and world. When the primordial will makes itself its own object, then it loses its original identity and must strive to bring it back; it loses its original freedom and must long for its recovery. This is the innermost secret of creation. The contrast between the object-will and the original subject-will engenders a strife between them in which their opposition widens, so that nature can emerge as a relatively self-dependent entity or realm. The opposition of the spiritual and the material is thereby brought about. Love and hate result. Only thus is God a living God, a willing and acting self. He is mysterious because his selfhood leads to the contrast of himself and nature.

Human desire and anxiety, tragedy and sin, are the consequences of this original duplicity. Boehme knows all these " existential " traits of human life. Indeed they impel him to seek for their ultimate cause. God and world are opposed to each other, but they are also united in God himself. Hence strife is the father of all things, as Heraclitus, his great predecessor, had said. Nature, he insists, " manifests itself through strife." " All things flee in the stillness of rest, but thereby they run only against each other."[26] The strange and bewildering clash between love and hate, joy and grief, strife and peace is the consequence of that original unity in difference, or identity in contrariety, which we meet in the selfhood of God as well as in the selfhood of man.

Out of unrest, the longing for rest comes; out of the longing for rest, unrest results. Out of the desire for peace, anxiety arises; and out of anxiety, the desire for peace. Everything at bottom fights itself. Nature is antagonistic to the free will.[27] But this very enmity

---

[25] *De electione gratiae,* ch. 1:10.
[26] *De signatura rerum,* ch. 2:4.
[27] *Ibid.,* 11.

generates the joy of triumph over nature. And thus spiritual life is born. The divine will reappears in the human will, but since man is a part of nature, selfhood turns in him into self-will, self-interest, selfishness, i.e., the root of all moral evil. This is at the same time the very root of goodness too, and goodness could never appear and defeat evil, if evil were not at its own root.

In all his books Boehme connects nature with the doctrine of the trinity. The primordial will is that of the Father, the begotten will is that of the Son, their union is that of the Spirit. The relation between the three persons is dynamic and cannot be fixed logically. It is a kind of love-strife that breaks into the creation, and this love-strife continues in all finite things and beings. It is the sameness and the discrepancy of the persons in God which re-emerges in man. Our life is as infinite as it is finite. We are all one, but we are also divided against one another. All the polarities and conflicts of human society spring from this underlying mystery. The dynamics of history is its consequence. The visible universe is the counterpart of its invisible ground. Occasionally Boehme calls the world the body of God and God its soul, thereby falling back to pre-Christian cosmotheism. "As the spirit of a man controls the whole body in all its arteries and fills the whole man, so also the Holy Spirit fills the whole nature and is the heart of nature." [28] Here one may hear Schelling speaking.

However, Boehme was not a cosmologist like Schelling or the Italian nature philosophers. While they identified God and cosmos, Boehme believed that nature is the effect of an emanation of the divine will, its self-manifestation, its outer appearance. Nature is the image of God, not God himself.[29] In a way nature with its permanent changes, its rhythm of growth and decay, corresponds to the primordial Nothingness; to that degree Boehme may be called a pantheist. But nature was to him only the outer periphery of the divine center, so that his "naturalism" itself was only the outer aspect of his inner and intrinsic spiritualism. God is not good and bad, although this contrast too can be traced back to the divine duality. But only in man does this duality develop into the moral opposites. "The bitter quality is in God too, but not as it is in man, rather as an everlasting,

---

[28] *Aurora*, ch. 2.
[29] E.g., *Mysterium Magnum*, ch. 11:33.

exalting, triumphing source of joy." [30]

God and Lucifer fight each other in order to conquer the soul of man.[31] In this gigantic war God is the victor in eternity. Through the Son who humiliates himself, God defeats the adversary and returns to heaven, i.e., to the original unity. Man lives in hell as long as he succumbs to the seductions of the tempter. Christ enables us to join the original center of love. " O men, you who believe yourselves to be wise and seek honor from each other, . . . how mad are you standing before the heavenly judge! Your own honor is a stench as compared with the all-embracing love of God, while he who seeks and respects and loves his neighbor, unites himself with the All." [32]

[30] *Aurora,* ch. 2.
[31] *De triplici vita hominis,* ch. 9:16.
[32] *Mysterium Magnum,* ch. 29:71.

IV

THE SOURCE OF CERTAINTY

THE MYSTICAL theosophy of Jacob Boehme is attractive to those who are inclined to speculation, but it is of doubtful value to those desiring certainty on which their understanding can rely. Boehme's theosophy is based upon a spiritual imagination, without which faith is indeed impossible, but which is an impure source of intellectual certainty and scientific knowledge. We now must turn to a thinker who made it his special duty to find the true source of that certainty and to base his system of thought upon that solid foundation. In the theosophy of the Protestant visionary shoemaker, revelation was predominant; in the epistemological meditations of Descartes, speculation sought a point of departure so absolutely certain that he could build a system that would withstand the most obstinate skeptic. Such an undertaking demanded a resolute and radical separation of revelation and reason, of faith and knowledge, of philosophy in the scientific sense and sacred theology. The two rivals might gain from such a divorce; religion might no longer be alienated from its true goal: the redemption of the sinful soul; and science would no longer be confused by nonscientific ends and aims. If religion is essentially personal and science essentially impersonal, their complete severance would be, after all, an advantage to both. Considerations like these influenced the origin of " scientific philosophy " in modern times.

It is clear that this whole trend was produced and favored by the mathematical foundation of modern physics. Galileo was the immediate forerunner of Descartes, Spinoza, and Leibniz. But even English empiricism was indirectly an outcome of the same rationalism that was predominant on the continent in the seventeenth century. Although mathematical physics does not need any philosophic basis to be conclusive, yet it raised some philosophic problems that cannot be answered by it. Galileo denied the possibility of penetrating the " inner substance " of things, but he did not prove this denial. Mathematical physics took for granted that the natural substances and processes that it investigates exist outside the human mind. Is this assumption justified? Can these questions be answered? And if so, where can we find the ultimate criterion for these answers? Furthermore, how do the senses and the understanding collaborate in order to bring about the results of mathematical physics? What is the ultimate relation between mind and nature? All these philosophic questions arise out of the new science, but are not answered by it.

René Descartes (1596–1650), more than thirty years younger than Galileo, felt the impact of these questions at an early age. He was still at school when he realized that the Scholastic sciences no longer satisfied the intellectual needs of the time and that a thorough revision of philosophic inquiry was imperative. In his *Discourse on Method* (1637) he tells us about his first philosophic scruples. " I found myself involved in so many doubts and errors, that I was convinced I had advanced no farther in all my attempts at learning than the discovery at every turn of my own ignorance." [1] Descartes belonged to a group of scientists, all of them disciples of Galileo; they met in Paris and discussed the new science, or they communicated by letters. Here the young thinker breathed the atmosphere in which his philosophic thoughts ripened.

DESCARTES AND MONTAIGNE

Descartes, however, was not simply impressed by the mathematical method of Galileo; his mind was also shaped by the powerful effect of Montaigne's *Essays*. In the beginning of his intellectual development the two sources blended. Besides Montaigne, other authors who had similar feelings aroused his doubts concerning the possibility of achieving objective knowledge in philosophic matters; e.g., such skeptics as Pierre Charron (1541–1603), whose book *Traité de la Sagesse* (On Wisdom) denied any theoretical doctrine about

[1] *The Method, Meditations, and Philosophy of Descartes,* tr. by John Veitch (Tudor Publishing Company, n.d.), p. 151.

ultimate problems and pointed to that self-examination which the moral consciousness demands, and Francisco Sánchez (1562–1632), who claimed complete ignorance in the field of metaphysical riddles. But Montaigne was the most impressive among them and the most original because he replaced metaphysical knowledge by his " existential " self-contemplation, and because of his conviction that in the realm of life only the individual, with his own inclinations and opinions, can give us certainty. Descartes, although he did not mention Montaigne, was evidently deeply influenced by him.

In the *Discourse on Method* two strikingly different conceptions of method vie with each other, the one following Montaigne's *Essays,* the other mathematical physics. Descartes did not notice the divergence of these two conceptions. He speaks as if only one method had been discovered. And yet, the two ideals of knowledge are worlds apart: the one exhibits the autonomy of the individual person, the other, that of mathematical reason; the one considers what is peculiar to Descartes himself, the other, what is universally true and demonstrable, binding every rational being. Montaigne and Galileo clash within the mind of Descartes. Of course, there is a kind of equation between them, in so far as Descartes's *personal* ideal was that of the *mathematical* method.

Montaigne's autobiographical self-portrait is the pattern and model of a sentence like this: " My present design is not to teach the method which each ought to follow for the right conduct of his reason, but solely to describe the way in which I have endeavored to conduct my own. . . . This tract is put forth merely as history, or, if you will, as a tale, in which, amid some examples worthy of imitation, there will be found perhaps as many more which it were advisable not to follow." [2] Here Descartes almost literally repeats what Montaigne says about his method. [3] The whole *Discourse* has an autobiographical character; " method " in this sense signifies the " way " by which he arrived at his position. It is Montaigne speaking when he writes: " I was aware that the grace of fable stirs the mind, that the memorable deeds of history elevate it." Or: " I entirely abandoned the study of letters and resolved no longer to seek any other science than the knowledge of myself, or of the Great Book of the world . . . making such reflection on the matter of my ex-

---

[2] *Ibid.,* p. 150.   [3] " I do not teach, I tell."

perience as to secure my improvement." [4] Or: " I at length resolved to make myself an object of study and to employ all the powers of my mind in choosing the paths I ought to follow, an undertaking which was accompanied with greater success than it would have been, had I never quitted my country or my books." [5] Like Montaigne he goes on to reflect upon the historical condition of all individuality: " I was thus led to infer that the ground of our opinions is far more custom and example than any certain knowledge. . . . Thus I found myself constrained, as it were, to use my own reason in the conduct of my life." [6]

This autobiographical touch in Descartes's most famous writings contributes to the persuasive charm that distinguishes them and makes them appear popular although they deal with the most profound and difficult problems of metaphysics. Descartes himself advises the reader to read his *Meditations* first " as he would a romance." [7] This combination of an " existential " and a " rational " approach is the more remarkable since the rational ideal of Descartes was mathematical — far removed from existential thought.

At the end of the *Discourse* the mathematical ideal prevails. Although Descartes was a skillful narrator, and although this trait gives his writing an individual character, he was, in the first place, a scientist who pursued the goal of an exact method that demonstrates the truth of his views. He was the discoverer of analytical geometry which transformed geometrical relations into numerical ones; he also wrote original contributions to optics and other physical sciences. Not " his own reason " but demonstrable reasons were the principles which his method established as the highest criterion; not the " conduct of his life " but the search for scientific truth was the real end of that method. The original title of the *Discourse* shows, however, the duplicity of Descartes's aim: " Project of a universal science which may elevate our nature to the highest degree of perfection." But the highest degree of perfection which Descartes desired did not properly concern human nature; it concerned the method by which the phenomena of physical nature can be

[4] Veitch, *op. cit.*, p. 154.
[5] *Ibid.*, p. 155.
[6] *Ibid.*, p. 159.
[7] In the Preface to *The Principles of Philosophy*.

accurately known. It is true that Descartes hoped that this method would also lead to absolute certainty in the field of metaphysics. This becomes apparent when he says: " I was especially delighted with the mathematics on account of the certitude and evidence of their reasonings." [8] Here he believed he had discovered the ultimate source of certainty.

From now on he was intent on finding the hidden truth of speculation by the same method. Philosophy must be rigorously separated from revelation and theology. Theology admits the " impotency of reason, the need for a special help from heaven," he says half ironically.[9] Philosophic speculation, on the contrary, should rely exclusively on demonstration of the kind Euclid offered in his geometry. In order to prepare such a foundation for the most obscure and the least secure of all sciences, Descartes contrived a new point of departure which would be absolutely certain. " I began to conceive the fundamental principle of a marvelous design," he wrote in his diary on November 10, 1619, pointing to the plan of his *Meditations*. This newly gained self-confidence merged his individual and universal reason. " I have never contemplated anything higher than the reformation of my own opinions, and basing these on a foundation wholly my own." [10] Here Montaigne comes once more to the fore. But what was the result of this personal reformation? It was the creation of a foundation that he regarded not at all as merely his own, but as universally certain. As an example of the new method, he annexed to the *Discourse* various treatises dealing with problems of mathematical physics and geometry.

Whereas Montaigne made himself the theme of his book, Descartes wanted to demonstrate propositions about physical processes as sure as those of Euclid's geometry. Galileo seemed to triumph over Montaigne. " In conclusion . . . this only I will say, that I have resolved to devote what time I may still have to live to no other occupation than that of endeavoring to acquire some knowledge of nature." [11] But this statement was as one-sided as the " existential " utterances. Descartes was not simply a scientist like Galileo, nor was he an individualistic writer like Montaigne. He was both a philosopher and a scientist and the uneven content of the *Discourse* dis-

[8] Veitch, *op. cit.*, p. 153.
[9] *Ibid.*, p. 154.
[10] *Ibid.*, p. 158.
[11] *Ibid.*, p. 203.

closes this double character of its author. In Part IV of his book Descartes develops some reflections that foreshadow the discussion of the *Meditations*.

DOUBT AND CERTAINTY

The full title of this book is: *Meditations on the First Philosophy in Which the Existence of God and the Real Distinction of Mind and Body Are Demonstrated*.[12] This title shows the ambitious end which Descartes, in contrast to both Montaigne and Galileo, pursued. It was the old but never satisfying science of speculative metaphysics which Descartes wanted to re-establish on a new basis. As Galileo had reformed physics, so Descartes thought that now the moment had arrived in which metaphysics could be based on an equally firm method.

Descartes begins in a style reminiscent of Montaigne. " Once in life I should radically overthrow all opinions and I should make an absolutely new beginning, in order to establish something permanent in the sciences." These lines are both a personal confession of a serious intention and an assurance that the author is going to demonstrate something valid for all who have a scientific mind. The first meditation is peculiarly fascinating; the reader is permitted to be present at a most dramatic scene: Descartes is sitting in his winter coat, during a campaign in Germany, brooding about the deepest questions, while warming himself at the fireplace. The dramatic effect is that the reader can understand Descartes's considerations, as though the reasons Descartes offers for the course of his argument were the reader's own. This " existential " method makes the reader believe that there is no difference between Descartes and any other person reasoning with him, and that therefore the conclusions drawn are not of individual, but of universal, validity. Descartes thus combines the mood of Montaigne with the certainty and demonstration of Galileo and that in a field where argument and demonstration is of the uttermost importance for every thinking being. The " I " of Descartes assumes a universal connotation and turns into the " I " of every reader — into the " I " of reason itself. In this " I," Descartes finds the ultimate source of certainty. Aesthetic empathy and metaphysical reason are joined together.

[12] The first (Latin) edition was published in 1641.

If all theories of the past are rejected, what remains? Nothing but doubt. But Descartes is not a skeptic. He doubts, not for the sake of doubt, but for the sake of certainty. If I start from doubt and do not allow any opinion to stay in my mind, I am at least protected against false or illusory assumptions. But how can I proceed to true and irrefutable statements? Can we imitate the method of physics in the realm of metaphysics? One thing seems evident: we cannot apply the method of Galileo in order to prove the existence of God.[13] Descartes proceeds from doubt to the certainty of his own existence. No fact of the outer world can give me the certainty I need; I cannot even know whether or not such facts exist in the outer world or in my own consciousness alone. Was Descartes in earnest when he doubted the existence of the outer world? Did not his whole report on the situation in which he composed his book show that he did not doubt this existence? And how can anyone in his senses doubt whether the world in which he exists itself exists? But such objections miss the mark.

Descartes sought a foundation that could be made the basis for further metaphysical reflections. He sought a principle that would enable him to determine the kind of existence that might be ascribed to the physical world. Since Galileo had declared that physics does not penetrate metaphysical substance, Descartes could not use it for his purpose. Moreover, the time was not far off when British philosophers were to doubt whether external objects corespond to our impressions and ideas. Hume denied that we can know anything certain of their existence. Descartes was thus obliged to inquire into the certainty of something less open to question. His fundamental doubt was the means of distinguishing the existence of the " I " from that of the external world. It was a methodical and productive doubt.

Another reason was even more urgent. Modern physics sprang from doubt about the reliability of sense perception. The Aristotelian physics and the Ptolemaic system were based on the observation of the senses. Both had been destroyed because the modern scientist

[13] Descartes, however, did try to fashion his proof of God in a geometrical way, thus anticipating Spinoza, in his " Reply " to the " Objections " which he had asked for from his friends, and which he attached to the *Meditations*. Cf. Veitch, *op. cit.*, pp. 363–371.

distrusted the evidence of this source. But if the objects of outer perception do not exist as they appear, how can he who seeks for the source of certainty take their existence for granted? Descartes had to find something that was not exposed to such doubt. Where could he find it? Where else than in that very " I " which doubted? Here indeed was the most certain principle. Descartes discovered the secret presupposition of all modern philosophy: the self-assurance of the thinking ego. World and God, the principles taken for granted by the cosmological and the theological age of speculation, may be doubted; but I cannot doubt that I who doubt exist. Here we have reached the frontier of all reasonable doubt, something that carries the certainty of its existence within itself. Here is the Archimedean point from which I can proceed with absolute certainty.

The principle at which Descartes arrived was already stated by Augustine, and a comparison of the two thinkers might be instructive. Augustine too had argued that he who doubts can be sure that he exists. Augustine too had confronted the outer world and the inner self. The outer world seemed to him less certain than the soul. He too had contrasted world and soul in order to turn to the soul alone. And yet the two thinkers are worlds apart. Augustine was interested in the soul as the place where God reveals himself. God, not the soul, was his real source of certainty. And the soul was not the thinking ego of Descartes, not that understanding which was able to know the outer world by means of mathematical analysis. Augustine turned inward because he was religious; Descartes turned to the *Cogito* because he took it as the source of rational certainty. The philosophy of Augustine was theocentric, that of Descartes was autonomous in the sense of mathematical reason. Augustine was the founder of medieval theology; Descartes, the founder of modern epistemology.

Descartes doubts the existence of the outer world. But what about the certainty of mathematics? " Arithmetic, geometry, and the other sciences of the same class, which . . . scarcely inquire whether or not the objects themselves exist, contain somewhat that is certain and indubitable." [14] Mathematics implies that geometrical figures exist not only in my mind but also outside. Is this implication justified? Mathematics cannot answer that question. And yet the meaning

[14] Veitch, *op. cit.,* p. 222.

of mathematical physics depends upon the application of geometry to the outer world. It is therefore necessary to pursue an epistemological inquiry in order to clarify this obscure point. From here Descartes directs his attention to God, although at first only in a disguised form. He asks whether we can trust our belief that geometrical figures have an objective reality or whether a " demon " may be deceiving us. Only if I can be sure that such a " malignant demon " does not exist, can I rely upon my assumption.

In the last analysis the quest for certainty issues in the quest for God. As long as I suspect that a deceiving spirit might be responsible for my belief in the objective validity of geometry and arithmetic, I cannot proceed beyond the initial certainty which I have found in the thinking ego. I can reach the desired certainty only by proving the existence of God. In this way Descartes resumes the tradition of Christian philosophy which was still alive in him, in spite of his universal doubt and in spite of his resolution to make an absolutely new beginning. However, the tradition is transformed by him, since his ultimate purpose concerns the scientific truth which he wishes to find. Not theology, but epistemology is the final end of his inquiry. Nevertheless, it remains important that Descartes believes he cannot reach that end without appealing to a veracious God. But before he proves the existence of such a God, he puts the question: Who am I? Who is the man who doubts and who thinks?

Who Am I?

Cogito ergo sum — I think and so I am certain that I am. " But I do not yet know what I am." [15] Before the inquiry begins, Descartes believes that he is a being composed of body and soul. He refers here to the Aristotelian doctrine, but he rejects it. The existence of a body is not any more probable than the existence of the outer world; the distinction of body and soul is based on the cosmological outlook according to which the world is the most certain principle and I belong to the world. The Aristotelian doctrine treats the person as it treats other " substances." My soul is then conceived in the same manner as the forms of other things; indeed, it is only a special " form " which is characteristic of man. Descartes is too much a Christian to accept this theory. I am not a special substantial form;

[15] *Ibid.,* p. 226.

I am, rather, a thinking being and only as such am I in contrast to the whole world of substances and forms. Only thus I am a self and know myself to be myself.

I am truly myself inasmuch as I am a thinking being. " Here I discover what properly belongs to myself. This alone is inseparable from me. I am as often as I think. . . . I am therefore, precisely speaking, only a thinking thing (*res cogitans*), that is, a mind or a soul (*mens sive animus*), understanding or reason, terms whose signification was before unknown to me." [16] What is completely new in this definition is the emphasis laid upon the self as not belonging to the world, in so far as I think of the world and thereby of myself as the subject of thinking, whereas the physical things (including the body) are objects of my thinking. The Christian inwardness is here interpreted as the unique position of the thinking subject in contrast to the objects thought. No thinker before Descartes brought the principle of modern philosophy, its epistemological subjectivism, so emphatically and definitely to light. In that respect he was the true initiator of philosophy in the modern world.

Descartes was, however, also influenced by the Renaissance. Although he radically and resolutely conceived of the thinking ego in noncosmological terms, his ultimate purpose was to comprehend the world. Before he published the *Discourse on Method* and the *Meditations,* he had begun to write a book that was supposed to have the title *Le Monde* (The World); but it remained a fragment and was not published until fourteen years after his death. Even in the *Meditations* themselves he was not quite sure whether his epistemological definition of the self as the thinking ego excluded cosmology or whether it only re-established a new cosmology which would conceive of the self as a " thinking thing," in contrast to the extended things of nature. Eventually he did fall back on such a cosmology, as we shall see. Descartes was not so much intent on confronting the self and the world as on contrasting two kinds of substances, thinking substance and extended substance. This distinction spoils the *Cogito ergo sum* principle. In the *Meditations* the epistemological problem stands in the foreground; but it is not completely victorious because the cosmological concern remained powerful. The idea of the thinking self is only instrumental to this ultimate

[16] *Ibid., p.* 227.

aim. It serves to distinguish two classes of substances in the universe as much as it secures the validity of scientific thinking. These two aspects are not clearly distinguished from each other and this lack of clarity finally weakens the discovery of the thinking self as the principle of certainty.

IDEAS AND GOD

The first step toward the stabilization of scientific objectivity is the distinction of the intellect in contrast to sensation and imagination. The core of thinking is to abstract from the content of sense perception and to abstain from imagination which copies that content in my mind. Thinking in the true sense is pure, i.e., it is neither sensuous nor imaginative, but instead solely rational or intellectual. Only when the mind produces " clear and distinct ideas " does it think properly. The concept of the thinking ego itself was made clear in the distinct idea of the *Cogito,* in contrast to everything that might become the object of thought. Through the elimination of sensation and imagination, this idea becomes even more clear and distinct. I can therefore conclude that the supreme methodical criterion of truth is this clearness and distinctness of my ideas.[17]

But ideas as such are not true or false; only judgments are. Some ideas are taken from the outer world, and some are innate to my mind, i.e., the idea of myself, of God, and of mathematical entities. If I judge that the outer world exists as I perceive it, I might be mistaken. The ideas of the outer objects may not correspond to those objects; they may be impressed upon my mind by an unknown power of my mind itself. But what about the idea of God? This also seems to point to a being that exists outside my mind; am I right in concluding that God really exists the way I conceive of him? This idea does not spring from sensation or imagination; it has no sensuous features. According to my idea, God is perfect. A perfect being cannot be perceived, and it also transcends the power of my imagination. Although I find it in my mind, it nevertheless cannot be produced by my mind. How could I, a finite being, liable to error and deception, produce the idea of a being that is absolutely exempt from all error and deception and therefore infinite? This idea can be originated only by God himself. He alone is able to impress upon

[17] Cf. *ibid.,* p. 234.

the finite mind of man an idea that corresponds to his infinity. " The whole force of the argument of which I have here availed myself to establish the existence of God consists in this, that I perceive I could not possibly be of such a nature as I am, and yet have in my mind the idea of God, if God did not in reality exist." [18] In other words: the finite mind depends upon the infinite mind, not the reverse.

What does the argument of Descartes imply? In a way, it reminds us of the ontological proof as given by Anselm. And yet there is a considerable difference between the two. Descartes derives his conclusion from the comparison of the human and the divine mind, not merely from the idea of God, as does Anselm. Descartes's proof is not ontological, but epistemological. Its real nature can be traced back to the original point of departure. The source of certainty was found by Descartes in the thinking ego. But this thinking ego started from doubt; it was in the beginning a doubting ego. Subject to error and illusion as it is, it was bound to doubt. We can therefore call it finite. A finite mind is a mind that can err. Although thinking is a power, it is nevertheless a limited power in a being whose thought might be false. But this is our true situation. We can find the source of certainty in our capacity to think and thereby to find the absolute truth; but as we are, we do not yet possess this truth, but are only striving for it. God guarantees, as it were, that such striving is meaningful. It is meaningful only if we can be sure that there is a reality which corresponds to the idea of absolute truth, or that this idea is not merely a phantom of our imagination. God is the guarantor of this reality. If he were not real, then our whole cognitive enterprise would be in vain. In this sense the reality of God is assured by our own reality, in so far as our argument is rooted in our existence as thinking beings. But objectively our own reality as thinking beings is possible only if God, as the guarantor of the meaning of thinking, himself exists. Finite thinking demands as its own presupposition infinite thinking, which itself does not need any guarantor, because it is the standard and measure of the degree to which we arrive at the truth.

I could not think of error, I could not even have doubted without the idea of an infinite mind that alone gives meaning to the idea of

[18] *Ibid.,* p. 248.

error, and thereby to the act of doubting. Descartes demonstrates the existence of God in this way from the existence of the doubting human mind. The will to know, the longing for truth, the faith that we can approach the truth by the effort of thinking, all this is possible only if God — who ultimately is the truth — exists. Instead of an ontological proof, Descartes offers a modern proof of God based upon the self-assurance of man as the subject that thinks and wishes to know. He does not begin from God, but from man; but he recognizes that man could not be man if God did not exist. Man could not pursue the goal of knowledge with confidence and certainty without trusting the objective reality which alone can ultimately justify his subjective endeavor. We may say that Descartes in this proof establishes a cognitive faith in God. We may also — using a Kantian term — say that faith according to the Cartesian doctrine is a "postulate" of the thinking intellect. This intellect loses all its function and even its meaning if God, as defined by Descartes, does not exist. The proof given in the third meditation is modified in the fifth. There it is assimilated to the ontological argument which shows that Descartes still felt the weight of Christian philosophy, although he abandoned, as indeed all modern thinkers did, the natural theology of Aquinas, with its cosmological proofs.

"Existence" as conceived in the *Meditations* is essentially cognitive; it is the existence of the knowing mind, finite or infinite. The *Cogito ergo sum* does assure not the existence of the individual person but that of the universal reason or intellect. As the existence of Descartes was in the main an intellectual existence, the existence of a scientist and a thinker who wants to guarantee the validity of scientific research and theory, so his whole argument is derived from this intellectual existence; his God is an intellectual God, a scientist God. I exist in the true sense, only inasmuch as I am able to reach the truth. Since I am always erring, I can never fully exist. God alone in this sense really and fully exists because he stands for the full and errorless truth.

Error is the outcome of impressions which deceive me. I must get rid of the impressions and the products of imagination in order to arrive at knowledge. Only to the degree to which I succeed, do I truly exist. Man can never absolutely overcome error and illusion. Descartes's argument from the *Cogito* is finally an argument for the existence of God: *Cogito ergo Deus est.* Descartes uses a religious metaphor in vindicating the ontological priority of God's existence. " In truth, it is not to be wondered at that God, at my creation, implanted this idea [of God] in me, that it might serve, as it were, for the mark of the workman impressed on his work." It is therefore " highly probable that God in some way fashioned me after his own image and likeness, and that I perceive this likeness in which is contained the idea of God, by the same faculty by which I apprehend myself; when I make myself the object of reflection, I not only find that I am an incomplete and dependent being, and one who unceasingly aspires after something better and greater than he is; but at the same time, I am assured likewise that he upon whom I am dependent, possesses in himself all the goods after which I aspire, and that not merely indefinitely and potentially, but infinitely and actually, and that he is thus God." [19] The Christian faith in that way becomes the faith of an autonomous scientist.

Descartes himself takes notice of this correspondence. " Just as we learn by faith that the supreme felicity of another life consists in the contemplation of the divine majesty alone, so even now we learn from experience that a like meditation, though incomparably less perfect, is the source of the highest satisfaction of which we are susceptible in this life." [20] Evidently Descartes was aware of the quasi-religious significance of his proof of God. His speculative approach to God, although not based on revelation, nevertheless does not contradict revelation but transforms it so that it can be accepted by the " scientific " philosopher. This speculative transformation leads to a contemplation of God which we can enjoy " in this life " and which is in harmony (as Descartes thinks) with the accuracy and logical exactitude of mathematics, but it enlarges the horizon of mathematics in the direction of the content of religious faith.

ERROR AND WILL

Although the approach of Descartes to the majesty of God is dictated and demonstrated by the thinking intellect, he also gives the will an important function in the fabric of knowledge. The epistemology of Descartes is not only a theory of knowledge, it is also a theory of error. Since Descartes begins his whole reflection

---

[19] *Ibid.*   [20] *Ibid.*, p. 249.

with an insight into the errors of the past, such a theory is not unexpected. Even the proof of God rests on the fact that man is an erring being and that he can never totally subdue error. In the fourth meditation Descartes turns to finite thinking and knowing. If we were immune from error, we would not need science or a theory of knowledge. As it is, we need not only a theory of knowledge but also a theory of error. Error is a kind of deception, and the first occasion for Descartes to prove the existence of God was the fear that a demon might deceive us. Now we no longer fear that all our knowledge is contaminated by deception because we have seen that it is not a demon but God, who stands for truth, who guides us and guarantees that we at least are able to approximate the truth. God cannot be a deceiver, since " all fraud and deception spring from some defect." [21] God is perfect. But what about the ideas which seem to come from an outer world? Can we now trust them too? No. The thinking ego has another relation to the ideas of external objects. Nevertheless, my belief in the existence of these objects cannot be entirely untrue. If I think accurately, if I proceed carefully with respect to the knowledge of these objects, it should be possible to arrive at truth too. " I possess a certain faculty of judging which I doubtless received from God, along with whatever else is mine; and since it is impossible that he should will to deceive me, it is likewise certain that he has not given me a faculty that will ever lead me into error, provided I use it aright." [22]

God helps me only if I help myself; and to a certain degree I have the ability to protect myself against erroneous arguments or conclusions. Knowledge is not only an intellectual achievement, it is also an achievement of the controlling power which warns me not to accept any thesis that is not examined and corroborated by my methodical principles. This power is the will, collaborating with the intellect in the achievement of knowledge. Here Descartes again is heir to Christian philosophy. It is true that the Stoics had a similar theory; they taught that we can suspend our judgment when we are not absolutely certain about its correctness. But only Christianity strengthened the element of will in the organization of the human personality so much that Descartes was able to connect his theory of error with his epistemological proof of God. The acceptance or re-

[21] *Ibid.*   [22] *Ibid.*, p. 250.

jection of theoretical statements is an act of the will, whereas the connection of subject and predicate as such is an act of the intellect. Both support each other in the cognitive act by which we accomplish the task of scientific knowledge. Intellectual assiduity must be accompanied by an intellectual conscience, if our labor can be crowned with success. Descartes knew this well since he himself had assiduously labored in order to find out optical and meteorological theories. Only the conscientious scientist can advance learning and enrich knowledge. Conscience, however, is not the function of the intellect as such, but of the will. Error is a kind of moral defect as well as of intellectual ignorance.

It is within the domain of my will not to err. I can refuse to affirm a theoretical predication. " Judgment " is always both a predication and an affirmation or negation. I can at any time withhold my approbation from an assertion that lacks accuracy. I should approve of it only if my conscience permits it. If I follow this advice, error can be avoided. Disciplining the will that works within the intellect is a condition for reaching the truth in physics as well as in metaphysics. To err implies at bottom lack of such discipline. Guilt is not ultimately error, as the classical theory said; rather, error is a kind of guilt.

Error springs from the concurrence of two factors: cognition and free choice. Cognition may be limited, for we are ignorant, but it is as such not responsible for error. Man's will is free to acknowledge the limitation of theoretical cognition instead of falling into error. Error is my fault, not the fault of my restricted knowledge. I am not forced to affirm or deny a theoretical thesis; I can suspend my judgment. This is the highest privilege of my selfhood which makes the ego the source of certainty. Doubt not only implies the absence of knowledge, it also implies the presence of wisdom. Although I am not omniscient, as God is, I can at least preserve my integrity by applying my freedom of judgment. " It is the faculty of will only or freedom of choice, which I experience to be so great that I am unable to conceive the idea of another more ample and extended; so that it is chiefly my will which leads me to discern that I bear a certain image and similitude of deity." [23] Not God, but I am the author of error as I am the author of sin. God has created me in such a

[23] *Ibid.*, p. 253.

way as to permit me to keep my intellectual innocence. "Whence, then, spring my errors? They arise from this cause alone, that I do not restrain the will which is of much wider range than the understanding, within the same limits, but extend it even to things I do not understand." The will "falls into error and sin by choosing the false instead of the true, and evil instead of good." [24] The epistemology of error thus results in an ethics of knowledge. Speculation joins revelation.

Intellectual failure and moral failure have the same source; indeed, intellectual mistakes are ultimately considered moral mistakes. God has created me so that I am able to keep my knowledge within the boundaries of my insight; therefore, "I have to thank the goodness of him who bestowed [this ability] upon me." [25] Since it is of higher value to avoid error than to grasp what transcends the horizon of my intellect, the insight that philosophy grants is of tremendous weight. "I deem that I have not gained little by this day's meditation in having discovered the source of error and falsity, since it is in being superior to error that the highest and chief perfection of man consists." [26] And with a new courage and a new confidence he goes on to explore the metaphysical problem which is still unsolved concerning the relation between man's intellect and the material world which physics investigates.

NATURE AND GOD

The scheme of the *Meditations* can now be seen in its entirety. Descartes is seeking the source of certainty. He discovers this source in the self-certainty of the thinking mind, proceeds from there to the certainty that he finds in the existence of God, then inquires into the source of error, and finally ends by discussing the source of the certainty of external knowledge. This is the final goal of the *Meditations*. Is knowledge of the outer world possible and how? Descartes wishes to protect mathematical physics from the snare of skepticism laid by men like Charron and Sánchez and later by David Hume. If it is false that outer things exist, i.e., that things exist outside the human mind, physics also cannot be true. The methodical doubt, from which Descartes began, concerned precisely this point. Since the senses err and since sense qualities do not per-

---

[24] *Ibid.*, p. 254.   [25] *Ibid.*, p. 256.   [26] *Ibid.*, p. 257.

mit objective knowledge, how can we be sure that things with those qualities exist outside the sense impressions? The British school took it for granted that such a certainty cannot be gained; it assumed, rather, that the objects we perceive are in reality our impressions and therefore not outside, but inside, the mind. If such a doctrine is called "idealism," then Descartes was not at all an idealist, but a realist (in the modern, i.e., non-Platonic sense of this term).

Mathematical physics is true only if the mathematical statements concerning the outer world are true, or if it is legitimate to apply geometrical and arithmetical symbols to the quantitative relations between physical entities. If the power that controls and transcends our intellect is not a deceiving demon, but a veracious and perfect God, then we can trust our intellectual judgments if they are evinced after conscientious examination. The sensuous qualities may belong to my own sensation and imagination, but the mathematical, numerical determinants are not subject to such doubt. The certainty of God is thus the mediator between the certainty of myself and the certainty of physical or scientific knowledge. Since I am allowed to trust God, the guarantor of conscientious knowledge, I must no longer doubt that the mathematical order extends to an objective world, that, in other words, this world has not only a physical, but also a metaphysical, reality.

Descartes establishes in this way a rational faith in the existence of things and relations as demonstrated by science. Science has a kind of metaphysical significance. It gives us a true picture of "the things-in-themselves," as Kant later called this metaphysical reality. But whereas Kant (like Galileo) denied a knowledge of such a metaphysical reality, Descartes believed he could establish it by means of his *Meditations*. This rational faith of Descartes has an epistemological and ethical basis. But Descartes also tends to renovate a cosmological metaphysics. On the one hand, he goes back to the ontological argument of Anselm, while on the other, he eventually falls victim to the restoration of cosmology by abandoning the deep insight of the first *Meditations*.

As we have seen, Descartes was inclined from the beginning to mistake the epistemological distinction between the thinking ego and the outer objects for a cosmological distinction between two contrary groups of substances existing in the world. The temptation to rebuild metaphysics by means of the new physics was very great indeed; it proved too strong for Descartes. After establishing the certainty that the mathematics of nature grants objective validity, Descartes does not doubt that this validity has metaphysical significance, that things exist absolutely as extended substances or mathematical entities. In *The Principles of Philosophy* he says: "The nature of body consists not in weight, hardness, color, and the like but in extension alone." [27] It is ironic that, although Galileo did not pretend to be a philosopher, he was much more critical than Descartes. The latter thought it possible to avoid error, and even regarded error as a moral deficiency. Yet it was Galileo who realized that physics does not penetrate into the inner essence of things, whereas Descartes held that the material objects perceived by the senses are from the standpoint of philosophy merely extended things.

The consequence of this fateful error is the further metaphysical doctrine that both extended and thinking things are metaphysical substances. This was indeed, as William Temple calls it, the Cartesian *faux pas*. The epistemological significance of the thinking I, the *Cogito,* was thereby sacrificed. The modern anthropocentric position was abandoned; instead, the pre-Christian cosmocentric principle was revived. Spinoza and Leibniz followed Descartes's lead. Renaissance naturalism marred thus the foundation of modern epistemology. The terms mind, intellect, reason, even self or ego were now understood as parallels to extension, as if they lay on the same plane. The superiority and primacy of the thinking subject in contrast to the objects thought was surrendered. The ego is here no longer what it was in the *Meditations;* rather, it is an objective entity that has to be investigated by a metaphysical psychology, as extended things are investigated by a quasi-metaphysical physics. The reflections on truth and error no longer have a logical and ethical meaning; they are merely psychological observations, although with cosmological implications. Certainty itself is no longer the principle that it was in the *Meditations;* it is a mere psychological datum. Of course, Descartes does not draw all these conclusions. He simply turns from epistemological and ethical theory to a bad cosmology.

[27] Parts II, IV. Cf. also Parts X ff.

Out of this mistake the tortuous debates concerning the " psycho-physical " causality subsequently developed. They first arose in the so-called school of the Occasionalists, disciples of Descartes who sought to explain why certain physiological activities arise together with or at the " occasion " of psychical actions. From the same mis-understanding Spinoza's " parallelism " between extension and thought sprang. The idea of God was now used to solve these " meta-physical " problems, which in fact were not metaphysical at all but grew out of false presuppositions. Mind and matter now seemed to be genuine metaphysical polarities because the true function of mind was forgotten. Kant alone was to clarify these misunderstand-ings and to dissolve the falsity of metaphysical solutions.

The idea of God that had played an epistemological and ethical part in the *Meditations* lost this function and was perverted into that reality which brings about the relation between the extended and thinking things. But such a perversion brought the idea of God into a distorted rivalry with nature. Does not nature comprise both kinds of entities? Nature now took on the meaning of the ancient cosmos, but at the same time it retained that of the object of the " natural " sciences. Thus it came about that God and nature seemed to be identical, as they really became identical in the system of Spinoza. The origin of the idea of God in revelation which was still evident in Descartes's reflections seemed thereby obscured, if not entirely denied. Pre-Christian speculation once more took the place of revelation. Descartes himself had already gone far in the wrong direction. The step from the first to the last Meditation in-dicates this deplorable transformation. Even more so does the step from the *Meditations* to *The Principles of Philosophy* (1644). Al-though the first part of this systematic treatise repeats the tenets held in the *Meditations,* paragraph VIII outlines the shift which we have noticed. Whereas Descartes in paragraph VII still says " that we cannot doubt of our existence while we doubt, and that this is the first knowledge we acquire when we philosophize in order," [28] the next paragraph goes on to distinguish " the mind and the body " or " a thinking and a corporeal thing." In paragraph XXV Descartes states " that we must believe all that God has revealed, although it may surpass the reach of our faculties," e.g., " the mysteries of the

[28] Veitch, *op. cit.,* p. 303.

incarnation and the trinity." [29] It is not impossible that Descartes added this admonition in order to avoid the criticism of his ecclesiastical enemies, but we have no definite basis for suspecting his sincerity. However, in the following paragraph Descartes ponders the infinity of God, as if it were identical with the infinity of extension, although he attempts to distinguish the two kinds of infinity by calling the second indefinite. In paragraph XXVIII he turns resolutely away from ancient cosmology by emphasizing that the natural light of our intellect cannot share the purposes of God's will and that it therefore " should examine, not the final, but the efficient causes of created things." [30] But in this context he avails himself of the dangerous phrase " God or nature," thereby making the whole discussion ambiguous.

From paragraph LI on, Descartes philosophizes about substances and distinguishes the finite from the infinite, so that even God becomes a kind of thing. If substance — his remarks foreshadow the system of Spinoza — " means, as it does in the precise sense, a thing that exists in such a way as to stand in need of nothing beyond itself," then God alone is substance.[31] He applies the term, nevertheless, to finite substances also because " they stand in need of nothing but the concourse of God." In paragraph LIII he calls both thinking and extension attributes of finite substances; God has thinking as his only attribute (in contrast to Spinoza's doctrine). But soon afterward (in paragraph LVI) he speaks of God's " attributes." It is evident from these passages that Descartes never fully understood the distinction between substance and subject, thing and self, neither with respect to man, nor with respect to God. The tendency toward such a distinction, which was observable in the *Meditations,* is abandoned in the *Principles.*

CONCLUSION

Two opposing motives are at work in Descartes's speculation: the one originating in Montaigne, the other in Galileo; the one existential, the other scientific. They are never reconciled to each other. In his epistemology Descartes tries to unite them, but he is not quite successful because the idea of the individual ego is swallowed up by that of mathematical reason. The desire to justify the validity of

[29] *Ibid.,* p. 310.   [30] *Ibid.,* p. 311.   [31] *Ibid.,* p. 320.

science is stronger than the wish to understand the self, as the center of the person. The *Meditations* go far in the direction of self-knowledge by making the free will responsible for error and by underlining rational faith in God as the supreme condition of finding truth. But this stress on the self is ultimately of no avail when Descartes moves in the direction of an all-embracing " scientific " metaphysical and cosmological system. In this system, which was never completed, mathematical physics is in the ascendancy.

The inner break and the critical defect in Descartes's position already mars his supreme principle. When he makes the statement: " I think, therefore I am," he does not clarify the meaning of that " I." Is it the individual person — is it Descartes himself — or is it that general intellect which reasons about itself and about God? Who is it that according to the supreme thesis does exist? The general intellect, after all, does not " exist "; this intellect is not a personal self. In the strict sense it is not the general intellect but only the individual person that is entitled to say: I exist. In his treatise on *The Passions of the Soul,* Descartes acknowledges that only the individual is the existing person. But if the *Cogito* points to the individual, then existence is not demonstrable! The existence of the person is more than the existence of the thinking subject; the individual exists in a fuller sense than the general; he is not merely a thinking subject but also an ego moved by desire and passion, by feeling and willing. Pascal realized this defect in Descartes; thought, therefore, became existential in a deeper sense.

It is true that Descartes did point to the will and included the will in the thinking ego. But what he calls " will " in the *Meditations* is a somewhat intellectualized will; it is the will to truth, although this will can fail in a quasi-moral sense when it falls into error. It is the will working within the intellect, not the individual, personal, concrete will of the existing man. The same ambiguity obscures the proof of God. Descartes identifies the general thinking mind with that intellect which is the thinking subject in mathematics and mathematical physics. But is the certainty of God really the same as the certainty in geometry and arithmetic? Is the reason that reasons in an epistemological and metaphysical context really the same as mathematical reason? To assume that it is, was the initial fault of all metaphysics built upon the sciences, whether that of Descartes,

Spinoza, or Leibniz. Only Kant saw through that self-deception. The source of certainty in speculation is not the same as that in mathematics. Scientific truth is not the same as truth in epistemology and ethics.

The existence of myself as a person cannot be demonstrated in that quasi-mathematical fashion in which Descartes wanted to demonstrate it. " Existence " in the sense of Kierkegaard is beyond the reach of any scientific demonstrability. It is the very contrast to everything that is known by physics or by metaphysics. Descartes did not yet realize that existence in that sense has any special significance. His real concern was not the proof that I exist, but the proof that it is impossible to deny thought whether scientific or speculative. It is the thinking ego in general that exists and whose existence cannot be denied, because in that case I could not even state that I exist in any meaningful sense. Descartes, however, did not distinguish the thinking I from the existentially existing I; that was his primary mistake, which Pascal corrected. I am not certain that I (the individual) exist, because I am a specimen of the genus " thinking subject "; rather, the reverse is true: I can conceive of myself as a thinking subject because I as an individual exist. Descartes's opponents sensed this mistake, but they were not able to correct it because they were too much influenced by older traditions of thought. Descartes was far more profound in his demonstrations than they understood him to be.

Descartes recognized that thinking is an essential attribute of the existing person. I would not be a human being if I could not think; and indeed I would not exist as a human being if I did not know myself to be such a being. That was the true kernel of Descartes's supreme thesis; Pascal adopted this thesis although he rejected the scientific restriction. Thinking does distinguish me from the beast. Thinking enables me to seek the truth. Thinking thus relates me to God. It is indeed the supreme source of certainty. But this certainty is not only as Descartes believed, of importance as the basis upon which science is built, but as the foundation upon which I as an existing individual relate myself to God, as Kierkegaard later saw.

Descartes did not give up ancient cosmology or medieval theology. He separated these traditional sciences from epistemology and ethics, but in order to establish his physical metaphysics he again blurred this line of separation. He was seduced into doing so because he conceived of his *Meditations* as " First Philosophy," using the Aristotelian term for metaphysics. He did not recognize the chasm between his epistemology and his naturalistic speculation. Therefore he was eventually tempted to identify nature and God.

V

THE PARADOX OF MAN

BLAISE PASCAL (1623–1662) made man the special subject of his inquiry in his *Pensées,* although he aimed in the first place at a new apologetics of the Christian faith. In Pascal the old rivalry between revelation and speculation was adjusted in favor of revelation. He recognized that Descartes had leaned toward speculation and that he had not done justice to revelation. Although Pascal was a scientist like Descartes and contributed important new knowledge to physics, he was infinitely more religious than Descartes, and this trait predominated in him on an increasing scale until he at last almost became a saint. Whereas Descartes relied upon mathematical reason to the point where he identified it with speculative reason, Pascal realized that mathematics can never give the key to the riddle of man, that it is rather itself subject to metaphysical criticism. Descartes tried to establish a kind of physical metaphysics; Pascal detested such a metaphysics. On the whole Pascal was the deeper man and thinker. The historians of philosophy never acknowledged this superior position of Pascal; they referred to him mostly in a footnote or treated him as a mystic who does not really belong to the history of philosophic thought; they did not understand the inseparable unity of philosophy and religion in him, of speculation and revelation, of reason and faith.

Pascal was in full agreement with the Reformers as to the impossibility of metaphysics' comprehending the mystery of God. In this sense he was more Biblical than the Aristotelian Scholastics. In his famous " Memorial " he denounces the " God of the philosophers and scientists " and appeals to the " God of Abraham, Isaac, and Jacob." Pascal was the most Protestant among the Roman Catholic philosophers. He never abandoned his church although he severely criticized many of its institutions; he was especially critical of the Jesuits.[1] Like Luther he went back to Augustine, laying stress upon the gratuitous divine grace. His sympathy with the Jansenists and his intimate friendship with Antoine Arnauld, the defender of Jansen's book on Augustine's anti-Pelagianism, manifest this trait. As Augustine lived about thirty years in the manner of the world, enjoying the pleasures and pursuing the ambitions of ordinary Roman boys, so Pascal too was fond of the goods which society can offer. " He insensibly became engaged in seeing society, in gaming, and in diverting himself to pass the time." [2] But in 1654 he had an ecstatic experience that forever changed his soul and the conduct of his life.[3]

There are, however, momentous differences between Augustine and Pascal. Whereas thought and faith in Augustine were in complete harmony and peaceful co-operation, Pascal was a modern in whom these two polarities competed and fought each other. He had to reconcile them and work in order to unite them in his own thought. Augustine believed in the agreement of metaphysics and Christianity, of Plato and the gospel. Pascal like Descartes was fascinated by mathematical reason, but he was also convinced that the mysteries of religion could not be mastered by reason at all. Reason and revelation thus were at odds in him and he had to decide which was to be trusted more. In Augustine human unrest was absolutely overcome when he was converted, whereas Pascal was torn by the antagonism of the world and God, of intellect and heart. He had to look for a philosophic position which would vindicate his faith and triumph over the doubt generated by his intellect.

He felt his main task was the critique of mathematical reason so highly admired and overrated in his century, so victorious in the field of physics, and so dear to him personally. Although he had rendered to science great services by the invention of a geometry of the cone and of a theory of probability, by treatises on the mechanics of fluids, and other similar treatises, he disliked the tendency of the

[1] Cf. Denzil Patrick, *Pascal and Kierkegaard* (Alec R. Allenson, Inc., 1948), Vol. I, p. 104.

[2] Morris Bishop, *Pascal: The Life of Genius* (Reynal & Hitchcock, Inc., 1936), p. 111.

[3] David E. Roberts, *Existentialism and Religious Belief* (Oxford University Press, 1957), pp. 20 f.

period to extend mathematical science to the universe at large and to speculation in general. The critique of mathematical reason was for him the steppingstone to the evaluation of man's capacities in their entirety; and this evaluation in turn enabled him to discover the meaning of faith. He became the founder of a philosophy of religion unsurpassed up to the present day.

Pascal was a religious thinker, but he distrusted any speculation about the mysteries of faith. His proper subject of thought was man, not God. He was not a mystic like Eckhart, nor a theosophic philosopher like Jacob Boehme. In the lucidity of his thought and the rational precision of his style he proved to be both a scientist and a Frenchman. But it was his peculiar greatness not to fall victim to any kind of rationalism or intellectualism; like Galileo he realized that mathematical analysis and scientific theory are confined to their own realm. We are not permitted to apply them to metaphysics, as did Descartes. Pascal thus directly anticipated the critique of Kant.[4] Like Montaigne he was a kind of existentialist. But in contrast to Montaigne he was not at all preoccupied with the peculiar character and nature of his own individuality, but he was prepared to repent and to atone for the laxity of his worldly life. Montaigne in spite of his wisdom always remained a courtier with an easy conscience; Pascal, on the contrary, recognized the perplexities and conflicts of life and longed for the salvation of his soul.

He was most sensitive to the consciousness of guilt and to the inner struggles of the human soul. "There is internal war in man between reason and the passions. If he had only reason without passions! If he had only passions without reason! But having both, he cannot be without strife, being unable to be at peace with the one without being at war with the other. Thus he is always divided against, and opposed to, himself."[5] Pascal was tormented by this inner combat, until he found peace in faith. "Every day of my life I bless my Redeemer, who . . . of a man full of weakness, of miseries, of lust, of pride, and of ambition has made me a man free from all these evils by the power of his grace, to which all the glory of it is due, as of myself I have only misery and error."[6]

[4] Cf. Bishop, *op. cit.*, p. 289.

[5] *Pensées* (first published in 1669). (Modern Library, Inc., 1941), No. 412, p. 130.

[6] *Ibid.*, No. 549, p. 174.

Whereas Descartes believed that error can be avoided by the conscientious thinker, Pascal does not believe that man out of his own power can rid himself of it.

He criticizes Montaigne, who was, according to his estimate, a pagan, not a Christian. " He suggests an indifference about salvation without fear and without repentance." " One can excuse his rather free and licentious opinions on some relations of life, but one cannot excuse his thoroughly pagan views on death." " Through the whole of his book his only conception of death is a cowardly and effeminate one." [7] Although Pascal was affected in his style and also in the choice of his topic by the *Essays,* as a personality he was almost the antithesis to Montaigne. But he was not less opposed to Descartes. He never could forgive Descartes for having made mathematics the model of philosophic thought and for vainly seeking to build his metaphysics on the basis of physics.[8]

Man is wretched without faith in God and Christ. This theme constantly recurs in Pascal's *Pensées.* It is his existential argument for the truth of faith, a truth rooted in man's spiritual situation, in his moral insufficiency, in his finite constitution. Here again Pascal has much in common with Kant, although Pascal's faith was not rational and moral, but Biblical and moral. To him Jesus Christ was not only his personal Redeemer but God in the fullest sense although always " truly hidden." " We know God only by Jesus Christ. Without this mediator all communion with God is taken away." [9] He was the Messiah whom the Jews had expected, but whom they did not recognize when he came, because he deviated from the pattern envisaged by those who prophesied about him. " Religion," he says, " is so great a thing that it is right that those who will not take the trouble to seek it, if it be obscure, should be deprived of it." [10]

Man cannot find the truth about himself without faith. The athe-

---

[7] *Ibid.,* No. 63, p. 20.

[8] " I cannot forgive Descartes. In all his philosophy he would have been quite willing to dispense with God. But he had to make Him give a fillip to set the world in motion; beyond this he has no further need of God." (No. 77, p. 29.) " To write against those who made too profound a study of science: Descartes." (No. 76, p. 29.)

[9] No. 546, p. 189.

[10] No. 573, p. 189.

ists are therefore right in complaining that they "have no light." [11] As long as man lives by his own natural insight, he is doomed to be miserable; he seeks in vain for that happiness which faith alone can grant. Man "without passions, without business, without diversion, without study . . . feels his nothingness, his forlornness, his utter insufficiency, his dependence, his weakness, his emptiness. There will immediately arise from the depth of his heart weariness, gloom, sadness, fretfulness, vexation, despair." [12] All merely temporal and transitory occupations and engagements cannot truly satisfy a heart that longs for the Absolute or the Eternal. "So wretched is man that he would worry even without any cause for weariness." [13] Diversion itself is "the greatest of our miseries. For it is this which principally hinders us from reflecting upon ourselves, and which makes us insensibly ruin ourselves." [14]

As compared with Pascal, worldly philosophers like Montaigne and Descartes lack that depth and earnestness which alone lead to the ultimate truth. They reach only a superficial and partial truth which cannot save them from their innermost misery. The logical evidence and rational necessity which persuaded Descartes to believe that he could thereby gain ultimate certainty are shallow from the perspective of faith. Pascal had suffered too deeply to accept those arguments. He was too strongly convinced that all human thought can at best lead to a half-truth about relative matters, but never to that religious truth which alone can really make a man happy and safe. That has to be admitted not only with respect to all scientific knowledge, but even to all metaphysical thought, and especially to all proofs of God. "The metaphysical proofs of God are so remote from the reasoning of men that they make little impression; and if they should be of service to some, it would be only during the moment that they see such demonstration, but an hour afterward they fear they have been mistaken." [15]

Pascal did not pretend that the truth of the Christian religion can be demonstrated. Such an undertaking is uncertain and even impossible because thought then meets unavoidable and insoluble con-

[11] No. 228, p. 78.
[12] No. 131, p. 47.
[13] No. 139, p. 51.
[14] No. 171, p. 60. Compare Augustine, *Contra academicos*, Book One, ch. 1:2.
[15] No. 524, p. 172.

traditions. Religion is not the result of reasoning and can never be assured by it. The Christian religion in particular is not accessible by argument or inquiry. But if that is so, why did Pascal labor so hard to write an apology of his faith? Why did he spend so much intellectual energy to persuade his readers that the Christian religion is true, and that this religion alone can grant man his salvation? Pascal was aware of this paradox. But he knew that Christian thinking is paradoxical through and through. His apologetic thought is accordingly a strange kind of dialectical synthesis of an admitted ignorance and a profound insight; it is an indirect and ironical pointing to the wisdom of faith. It reminds one of Kierkegaard, and indeed Pascal is his most penetrating and sagacious forerunner. But in spite of this spiritual similarity between the two apologetic writers there is also a great chasm between them. The philosophic and intellectual means of the seventeenth-century French scientist and Catholic and those of the nineteenth-century Danish romantic and Protestant were so different that their language, their method, their arguments and reasons were bound to be very different too.

VIEW OF MAN

Two topics are foremost in Pascal's *Pensées:* the paradox of man and the embarrassing relation between reason and revelation, between thought and faith. The *Pensées* are not a well-organized book and do not give a sustained discussion of these problems. On the contrary, they are a kind of diary in which Pascal put down various thoughts about these subjects in an aphoristic and incoherent form. Although there is a consistent and systematic body of ideas in the background of these thoughts, Pascal never arranged them in a logical order. He never published them. After his death they were found and prepared for publication, and then not always in the same sequence.

What is man? This typically modern concern is in the foreground of all Pascal has to say. Pascal like Descartes held that at bottom man is a thinking being; but in contrast to Descartes, Pascal did not believe that thinking is mainly or in principle scientific. According to Pascal, thinking is a much more comprehensive activity, a much broader and wider capacity; only because of the extensive range which thinking controls does it characterize man as man, in all his aspects and in all his deeds. Thinking distinguishes man from all other beings. Man is a thinker not only when he methodically inquires into some special subject or when he forms theories or doctrines; he is a thinker wherever he goes and whatever he does. He is a thinker most of all because he cannot be a self without thinking himself. This is the basic and primary thinking which precedes all scientific or philosophic thought. This fundamental thinking is not logical, but constitutes man's peculiar consciousness without which he cannot act or react as a man. The peculiar being of man is permeated by this thinking so that they define each other. Man's special dignity, his moral stature, his very selfhood are conditioned by his thinking. " All our dignity consists in thought. By it we must elevate ourselves and not by space and time which we cannot fill. Let us endeavor then to think well; this is the principle of morality." [16]

This dignity stands in sharp and striking contrast to the fact that man although a thinking being is also an animal, a product of natural forces, a material substance, a " creature of a day " (Aeschylus), weak and vulnerable, the victim of desire and passion. " Man is neither angel nor brute, and the unfortunate thing is that he who would act the angel acts the brute." [17] Man is too much like an angel to be a brute, but he is too much a brute to be an angel. Thus he is always suspended between these two alternatives. He has to arrange his life by balancing himself, by bringing about an equipoise of the extreme polarities of his being. He is condemned to remain forever unsteady; he can never fully and perfectly solve the task set by himself as a self. " Since man is infinitely removed from comprehending the extremes, the end of things and their beginning are hopelessly hidden from him in an impenetrable secret; he is incapable of seeing the Nothing from which he was made, and the Infinite in which he is swallowed up." [18] Man living between Nothingness and Infinity is constantly threatened and can never conquer and control those extremes.

It is indeed the capacity for thinking and knowing which generates the instability, uncertainty, and disharmony of man's existence. He knows too much to live solely by instinct, and he knows

[16] No. 347, p. 116.   [17] No. 358, p. 118.   [18] No. 72, p. 23.

too little to live by reason alone. He therefore never attains his goal, is never perfect, never at rest and at peace with himself. He is himself " a Nothing in comparison with the Infinite, an All in comparison with Nothing, a mean between nothing and everything." [19] By virtue of his knowledge he not only *is* in this queer and uncomfortable situation, but he is *aware* of its oddity (whether philosopher or not) and thus he is seeking for a way out of his perilous imbalance.

But man's greatness and smallness are the inescapable consequences of this status or lack of status. " The greatness of man is so evident, that it is even proved by his wretchedness. For what in animals is nature, we call in man wretchedness." [20] " Man knows that he is wretched. He is therefore wretched because he is so, but he is really great because he knows it." [21] His very greatness enhances his misery, while his misery is the outcome of his greatness. Man is infinitely smaller than the universe, but he is also infinitely greater because he knows himself to be smaller while the universe does not know its greatness. Man excels everything in nature, but at the same time he is the most miserable of all created things — both because he knows himself and because he " cannot stay quietly in his own chamber." [22]

But the deepest reason for man's misery is his inability to understand life and the world. This ambiguity of his situation makes him not only unstable and restless, but gives him the dizzy feeling that for all his self-knowledge he does not really know who or what he is. It is precisely by means of his self-knowledge that he can become a riddle to himself. Only a thinking being can conceive of a riddle, because riddles exist only for the mind that wishes to solve them. Renaissance thinkers taught (as the Stoics had done already and as Leibniz taught later) that man is a microcosm, embracing and comprehending the whole world within himself, indeed that man himself is the world in a minuscule reproduction, the world reflected in an image. Is such a doctrine true? Are we really able to call ourselves little worlds? Are we mirrors of the universe? Pascal doubted such a view. We are hovering between the extremes of Allness and Nothingness, but we do not understand either. " We sail within a

---

[19] No. 72, p. 23.
[20] No. 409, p. 129.
[21] No. 416, p. 131.
[22] No. 139, p. 48.

vast sphere ever drifting in uncertainty driven from end to end." [23]
Descartes was right after all when he sought for the source of certainty. But the trouble is that we can never find it, because we do not know who we are. Man is to himself the greatest, although the most familiar, mystery.

"What a chimera is man! What a novelty! What a monster, what a contradiction, what a prodigy! Judge of all things, imbecile worm of the earth; depository of truth, a sink of uncertainty and error; the pride and the refuse of the universe; . . . know then, proud man, what a paradox you are to yourself . . . ; be silent, foolish nature, learn that man infinitely transcends man, and learn from your master your true condition, of which you are ignorant: Hear God! " [24] Pascal here rises almost to the stature of one of the prophets of the Old Testament. The brilliant evocation throws the brightest light upon his whole philosophy. It may be called a Renaissance philosophy, but it points to a faith missing in the Italian cosmological thinkers. This view is the center of Pascal's apologetic doctrine, unfolding in the gloomy picture of man's ignorance and his inability to escape his plight by his own resources. Since man is this monstrous mongrel he cannot understand himself; he has to turn to God in order to learn from his Lord what he is and what he is to think and to do, and how he can be saved. He needs revelation, since his own speculation leaves him in the dark and in despair. God alone can help him to bear his anxiety; God alone can brighten him and lead him on to a better life; God alone can warn him not to fall into the trap of the tempter: God alone can assure him that there is an ultimate solution of the contradictions, the perplexities, the conflicts and tragedies of life, a solution which surmounts all merely rational insight. The extremes " meet and reunite by force of distance, and find each other in God, and in God alone." [25]

REASON AND FAITH

Man knows himself, but he does not understand himself. He knows his dignity, his freedom, his autonomy, his glory, but also his deficiency, his slavery, his misery, and his shame. Human dignity and guilt, human greatness and pettiness, are impossible without

[23] No. 72, p. 25.   [24] No. 434, p. 143.   [25] No. 72, p. 24.

such twofold knowledge. But even this knowledge man has to learn from God's revelation; the pre-Christian thinkers, for all the profundity of their insight, all the sagacity of their mind, all the logical consistency of their thought, did not yet know this most important and hidden truth about themselves. Christianity infinitely deepened man's self-understanding. The Socratic " Know thyself! " could be heeded only by those who had been taught by Christ. Only now was the full scope of man's moral imperfection and merely relative perfectibility revealed. But at the same time the only possible remedy, the only possible consolation and comfort was disclosed. Man's self-confidence had to be broken completely so that his eyes could see the eternal glory and his heart could feel the eternal joy. Man could be exalted by being humiliated; he could be redeemed only by contrition and surrender.

The Biblical God as he appears in Christ can save man and help man only because he knows man's plight and knows how to cure his evil. He would not be the God of faith if he were not both superhuman and human. The God of faith is not the God of reason. There is an infinite chasm between faith and reason. No human intellect, regardless of its creativeness and brilliance, could have been able to discover and excogitate by speculation the God who has revealed himself in momentous events, through the mouth of prophets and through the appearance of his son. The paradox of man is dissolved by this revelation.

Pascal proceeds consistently to vindicate and verify this truth. First he proves that reason is restricted, and that it is therefore reasonable to inquire into the source and the reach of that restriction; then he shows that faith transcends reason without harming its privileges. Faith does not violate the prerogative of reason; rather, it transcends the limit of reason: it is of another " order." And finally, reason makes an ironical proposal for the sake of faith. In this whole course of thought the term " reason " signifies primarily the human intellect at work in the sciences, most successfully in mathematics; secondarily it means the arguing and concluding faculty: dialectical reason, which enables us to establish speculative systems of cosmology and theology, but which also has the capacity to criticize itself and to inaugurate its own limitation and self-restriction. This last ability is the zenith of the human thought before it defends faith and revelation. No philosopher before Kant has seen so clearly the necessity of a " Critique of Reason."

Pascal begins with the distinction between discursive and intuitive knowledge. This discussion is superior in epistemological insight to anything Descartes had said. Mathematical reason, Pascal insists, is discursive or deductive. It begins from clearly defined concepts and axioms and arrives by conclusive demonstration at propositions so that error is almost impossible in its field. The intuitive reason, on the other hand, needs a " good eyesight," for although its principles are less hidden than those of mathematics, they are nevertheless " so subtle and so numerous that it is almost impossible but that some escape notice." [26] This distinction can be called classical. Pascal sets forth here a significant doctrine regarding the difficulty which mathematical minds experience in familiarizing themselves with intuitive methods while intuitive minds on the other hand abhor the way " through definitions and axioms so sterile . . . that they are repelled and disheartened." [27] It was the genius of Pascal which enabled him to move easily in both realms and to attain mastership in both mathematical physics and an intuitive philosophy of faith, and which finally permitted him to compare the two sources of knowledge and to decide what kind of reality should be ascribed to each.

Each has its own authority and its own territory over which it is allowed to rule. Therefore neither should be disparaged; neither should scorn the other. Pascal appreciated as highly as Descartes did the enormous accomplishments of modern science. And he was the first Christian apologist to do so. But in contrast to Descartes he saw not only the limits of science, but he also envisaged with a degree of clarity and succinctness extremely rare the specific function of religious faith in an area in which the heart and even ecstasy and inspiration are more at home than thinking reason. He discerned the virtues and the defects of both scientific and religious cognition. He was fully aware that from the perspective of exactitude and accuracy mathematics and mathematical physics are by far superior; he acknowledged the risk inherent in religious belief. But he insisted that the nature of the object demands the duality of methods and that each method is peculiarly adequate in the different realms in which it is applied.

Religious knowledge is regrettably insecure when measured by

[26] No. 1, p. 3.   [27] No. 1, p. 4.

the ideal of rational precision. However, mathematical physics cannot perform what religion does perform. Mathematics not only fails to answer the questions which religion answers, but it also fails to satisfy completely even the intellect. There are problems in the realm of geometry and arithmetic which these two sciences cannot solve, and which point to an area unknown and unknowable by mathematical reason. Paradox marks not only philosophic and religious thought, it emerges in the very realm in which mathematical reason triumphs. We can compute neither with zero nor with the infinite without meeting paradoxical contradictions. " As we know it to be false that numbers are finite, it is therefore true that there is an infinity in number. But we do not know what it is. It is false that it is even, it is false that it is odd, yet it is a number and every number is odd or even. . . . So we may well know that there is a God without knowing what he is." [28] Here Pascal anticipates the " antinomies " in Kant's transcendental dialectic in the *Critique of Pure Reason*. Even more directly does he do this, when he speaks of the contradictions arising out of the attempt to conceive of the world. " The whole world is only an imperceptible atom in the ample bosom of nature. No idea approaches it. We may enlarge our conceptions beyond all imaginable space; we only produce atoms in comparison with the reality of things. It is an infinite sphere, the center of which is everywhere, the circumference nowhere. In short, it is the greatest sensible mark of the almighty power of God that imagination loses itself in that thought." [29] The same is true with respect to the beginning and the end of the temporal world.

It is noteworthy how different are the conclusions that Giordano Bruno and Pascal drew from the modern idea of mathematical infinity. Bruno thought that the visible universe is itself divine, a work of art identical with its artist; Pascal, on the other hand, inferred that the human intellect falters when it tries to embrace the physical infinite and that God transcends those contradictions which the intellect encounters. Bruno was a modern cosmologist, Pascal a modern Christian philosopher. How can the atheist uphold his thesis if he considers that we cannot even think of mathematical and physical infinity? The atheist cannot prove his thesis better than the theist can his. Our intellect fails when we soar so high.

[28] No. 233, p. 80.   [29] No. 72, p. 22.

God transcends all finitude, that of the world as well as that of our intellect.

When we try to conceive of God and to prove his existence contradictions again bar the way. " It is incomprehensible that God should exist, and it is incomprehensible that he should not exist." [30] When we try to answer the questions concerning the nature of the soul or of original sin we again meet insoluble contradictions. Pascal's philosophy of faith is a " learned ignorance," as Nicholas of Cusa called the essence of speculation. But Pascal is more advanced; he sees more clearly that even mathematical reason is itself caught in a net of unanswerable questions, and that therefore speculative reason has no chance to comprehend the content of faith. This content transcends the limits not only of mathematical and scientific reason but of reason in general. But whereas reason is left in the lurch when it deals with the Absolute, faith has its own legitimate sphere which reason cannot reach. Faith does not need the support of reason; on the contrary, faith rejects it because it has its own source of certainty. Reason, by its failure to transcend its own limits, only corroborates the claim of faith and makes it possible to understand the part of revelation. When our reason climbs to the lofty realm of the Infinite, it is consequently destroyed; the power of this destruction is the power of God working within reason. " The finite is annihilated in the presence of the infinite, and becomes a pure nothing. So our spirit before God, so our justice before divine justice." [31]

It is absurd to prove or to refute the existence of God; it is likewise absurd and antireligious to prove the validity of faith or of revelation. Faith is faith precisely because its truth can be known only by the word of God himself and not by reason or human demonstration. It can be learned only by inner experience, by growing wisdom, by suffering and humiliation, and it is by this existential way that revelation proceeds. Events that are historical, although with superhistorical significance, and not rational proofs are the " method " which God himself applies. Biblical religion is sublime because it is the only religion that teaches through events of that kind. " Who will blame Christians for not being able to give a reason for their belief, since they profess a religion for which they can-

[30] No. 230, p. 79.   [31] No. 233, pp. 79 f.

not give a reason? They declare in expounding it to the world that it is a foolishness, and then you complain that they do not prove it!" [32]

To establish a "natural theology," as the Scholastics did, is just unchristian. If it were possible to carry out such an undertaking, prophets and Christ would not have been necessary; the tortuous method of learning by sin and punishment, by disloyalty and the wrath of God, by revolt and alienation, by contrition and suffering would then appear as merely cruel and unworthy of the divine omnipotence and omniscience. But as it is, the defeat of reason by reason itself is perfectly adapted to the incomprehensible majesty of God. "There is nothing so conformable to reason as this disavowal of reason." [33] "If we submit everything to reason, our religion will have no mysterious and supernatural element. If we offend the principles of reason, our religion will be absurd and ridiculous." [34] Philosophy must render to reason the things which are of reason and render to faith the things which are of faith. Pascal is here in full agreement with the spirit of Kant and Kierkegaard.

Pascal will not demolish; on the contrary, he will establish a philosophy of faith. It is the task of that philosophy to demonstrate why God and the soul and the world are incomprehensible. This is indeed a paradoxical task. But the "intuitive mind," the mind of the believer, perfectly understands this paradox out of its own inner experience. And the believing mind alone is able to undertake such a demonstration. As it is ridiculous to expect that a man without any sense of beauty and without any appreciation of art (if there is such a man) should write an aesthetics, so it is also absurd to expect that anyone who has no religious belief should produce a philosophy of faith. Only the man of faith can conceive faith; only the man of faith can intelligibly write on God. The philosopher who dares to comprehend the nature of religion must have both an acute speculative mind and a profound religious devotion. Pascal possessed both to the highest degree.

"Faith is a gift of God; do not believe that we said it was a gift of reasoning." "It is the heart which experiences God, and not reason." [35] Out of this fundamental insight, so simple and so self-

[32] No. 233, p. 80.   [34] No. 273, p. 94.
[33] No. 272, p. 94.   [35] No. 279, p. 95.

evident to the believer, but so seldom heeded and understood by the speculative philosopher, Pascal arrived at his famous statement that "the heart has its reasons, which reason does not know." [36] There is an intrinsic logic in matters of faith, but it is not a logic that reason unsupported by faith could find. "The heart has its own order, the intellect has its own." [37] "Men will never believe with a saving and real faith unless God inclines their heart; and they will believe as soon as he inclines it." [38] Pascal does not deny that some persons have a "natural" inclination to believe in God and to love him while others have not. But if they are so inclined, they do not believe that "nature" has inclined them, just because they have faith in God and not in nature.

The believer whose heart God has filled with humility and thankfulness, with trust and joy, with faith and love does not complain that God is hidden and that our reason cannot understand him. He will rather exult that God does not reveal himself to "haughty sages unworthy to know so holy a God." [39] "Jesus Christ and St. Paul employ the rule of love, not of intellect, for they would warn, not instruct. It is the same with St. Augustine." [40] Pascal endorses what Augustine has God say to man: "Thou wouldst not seek me, if thou didst not possess me." [41] So paradoxical is the logic of faith.

Pascal calls that logic the "logic of the heart"; this logic is well suited to the inwardness of faith, the contrite conscience, the mystery of God's presence. Only this logic understands faith and accepts revelation. Only this logic is able to think about God. Since the order of the heart and the order of reason vary so profoundly, it is not surprising that they sometimes clash, although they are at bottom compatible with each other, the one ceasing to be valid where the other begins. In the sphere of the living faith contradiction does not condemn knowledge as it does in that of reason alone. "Contradiction is a bad sign of truth; several things which are certain are contradicted; several things which are false pass without contradiction." [42] Chastity is good, but it is also bad. To kill is for-

[36] No. 277, p. 95.
[37] No. 283, p. 96.
[38] No. 284, p. 97.
[39] Cf. No. 288, p. 98.
[40] No. 283, p. 97.
[41] No. 554, p. 179.
[42] No. 384, p. 124.

bidden, but not killing may entail lawlessness and promote crime. "We possess truth and goodness only in part, and mingled with falsehood and evil." [43] "All these contradictions which seem most to keep me from the knowledge of religion, have led me most quickly to the true one." [44]

Was Pascal a Catholic or a Protestant? It is difficult to answer this. On the whole he wanted to be a loyal son of his church. He clung to tradition and held it binding upon every believer. But this does not imply that he was willing to subscribe to all decrees of the popes and to all tenets of Catholic doctrine. On the contrary, he most emphatically insisted that in points of fact and scientific truth the church was not competent. To the Jesuits he said: " It was to little purpose that you obtained against Galileo a decree from Rome, condemning his opinion respecting the motion of the earth. It will never be proved by such an argument as this that the earth remains stationary; and if it can be demonstrated by sure observation that it is the earth and not the sun that revolves, the efforts and arguments of all mankind put together will not hinder our planet from revolving nor hinder themselves from revolving along with her." [45]

Pascal was utterly opposed to casuistry. It was his conviction that concrete life is too inexhaustible to permit the making of prescriptions for individual situations and individual decisions. Every person has to act according to his conscience; inner conflicts can by no means be eliminated. God wants us to struggle, and each individual has to seek his own way. There is no system which could prevent religious and moral error or wrong actions. The Christian religion is a religion for sinners. It awakes the sense of sinfulness and sharpens man's conscience. But reason is no guide in the darkness of life; only insight into the fallibility of judgment can cure those ills by generating distrust in our own power, and trust in the mysterious will of God, his mercy, and the redemption wrought by Christ. No doubt there is a Protestant spirit in these convictions.

Pascal severely criticizes the papal regime. " The pope is head. Who else is known of all? Who else is recognized by all, having

---

[43] No. 385, pp. 124 f.
[44] No. 424, p. 133.
[45] *The Provincial Letters*, Letter XVIII, p. 615.

power to insinuate himself into all the body because he holds the principal shoot. . . . How easy it was to make this degenerate into tyranny." [46] "Men like certainty. They like the pope to be infallible in faith and grave doctors to be infallible in morals, so as to have certainty." [47] The truth is that no human being can ever be infallible and that no institution can save man from being mistaken. Christians therefore should never be coerced into submitting to any statement or opinion they regard as wrong. " The saints were never silent. It is true that a call is necessary, but it is not from the decrees of the Council that we must learn whether we are called, it is from the necessity of speaking. Now, after Rome has spoken, and we think that she has condemned the truth . . . , we must cry out so much the louder, the more unjustly we are censured, and the more violently they should stifle speech, until there come a pope who hears both parties." [48] How much like Luther does Pascal here feel and speak! There was a strong sense of the rightness of revolt in his mind when truth was at stake, the truth which he saw and in which he believed.

THE WAGER

The content of faith cannot be demonstrated like the content of geometry or mechanics; from the point of view of mathematical reason it is forever uncertain and therefore involves risk; the pilgrimage of the believer is an adventure. Pascal agreed to a large extent with the skepticism of the French Renaissance philosophers. He chose a kind of simile or metaphor to express his skeptical but also religious sentiment, when he compared believing to betting. Some historians were bewildered by this comparison. In order to understand and to appraise it we must remember that Pascal, the mathematician, had written a theory of probability, so that the notion of the probable was in the foreground of his mind. One section of the *Pensées* argues strongly against the part probability plays in Catholic morals. " Can it be anything but compliance with the world which makes you find things probable? " [49] His fight against the Jesuits was a fight against the principle of probability in their casuistic code. What is of great importance in worldly life and in

[46] No. 871, p. 309.   [48] No. 919, p. 319.
[47] No. 879, p. 310.   [49] No. 909, p. 317.

mathematics appeared to him as dangerous and offensive in the moral and spiritual sphere. Probability does not give us that assurance which we need there. " Nothing gives certainty but truth; nothing gives rest but the sincere search for truth." [50] " The earnestness of the saints in seeking the truth was useless, if the probable is trustworthy." [51]

We are therefore greatly puzzled to read that Pascal himself recommends a kind of spiritual probability when he describes faith as a sort of wager. But this comparison is, no doubt, a witty form of repeating that the truth of faith cannot be ascertained by means of scientific demonstration. A wager, of course, presupposes that we cannot know the result by rational inquiry. This is the common ground of faith and betting. " You must wager. It is not optional. You are embarked. . . . If you gain, you gain all; if you lose, you lose nothing. Bet then without hesitation that He is. . . . There is an infinity of an infinitely happy life to gain . . . against a finite number of chances of loss, and what you stake is finite. . . . Wherever the infinite is . . . there is no time to hesitate, you must give all." [52] This is spoken to the doubtful, the forlorn, the desperate — spoken in a worldly language, the language of the races and of daily life.

Pascal's true intention is manifest when he speaks of a man who boasts that he does not believe in God as if this were a matter to be taken lightly and better assured than the belief in God. " Does he think that he has thus brought us to have henceforth complete confidence in him, and to look to him for consolation advice, and help in every need of life? . . . Is this a thing to say gaily? Is it not on the contrary, a thing to say sadly, as the saddest thing in the world? " [53] Pascal pitied those who are without God, and who do not boast of their unbelief but are rather seeking in vain. To them he turns when he speaks of faith as a wager.

" What harm will befall you in taking this side? You will be faithful, honest, humble, grateful, generous, a sincere friend, truthful. Certaintly you will not have those poisonous pleasures, glory and luxury. . . . I will tell you that you will thereby gain in this life and that at each step you take on this road, you will see so great

[50] No. 907, p. 316.　　[52] No. 233, p. 81.
[51] No. 916, p. 318.　　[53] No. 194, p. 70.

certainty of gain, . . . that you will at last recognize that you have wagered for something certain and infinite, for which you have given nothing." [54] Thus Pascal gently and graciously tries to persuade the honest and modest skeptic that it is the best for him to undertake this " wager," although he will win the good chances promised by him only if he really gives up his doubt and embraces faith. We cannot attain any rational certainty when we face the Infinite. " If we must not act save in certainty, we ought not to act on religion, for it is not certain. But how many things we do on an uncertainty. . . . We must do nothing at all, for nothing is certain. . . . There is more certainty in religion than there is as to whether we may see tomorrow." [55]

[54] No. 233, p. 83.   [55] No. 234, p. 84.

VI

THE LOVE OF GOD

WHEREAS Pascal criticized any metaphysics that would use the method of mathematics and rejected all natural theology, Spinoza may be regarded as the champion of such a metaphysics and such a theology. Benedict (Baruch) de Spinoza (1632–1677) eliminated revelation completely for the sake of speculation, whereas Pascal did exactly the reverse. But while this is the overt fact, and while Spinoza himself laid greatest stress upon the purely demonstrative method of his system, the Old Testament God was nevertheless secretly the Lord of his heart and thought. The consistency of his demonstrations, therefore, breaks down eventually in a most challenging and dramatic way. Spinoza, who wanted to transform theology into a kind of geometry, was at bottom a mystic, and his system attests clearly enough to this main and dominant note of his personality. The mathematical and deductive surface covers an ardent and passionate love of God, and this love is the real source and the true agent of all his doctrines. The outer appearance and the inner substance of the system thus contrast in an almost alarming fashion. But this contrast generates a very productive tension, which only makes the system the more attractive and fascinating. With respect to method and external form, Spinoza was a genuine child of his age, the disciple of Descartes, and even more rigid and radical in his Cartesian principles than the master had been. But in the heart of his heart, Spinoza was the child of Old Testament religion. It is the God of Abraham, Isaac, and Jacob, who in him, as in Pascal, was more powerful than geometry and the ideal of strict and precise demonstration.

Besides being influenced by modern thinkers, Spinoza was also influenced by antiquity, especially by Stoicism. To some extent, he was a Stoic himself in many tenets that he held. He was utterly autonomous in his whole attitude, but this autonomy was basically cosmocentric and theocentric, like that of the ancient Stoics. And like the Stoics his religiosity seems to be pantheistic, since he identifies God and Nature. But here again we must distinguish between essence and appearance. The surface is pantheistic, but the essence is theistic. In spite of the identification of God and Nature, it is God who prevails, as was also the case in Stoicism. Spinoza's system is outwardly cosmological, but inwardly only God exists. Hence the German romantics could call Spinoza the "God-intoxicated" thinker while most historians and critics of the seventeenth and early eighteenth centuries regarded him as a naturalist and even as an atheist; Hegel spoke of the system as being "acosmistic," because Spinoza denies not the existence of God, but the existence of the world or replaces the world by God.

It is obvious that a system like this must be full of inner tensions and cannot be understandable. Spinoza was utterly intent on denying the existence of a personal God; he even denied the existence of any purpose in the universe; he considered human affections and virtues from an absolutely detached point of view, as if they were lines or triangles — how could such a man be at the same time so deeply religious, so animated by the love of God that this trait in him overwhelmed the entire outer frame of his thought? Only the study of his speculation can give an answer to this puzzling incompatibility.

Spinoza was also influenced by the Scholastics. He had read widely in medieval literature and there is even a certain analogy between him and Aquinas inasmuch as both were to a large extent intellectualists, and yet also religious in their general outlook. Both asserted that the will is one with the intellect and that for God it is the same to be and to will and to act. Spinoza was, if we abstract from his mathematical leanings, the least modern of the three great metaphysical systematicians of the seventeenth century. It was either the world or God, and not man, that was in the foreground of his speculative interest and of his whole philosophy. And yet with the exception of the first book all discussions circle around man, his passions and his actions, his knowledge and his felicity. Therefore his book was called *Ethics* when it was published after his death.

It is true that this so-called ethics is not an ethics at all, if we think of a science that deals with the moral law, moral norms or rules, but it is an ethics in the sense in which the ancients and also the Scholastics treated questions of human virtue and vice, of human wisdom and happiness. But even here the theocentric perspective prevails, as we shall see. In this way modern, medieval, and pre-Christian speculation are fused in Spinoza's system. But the whole system culminates in the love of God, i.e., in the love with which man loves God and in the love with which God loves himself. " Sacrifice a lock to the manes of the holy Spinoza," Schleiermacher demands in his *Speeches on Religion to the Cultivated Amongst Its Despisers.*

Outwardly viewed, Spinoza's system almost slavishly imitates the Euclidean method. It starts with definitions and axioms, then proceeds to propositions each of which is proved by pointing back to the definitions, axioms, and propositions previously demonstrated; finally corollaries and notes are added. Thus the maximum degree of certainty seems to be reached. Indeed, all propositions seem to be irrefutable, if the presuppositions are agreed upon. Spinoza's work is divided into five parts: the first deals with God; the second part is entitled " Nature and Origin of the Mind "; the third, " On the Origin and Nature of the Emotions "; the fourth, " Of Human Bondage, or the Strength of the Emotions "; the fifth and last part, " Of the Power of the Understanding, or of Human Freedom." The Cartesian philosophy is thoroughly dualistic: there is the duality of the thinking subject and the objects of thought; the duality of the extended and the thinking things or substances; the duality of body and soul, of qualities and quantities, of reason and sensation or imagination, of distinct and confused conceptions, of intellect and will, of passion and freedom. In Spinoza's system these dualities are not absent, but they are finally united and surmounted by the oneness of God in whom all things are. In Descartes, on the contrary, all these polarities are never systematically overcome, although Nature contains them. But the concept of nature is vague in the Cartesian system, and the question whether there are many substances or only one remains unanswered. Spinoza's philosophy, on the other hand, is thoroughly monistic. God or the only Substance is the fundamental principle from which everything else is derived and by which everything else is conceived.

Spinoza, at the beginning of his intellectual development, was a loyal disciple of Descartes. He expounded the Cartesian system in a special treatise.[1] Here he arranged the doctrine of his teacher in a geometrical fashion. He followed him in accepting the concept of extended substances. But later he gave up this concept and recognized the existence of only one substance: that of God. God is the unity of all dualities; in him extension and thinking are attributes. Since all finite things are in God, they are not substances but only *modi* of the divine substance, modifications of the infinite being, and they have no self-existence. Like Pascal, Spinoza distinguished two kinds of knowledge: one rational, discursive, and demonstrative, the other intuitive and immediate. But Spinoza did not distribute these two kinds of knowledge into two different spheres, the one mathematical, the other spiritual; instead, he unified them within speculative comprehension. Intuition precedes demonstration in time and rank; it is the fundamental presupposition of all knowledge; it underlies the whole vision which unfolds by means of demonstration. Intuition is common to speculation and life; it is akin therefore to revelation; it is the presupposition not only of all rational proofs and propositions but also of a virtuous and happy (blessed) life. Therefore objective, systematic, speculative truth and the truth which we live, as it were, when we live in accordance with the speculative insight, i.e., when we live a wise, free, and virtuous life, are harmoniously united by intuitive knowledge. Essential and existential truth, as we would say today, are thus completely and perfectly united. Spinoza lived his system, he did not merely excogitate it. This makes his philosophy as attractive as it is and probably persuades many to believe in its truth.

Intuition enables us to perceive our own life and all finite things, as it were, with one glance, to look at the world *sub specie aeternitatis* (under the aspect of eternity). Time seems to be effaced or conquered by the all-embracing mind. Transiency is surpassed by the perfect stability of truth in its ultimate sense. We cannot doubt that this glance is akin to the way the religious believer sees the world when he sees it in God. But Spinoza was convinced that speculation

[1] Benedictus de Spinoza, *The Principles of Descartes' Philosophy,* tr. by Halbert Hains Britan (The Open Court Publishing Company, 1943).

had exactly the same power: there was not the slightest rift between speculation and faith, or reason and intuition, in his thought and life. Like the Existent of Parmenides, the One of Plotinus, or Being in the philosophy of Augustine, Spinoza's Substance is identical with God — whether He is the God of knowledge or of existence. As in the speculation of Parmenides the Existent is at perfect rest, so also Spinoza's Substance is eternally stable and infinite, absolutely self-sufficient, self-existent, and self-dependent. Unrest, movement, change, coming to be, and ceasing to be are in the last analysis nonexisting, just as they are in the Eleatic system. Therefore there is no real causality, no real becoming in the divine substance; only the relation between concepts and propositions exists. In this respect an analogy between Spinoza's system and that of Euclid truly characterizes the eternity of existence in both, as Parmenides also compared his Existent with the geometrical figure of a sphere. There is no antagonism, no dialectic, no dynamism in Spinoza's God-Nature as there was no ultimate tension, no ultimate struggle, no ultimate contradiction in Spinoza's soul and mind. Speaking in religious terms: his faith was not troubled or disturbed by doubt. It is amazing to read in his letters how unshakable was his conviction that his philosophy is true. Without any arrogance or immodesty he simply trusted his intuition and the demonstration of his quasi-geometrical method. If there is a deficiency in Spinoza, it is a deficiency of insight, not of certainty which is ultimately rooted in his imperturbable love of God.

All troubles of life are ultimately absorbed by the contemplation of the majestic and infinite substance of God or Nature. Intuition embraces the All, as the cognate intuition did in the pre-Christian systems. All earthly sorrow, all finite misery is surpassed and, as it were, extinguished by the light of truth outshining error and falsity, vice and weakness, hate and adversity. Spinoza studied the human emotions as carefully and painstakingly as he did because he wanted to defeat all passions and infirmities of the soul intellectually as well as emotionally. All individuality is finally swallowed up by the universality of the One God who alone truly Is. There is a religious ardor in the apparently cool and objective sequence of the propositions and proofs. Never was a speculative system more religiously conceived and more religiously carried out than that of this lonely thinker who had to flee from city to city because he was persecuted as an atheist or materialist. Spinoza was persecuted also by his own Jewish community which excommunicated him by the most severe anathema the synagogue could impose. Spinoza had intimate connections with some Christian sects, but he could never make up his mind to join them completely, although he was several times on the point of conversion.

Perhaps in no other philosophy did mysticism and rationalism ever contract so close an alliance as they did in Spinoza's system. Neither was mysticism as personal and passionate nor rationalism as mathematical as they were in this geometry of God. To be, according to his system, is to be conceived. Both are as intimately and firmly identified as they were in the system of Parmenides. " By substance I mean that which is in itself and is conceived through itself." [2] These two predicates " to be " and " to be conceived " mean the same thing, since the substance is what it is only in so far as it is thought to be what it is. Therefore the system is utterly " dogmatic " (in the Kantian sense), utterly rationalistic, and thereby utterly monistic.[3] " Conceiving " is not merely a human activity, it at the same time belongs to the nature of things.

This extreme rationalism and monism nevertheless provides for the world of particular existence, of process and change, of causality and action, at least according to Spinoza's explicit intention. The all-embracing and all-pervading deity, in spite of its indivisibility and infinity, is itself multifarious and divided into parts. By an ingenious stroke of thought Spinoza introduces together with the concept of substance, that of attribute and mode. The latter are defined before demonstration begins. The God-Nature has infinite attributes and infinite modes as Space has infinite directions and infinite configurations within itself. Spinoza distinguishes therefore, as Bruno had done, *natura naturans,* the active nature, from *natura naturata,* the passive nature; thus he distinguishes God from Nature after all, though in an oblique way. The comparison between the divine Substance and Space is more significant than a mere comparison be-

[2] *Ethics,* tr. by R. H. M. Elwes, *Philosophy of Benedict de Spinoza* (Tudor Publishing Company, n.d.), Part I, def. 3.

[3] Here again the kinship between Spinoza and Parmenides is striking. Cf. Richard Kroner, *Speculation in Pre-Christian Philosophy* (The Westminster Press, 1956), pp. 111 ff.

cause Spinoza explicitly proceeds after the fashion of geometry (*more geometrico*).

In this way a " coincidence of opposites " is achieved, but not in the sense of Nicholas of Cusa who realized the contradiction, rather inadvertently. Eternity and Time, God and World, the Universal and the Individual, even Necessity and Freedom are ultimately reconciled to each other, at least if we accept Spinoza's definitions and propositions. The world is ultimately inherent in God and so indirectly participates in his eternity and infinity. This relationship has the gravest consequences for man's cognition, freedom, and felicity, as we will see. Spinoza himself felt blessed and protected by this participation. In a letter he says: " I try to spend my life not in mourning and moaning, but in hilarity and joyfulness."

GOD AND WORLD

God-Nature (as Goethe translated the duplicity of Spinoza's supreme principle) is both thinking and extended. Thought (*cogitatio*) and extension (*extensio*) are his attributes in so far as we know them; in fact, God has an infinite number of attributes, but we do not know the others. Since the two attributes are co-ordinated with each other, God's thoughts and his corporeal affections correspond with each other. He is both Mind and Nature in one. Therefore Nature is animated throughout, and Mind is corporeal or inseparable from the divine body.[4] Here Spinoza is in agreement with Jacob Boehme whom he, however, did not know. The modes of the divine being are also double: partly ideas, partly physical entities. Modes are " particular things . . . which are finite and have a conditioned existence." [5] They are conditioned inasmuch as they depend directly upon each other and indirectly upon the infinite substance of which they are modifications. Spinoza nowhere says how and why these finite modifications arise within the divine eternal, and infinite being. He takes their existence for granted, as the geometrician assumes without question the possibility of drawing lines and figures in the infinite space.

The existence of modes implies a partial negation of the divine substance, since this substance is infinite while they are finite. What is the source of this negation? Does the divine Mind negate itself?

---

4 Elwes, *op. cit.,* Part II, prop. 13, note.   5 Part II, def. 7.

Spinoza remains silent on this point. He only states that God is absolute affirmation; in the so-called *Tractatus Brevis* (a short outline of his principles) he expressly states: " Of all imperfections the greatest is nonbeing," as Plato and Augustine had done before him.[6] Why then does God, who is absolutely perfect, make himself imperfect by partly negating himself? Or else if he is not the author of this negation, who is the author, since there is nothing besides God? Of course we could also ask why there is a duplicity of God and Nature. We are never informed about either question; they are the " dogmatic " presuppositions of the whole system which, however, make this very dogmatism itself questionable.

In Bruno's aesthetic cosmotheology the duality of a Creator-Artist and his created work was meaningful, partly because we can understand that such a God creates and because action and movement belong essentially to the infinite universe of the Italian philosopher of nature. In Spinoza's scheme, where all action and movement is ultimately denied, such a double character of God is less understandable. The claim to comprehend Him stands in harsh contradiction to the incomprehensibility of his relation to his attributes and modes. Only those who are impressed by the outer perfection of the system or those who are inclined to accept it out of the same love of God which impelled Spinoza to create it can overlook the lack of logical consistency and the fact that Spinoza did not make good his claim of logical demonstrability and rationality. Of course, the moral grandeur, the mystical piety, the sublime loftiness of his character are not impaired thereby. One may even say that the intuition which generates the demonstration is beyond all contradictions, and that the whole system is sound if one takes the definitions and the axioms for granted.

In order to mitigate the gulf between the infinite substance and the finite modes, Spinoza interpolated the concept of the infinite modes which have caused trouble for his interpreters. There are two infinite modes, the infinite intellect and the infinite motion. However, the distinction between finite and infinite modes is by no means clear. An infinite mode pertains to the divine being, inasmuch as it is infinite; but as a mode it seems to belong to the finite world. It is obvious what Spinoza wished to do by introducing such

[6] Part I, ch. 4.

a concept, but the concept does not truly attain the synthesis of infinity and modality that it is supposed to achieve. Rather, the incompatibility between those opposites stands out all the more. The infinite intellect is a mode because it thinks, and thinking entails acts that cannot be combined with the eternal and perfect essence of God; the infinite motion again is a mode because it implies becoming and change, while God is immutable and stable. But the mere synthesis of the two mutually exclusive features — infinity and mutability — does not heal the break.

In an Appendix to Part I, Spinoza vehemently attacks teleology and theism. God cannot be a providential will, for " experience day by day . . . showed by infinite examples that good and evil fortunes fall to the lot of the pious and impious alike." Theologians therefore laid down as an axiom that God's judgments far transcend human understanding. Such a doctrine might well have sufficed to conceal the truth for the human race for all eternity, if mathematicians had not furnished another standard of verity in considering the essence and properties of figures without regard to their final causes. So strong was Spinoza's mathematical bias, so strong the impression wrought upon his mind by the victorious triumph of modern physics and the breakdown of the Aristotelian teleology that he did not realize how little the method of mathematics and physics could help a theologian to think out the mysterious essence of God! How could he believe that his mechanistic theology could explain the sufferings of the innocent, although this theology culminated in the idea that God loves himself, including his finite modes, and that man should love God?

The Human Mind

A positive answer to the question raised is given by Spinoza's doctrine of man, who is a mode within the divine substance and therefore also an idea in the divine mind. Man, as such an idea, is a finite entity caused by other finite entities of the like sort and causing in turn other ideas. This idea corresponds to a finite body which is a mode of the infinite body of God, so that " the order and connection of the ideas is the same as the order and connection of (extended) things." [7] In this thesis the epistemological relation between the

[7] Part II, prop. 7.

knowing subject and the objects known is definitely perverted and completely adulterated into an ontological or cosmological relation between existing entities. The proof of this proposition unmistakably discloses this fateful confusion: " The idea of everything that is caused depends on a knowledge of the cause, whereof it is an effect." [8] The lapse from epistemology into cosmotheology, already committed by Descartes, was now even more overtly perpetrated by Spinoza. The thinking self of man was identified with one of the fleeting ideas in the mind or intellect of God. The relation between subject and object was replaced by and confused with the relation between mind and body. The thinking subject was thereby deprived of all selfhood and responsibility; knowledge was degraded to the causal nexus of the ideas. Spinoza never reflected upon the all-important difference between the sphere of cognition and the sphere of causality. In this respect he really approached dangerously near the materialistic speculation of men like Gassendi whose views Descartes had victoriously refuted.

Another fateful mistake was connected with this misunderstanding of the epistemological relation between the thinking subject and the objects known. The difference between the intellect and its ideas was given up. The intellect was conceived as the causal nexus of the ideas (as later by Hume too). But Spinoza was not quite consistent in this, since he teaches that there is an idea in the divine intellect which corresponds to the human intellect. The impossibility of ascribing to God single ideas and even a concatenation of ideas, in analogy to the human intellect, here comes to the fore. On the one hand, the human intellect is merely such a concatenation, on the other hand, there is a special idea in the divine intellect which corresponds to the human intellect (as also to the human body). These two elements of the doctrine cannot be brought together. If the human intellect is merely a succession of ideas, then no special idea can correspond to it. If, on the other hand, such a special idea does correspond to it, then it is more than a mere succession of ideas. What is it?

The truth brought out by Descartes is that the intellect is not a

---

[8] The same confusion occurs when Spinoza identifies the object of the idea which represents the human mind with the human body (Part II, prop. 13), whereas according to his system the idea of the human body in the divine intellect belongs to a mode different from the idea of the human mind. Cf. the note of that prop.

mere sequence of ideas, but a thinking self or subject which is *toto genere,* i.e., by nature absolutely different from that sequence. Spinoza sacrificed the knowing self for the sake of his cosmotheological scheme. The human intellect is not an intellect at all, but merely an object in the mind of God; it loses its subjectivity, its freedom, its activity, i.e., that mark which distinguishes it categorically from all objects. The very essence of knowledge was thereby destroyed. Only divine knowledge was upheld. But as we have seen the concept of an infinite mode is so precarious that even the divine mind or intellect loses its meaningful function.

Spinoza's interest was not directed toward an understanding of the epistemological questions, but only toward the knowledge of God. Man was considered as secondary. Even so, the ethical and religious aspect were important enough so that he had to revindicate selfhood and freedom, at least in a certain sense. In order to arrive at this goal, Spinoza argues that ideas "differ one from another, one being more excellent than another and containing more reality." [9] By this artifice he restored, as it were, the world of values which was threatened by the principle of causality and determinism. Secondly, he admits that "the idea which constitutes the actual being of the human mind, is not simple but compounded of a great number of ideas." [10] Thus he restored the unity of the mind and its difference from the sequence of ideas. And thirdly he distinguishes, as Descartes had done, adequate (clear and distinct) ideas from inadequate ones, a distinction pointing to the truth value of knowledge in contrast to the error arising out of sensation and imagination.

By means of these concessions Spinoza could rehabilitate the epistemological dignity of intellect and knowledge. However, he had to pay a high price for this correction of the original scheme. The adequacy of ideas is guaranteed only if they do not merely exist on the level of the finite mode but participate in the infinite mode of the divine intellect; in other words, if they are not merely subject to causality but belong to the order of eternity. In order to enjoy the value of truth the ideas in the human mind must be also ideas in the divine mind. The adequate ideas cannot be so fleeting and transitory as the inadequate ideas, they must rather be understood as perma-

[9] Part II, prop. 13, note.   [10] Prop. 15.

nently valid. How can ideas in the finite human mind, which is only a mode and, being such, belongs merely to the temporal order, yet also be eternal and belong to the infinite divine mind? We met this question before but in the reverse sense. We asked how the divine substance can divide itself into finite modes. Now we ask: how can the finite modes, at least in so far as they are human and harbor adequate ideas, surmount their finitude and return as it were to the divine substance? Both questions are equally unanswerable when we remain within the framework of Spinoza's system.

But Spinoza at least recognizes, although inconsistently, the value difference first between the material world and the thinking self, and second between the two kinds of modes, i.e., the higher rank of thought and mind. Whereas the body is merely an infinitely small part of the extended physical world, the human intellect, inasmuch as it strives after truth and attains knowledge, is on the level of the infinite intellect of God. Spinoza bluntly grants that the human mind thinking of God cannot err because God is himself the truth.[11] "As light displays both itself and darkness, so is truth a standard both of itself and of falsity."[12] Schelling remarks on this thesis: "Nothing surpasses the serene joy expressed in these words." Indeed, here the source of Spinoza's speculative certainty shines most brightly: his love of God. However, this love itself is not the result of his speculation, but its presupposition.

KNOWLEDGE AND PASSIONS

The last three parts of the *Ethics* deal with the nature of the human passions and with the bondage which is involved in the power of the passions over the human soul and mind, but which is finally broken by the power of the intellect over the passions. The whole system reaches its summit in the last part which establishes this intellectual hegemony; it would seem that the entire system is founded emotionally upon this last part and that Spinoza would never have written the first four parts without possessing within himself the intellectual power which is finally derived from the premises in a logical form.

The third part develops an elaborate analysis of the human emotions. In the Preface we find the famous sentence: "I shall consider

[11] Cf. Part II, prop. 41.   [12] Prop. 43, note.

human actions and desires in exactly the same manner as though I were concerned with lines, planes, and solids." Indeed, seldom, if anywhere, were the emotions, which are the most stirring and agitating forces in the human personality, defined and systematized with more poise and equanimity. Spinoza himself says that his doctrine is " as necessary for speculation as it is for the wise institution of life." [13] The quasi-mathematical objectivity therefore has a specially heightened significance when it is exhibited in the system of the emotions. The moral drawn from this detachment is this: the wise man should look at his own passions as if they were nothing but geometrical entities; to the degree to which he succeeds in applying this principle, the passions will no longer enslave him.

In the second part Spinoza made the astounding statement: " *Voluntas et intellectus unum et idem sunt* " (" Will and intellect are one and the same thing ").[14] No other statement illustrates better how deeply Spinoza was immersed in the ancient and Scholastic tradition, for the identity professed implies the primacy of the intellect. The will (in contrast to the impulses, desires, and emotions) is not merely the finite cause of action, but it is one with that intellect which can rise to the level of God. The will can therefore control the emotions and their tyranny by means of insight and knowledge. The intellect stands outside and above the sphere in which the human soul is enslaved; the will, being identical with the intellect, enjoys the same privilege.

" Everything," Spinoza defines, " in so far as it is in itself, endeavors to persist in its own being." [15] One might render this statement in another way: everything that exists endeavors to be as infinite as the divine substance. This version would be in agreement with the definition of the substance which alone is " in itself," whereas all other entities are not " in themselves," but in the infinite substance and therefore modes. The statement has still another origin. It is derived from the mechanical principle of Descartes, according to which movement persists in its direction and velocity if nothing interferes with it: the so-called law of inertia. And third, Spinoza was probably also affected by the doctrine of Thomas Hobbes, who taught that the first principle of life is its self-preserva-

---

[13] Part II, prop. 49, schol.
[14] Part II, prop. 49, corollary.
[15] Part III, prop. 6.

tion. This principle points to how Spinoza could conceive of man as a mode and yet maintain that man to a certain degree at least is self-dependent and self-existing — a self and not merely a compound of ideas. Spinoza used this principle in order to arrive at his final doctrine of the intellectual power of man.

In so far as we are merely modes, we are not active but passive, not moving but moved. As being moved we have emotions or passions. It makes us mere effects of causes outside ourselves and therefore impotent and enslaved. Man as a part of nature (*natura naturata*) is thus "always a prey to his passions." [16] In so far as man is not merely such a mode, but participates in the infinite and eternal power of God, he can discipline himself, i.e., subject his passions to his knowledge and will. Since Spinoza fails to discriminate between the order of cognition and that of causality, he can say that there are adequate and inadequate causes of human actions. They are adequate when man acts not by being moved but by moving out of himself, or when man acts not by passion but by thinking. " By an adequate cause I mean a cause through which its effect can be clearly and distinctly perceived; by an inadequate cause I mean a cause through which, by itself, its effect cannot be understood." [17] I am the author of my actions only if I can understand them out of myself alone as an intellectual being, or if they are brought about by my will. Only then are they not contingent as are all other effects and causes, but conditioned by myself — they are not actions at all in the proper sense, but rather acts of knowledge. The most adequate act is therefore the speculative insight into the truth of God; this insight elevates me above the whole sphere of causes and effects and makes me a participant of eternity; then I look at myself *sub specie aeternitatis*.

Only then am I the adequate cause of my motives and actions because I am no longer driven by the world, by other people, or by my own emotions, but by truth or God alone. Only then I am not merely a mode, but a real self, precisely because I am no longer an individual and finite being, but as universal and infinite as God is. Only then do I truly and adequately " preserve my own being." I preserve it when I lose it in the all-embracing totality of being which is God, and I can lose it that way by understanding myself out of God and

[16] Part IV, prop. 4, corollary.   [17] Part III, def. 1.

by not acting out of particular reasons or motives.[18] This is the paradoxical conclusion Spinoza derives from his doctrine, without, however, remarking that it is paradoxical, perhaps even without ever realizing its paradoxical character. Spinoza applies here as elsewhere not the geometrical logic of his method, but — to speak with Pascal — the logic of the heart. Thus Spinoza rectifies his one-sided cosmotheological perspective and acknowledges after all the personality and dignity of the individual human subject. It is this inconsistency which makes Spinoza's speculation as rich and deep as it is. It shows that Spinoza loved God and truth more than his " scientific " demonstrations.

The human mind is active, in so far as it possesses adequate ideas; it is passive and suffering, in so far as it is possessed by inadequate ideas. Truth and error are therefore the cardinal source not only of knowledge, but also of volition and action. Metaphysical knowledge is wisdom that enables me to act in accordance with the ultimate truth. By that wisdom I am both human and divine. In his system of passions Spinoza tried to be strictly psychological, inquiring dispassionately into the concatenation of emotions and motives. It is a marvelous account of this subject, which has rarely been treated in such a full and satisfactory manner. The English physiologist Maudsley says of it that it "was never surpassed and will probably be never surpassed." [19]

Spinoza uses in his system of human emotions the terms " good " and " bad " not in a strictly moral but in a utilitarian sense. " In no case do we strive for, wish for, long for, or desire anything because we deem it to be good, but rather we deem a thing to be good because we strive for it, wish for it, long for it, or desire it." [20] He would not have said the same about truth and falsity! [21] It is interesting that Spinoza denounces hope, fear, confidence, humility, and repentance as arising out of man's weakness, and not out of his intellectual strength. In such places Spinoza's Stoicism seems to prevail over his Biblical piety.

[18] Cf. the saying of Jesus: "He that loseth his life for my sake shall find it" (Matt. 10:39).

[19] Cf. J. Freudenthal, *Spinoza,* II, p. 239.

[20] Part III, prop. 9, note.

[21] Cf. above, p. 155.

Freedom and Virtue

The phrase "some action which we believe we have performed by the free decision of our mind" is full of implications.[22] Our mind, according to Spinoza's system, is not free if driven by desire or emotion. In that case we do not act by the will but merely by appetite. We are really free only if we act adequately, i.e., guided by the intellect disciplining the passions. "Inadequate" causes generate inner bondage; "adequate" causes, freedom. The outcome of inner bondage is enmity and strife between human beings; the outcome of freedom is agreement between them, since they do not differ with respect to their relation to truth. "In so far only as men live in obedience to reason, do they always agree in nature."[23] Thus a moral perspective finally triumphs over the utilitarian doctrine, although it is re-established only on the ground of Spinoza's ultimate intellectualism. Only if the will is identical with the intellect and actions are no longer real actions, can men agree. The dictum of Plato that the state will be well organized only if philosophers are kings can be transposed to the system of Spinoza, when we say that an agreement between people can be obtained only if all men become philosophers and replace action by thought. One can hardly go farther in the direction of intellectualism.

Spinoza's ethics is therefore strangely meta-ethical. In the last analysis it is not an ethics at all but instruction on how to achieve unity with God. If the will is ultimately intellect, if actions are to be replaced by thoughts, then moral life is in fact abolished. Instead of action contemplation alone remains, as it really did in Spinoza's life. This was the price Spinoza paid in order to uphold his extreme intellectualism. Man is free, not because he can make moral decisions for which he is responsible, nor because he can choose good instead of evil, nor because he is able to pass moral judgments; rather, he is free when he is no longer a being that wills and acts, but is instead one that thinks and contemplates. He is free not as a moral self, but as that "mode" which by means of intuition and rational deduction can take the place of the divine substance. He is free then from the pressure of passions, from the causality of emotions, indeed, from all causality and from the whole world — he is free, not

[22] Part III, defs. 26 f.   [23] Part IV, prop. 35.

in the moral, but in the religious, sense. Spinoza's ethics is thoroughly intellectual as well as mystical.

However, Spinoza insists that his system permits ethical thought and moral virtue. But even the term " virtue " does not have a truly ethical, but — in Aristotelian terms — a dianoetical meaning; it is a virtue not properly of the human will, but of the thinking mind. It is akin to the Stoic virtue of apathy and ataraxia, of imperturbability and serenity. It is not so much a moral virtue as an intellectual power. " By virtue and power I mean the same thing," he can say.[24] The virtuous man is identical with the wise man, but the wise man is the man who thinks and understands instead of willing and acting. " Man, in so far as he is determined to a particular action because he has inadequate ideas, cannot be absolutely said to act in obedience to virtue; he can only be so described, in so far as he is determined to action because he understands." [25] Spinoza should have said, " In so far as he is not determined to action but instead understands," for this is the real doctrine which he defends, since man is not " determined " to any action precisely when and inasmuch as he understands. That this is Spinoza's real opinion can be confirmed by his own words: " Whatever we endeavor in obedience to reason is nothing further than to understand; neither does the mind, in so far as it makes use of reason, judge anything to be useful to it, save things as are conducive to understanding (*ad intelligendum*)." [26] This sentence is precise and unequivocal, because it is as thoroughly intellectualistic as Spinoza's entire system.

But this system is at the same time thoroughly mystical; indeed, its very intellectualism is of a mystical kind. What Spinoza calls " power " in defining virtue rests ultimately not so much upon the ability to think or to demonstrate, but to know and to love God. " The mind's highest good is the knowledge of God and the mind's highest virtue is to know God." [27] But to know God means ultimately to be united with him or even to be completely absorbed by him. What Spinoza here calls " power " is therefore in the last analysis what the Christian faith calls grace. But his pre-Christian intellectualism kept him from understanding it as grace, as it restricted his entire religious horizon.

Spinoza's " freedom " is therefore not a moral idea, but a religious

---

[24] Part IV, def. 8.
[25] Part IV, prop. 23.
[26] Part IV, prop. 26.
[27] Part IV, prop. 28.

or metaphysical one. There is a certain kinship between Spinoza's and Augustine's idea of freedom, but the difference is that according to Augustine freedom from the lust, passions, and desires of the natural man is due to the grace of God, while Spinoza thought that man can achieve it himself by his own intellect.[28] However, in so far as man's power of understanding is ultimately a part of God's own power, this difference between Augustine and Spinoza is of no great significance. What is really different is the religious background: that of Augustine is determined by Biblical faith, that of Spinoza, by an intellectualistic mysticism. That Spinoza's concept of freedom is not moral, but mystical or spiritual (if this word may be applied), can be corroborated by a sentence like the following, " If men were born free, they would so long as they remained free, form no conception of good and evil." [29] Free men have, like God, only adequate ideas and consequently none corresponding to evil; since, however, good and evil are correlative, they also have no conception of good. Free men, in other words, live " beyond good and evil," to use the expression of Nietzsche, a great admirer of Spinoza.

THE LOVE OF GOD

Spinoza's doctrine is consummated in the idea of love. Pleasure and pain are emotions which underlie all other emotions. Pleasure is defined as " the transition from a less to a greater perfection," pain as that " from a greater to a less perfection." [30] Perfection points to the degree of power, freedom, and virtue, i.e., of the victory achieved by the intellect over the passions. The word " pleasure " is ambiguous; it may mean sensuous enjoyment, but it may also mean the freedom from this enjoyment. It may mean either the attainment of goods useful to man in satisfying his appetites, or of a happiness superior to all usefulness. Spinoza oscillates constantly between these two meanings. He succeeds thereby in preserving the appearance of a systematic unity and coherence which in fact does not exist. The contradistinction between passion and action makes the inner break manifest; it elucidates the duality which cannot be derived from the unity of the divine substance.

Ultimately pain is the outcome of passion, action generates pleasure

[28] See Kroner, *Speculation and Revelation in the Age of Christian Philosophy*, p. 137.

[29] Part VI, prop. 68.

[30] Part III, defs. 2 and 3.

or happiness (*beatitudo*). Inadequate or contingent ideas cause pain, while the thinking activity of the mind and its adequate ideas cause beatitude. If the mind recognizes how passions are aroused, their power over the soul is defeated. Beatitude is therefore the effect of knowledge, of that knowledge which understands the causal nexus of the world (*natura naturata*). " The mind has greater power over the emotions and is less subject thereto, in so far as it understands all things as necessary." [31] Here it is clearly stated that the mind itself does not belong to the world, otherwise it would not be able to transcend the whole horizon of things connected with each other according to the principle of causality. The mind can grasp the very essence of all particular things, for this essence is identical with the concepts which govern the *Ethics*.[32]

The ability to know and understand causes the greatest pleasure; " in so far as we understand the causes of pain, to that extent pain ceases to be a passion, that is, it ceases to be pain." [33] The cause of this pleasure must be traced back to the origin of all things, for it is by knowing this origin that we feel our own intellectual power. This origin is God. From him all things are derived and upon him they all depend. Since Spinoza defines love as " pleasure, accompanied by the idea of an external cause," we must love God who is the cause of the greatest possible pleasure, namely, that which is aroused by knowledge.[34] This love is intellectual (spiritual), inasmuch as it is rooted in the idea of God. This greatest pleasure is beatitude; it cannot be separated from the contemplation of God. Thus Spinoza in his own way and by means of his own " geometrical " system arrives at a result that reminds us of medieval doctrines.

The union of contemplation and love is the zenith of the human mind, the fulfillment of all its aspirations, the consummation of its entire life and thought. Seen from the vantage point of this love, Spinoza's whole system is based upon that beatific vision which the church fathers and Christian mystics always regarded as the root of faith and as its highest attainment. And yet the Christian doctrine and Spinoza's system differ so widely that the analogy is deceptive;

[31] Part V, prop. 6.
[32] Cf. Part II, prop. 11; Part V, prop. 9, proof.
[33] Part V, prop. 18, note.
[34] Part III, def. 6.

in Spinoza's system all knowledge and insight rest upon man's own activity, his own power, his own victory over the passions, while the beatific vision of Christian mystics is the work of God alone. " He who clearly and distinctly understands himself and his emotions feels pleasure and this pleasure is accompanied by the idea of God; therefore such a one loves God, and so much the more in proportion as he more understands himself and his emotions." [35] This understanding is " the mind's highest virtue." [36] Virtue and happiness here coincide: " Beatitude is not the reward of virtue, it is virtue itself." [37] A triumphant and proud sentence!

However, this result must not conceal the inner ambiguities that mar the whole system. Although the supreme knowledge, the supreme happiness, and the supreme virtue are achievements of man's own activity and power, they are supreme only because they are at the same time the achievement and power of God himself. Only because man and God unite on this summit can man be blessed; only thus can his ideas be adequate, i.e., not particular or individual, but universal and eternal. The barrier between substance and mode, between the eternal and the temporal, the divine and the human dissolves where the highest goal of all aspirations is reached. This is the very essence of beatitude. But if that is so, how can we avoid concluding that God himself is the real author of this activity? And if so, can God be exempt from action and even from emotion? Two views clash in the system. That suggested by the first part describes God as one with the absolute necessity of all things. Then he is beyond all becoming and change, eternally the same, enthroned above all particular things and relations, and, as we have seen, above the level on which the difference between good and evil matters. His infinity excludes all finite causes and effects, motives and emotions. Only on that basis is the geometrical method meaningful.

But there is another line of thought which increasingly gains momentum and is finally victorious. God is not sheer necessity, but an infinite intellect which knows necessity and which thinks the truth. Then God's intellectual superiority outshines extension and nature, which are the mere objects of the divine intellect. His true substance is selfhood and action. But he is not unemotional nor is he beyond

[35] Part V, prop. 15.   [37] Part IV, prop. 42.
[36] Cf. Part IV, prop. 28.

good and evil; he is, at least in a certain way, involved in man's own struggle to defeat his passions. He is not indifferent with respect to man's virtue and knowledge; and he is implied in man's supreme happiness or beatitude.

The full antagonism between these two approaches comes to light when we compare two incompatible statements in the last part of the *Ethics*. In proposition 17 we read, "God is without passions, neither is he affected by any emotion of pleasure or pain." In the corollary to that proposition Spinoza emphatically asserts, "God does not love or hate anyone," a thesis that is in agreement with the definition of love as an emotion. But in proposition 35 we read, "God loves himself with an infinite intellectual love." How can we bring together these two statements? It is the clash between the geometrical and the mystical aspects of the system which is here apparent, as indeed it was bound to occur somewhere. The naturalistic view of the divine substance and the spiritual view of God as eternal love collide in a dramatic fashion.

Doubtless, it is the second view that is more deeply rooted in Spinoza's personality, while the first view is characteristic of the age in which he lived and thought and composed his system. The true God of Spinoza, the man, is personal and resembles the Old Testament Creator, while the God-Nature of his definition in the first part is an adaptation to the Cartesian *Principles of Philosophy*. The inevitable encounter of the two ideas of God indicates the impossibility of constructing a system that could unite them. It shows the incompatibility of a naturalistic outlook and a mystical or religious faith, of the discursive demonstration and the immediate intuition — of speculation and revelation the way they are conceived by Spinoza.

The rest of Part V expounds more explicitly Spinoza's personal faith. He says in proposition 19 that " he who loves God, cannot endeavor that God should love him in return " (because he who loves God knows that God is without emotions) but in proposition 36 he says that " the intellectual love of the mind toward God is that very love of God whereby God loves himself, not in so far as he is infinite, but in so far as he can be explained through the essence of the human mind, regarded under the aspect of eternity (*sub specie aeternitatis*). In other words, the intellectual love of the human mind toward God is part of the infinite love wherewith God loves himself." This proposition reveals fully the profoundly mystical spirit of Spinoza's doctrine concerning the love of God. Nowhere else does he so plainly identify the divine and the human mind: they are united in love, so much so that it is not possible to separate the love of man for God and God's love for himself. They are at bottom one and the same thing.

By loving God we participate in God's own eternal life. Through our love we make ourselves a part of God himself. The statement, according to which we should not expect God to love us if we love him, is surpassed and indeed negated, since the identity of man's love for God and God's love for himself implies that God does love man, since man's love of God is the manifestation of God's love of man. It is not only to be expected that God returns my love to him, but my own love is at the same time his response to my love. As beatitude is not the reward of virtue, but virtue itself, so the love to God is itself his love to me! We could not explain God " through the essence of the human mind " if this mystical identity between the two did not exist. In addition to this unavoidable conclusion, I will add that Spinoza, in contrast to what he has said about God being unable to be affected by any emotion, in the note to proposition 36 himself speaks of " God's love toward man." " From what has been said we clearly understand wherein our salvation, or blessedness, or freedom consists: namely, in the constant and eternal love toward God, or in God's love toward man. This love or blessedness is in the Bible called glory, and not undeservedly." Nowhere else does Spinoza quote the Bible with such approval and identify his own speculative view of God with that of revelation.

The spiritual love toward God derives from intuitive knowledge which underlies speculation, but does not need demonstration, so that the common man who does not study philosophy yet can love God and feel that he is loved by God.[38] Virtue and freedom too are based upon that intuitive knowledge and therefore are accessible to every man — " He who knows things by this kind of knowledge passes to the summit of human perfection." [39] Intuition in Spinoza's system corresponds with the Christian Gnosticism of Clement of Alexandria. Although the system is intellectualistic in appearance,

---

[38] Cf. Part V, prop. 32, corollary.   [39] Part V, prop. 27.

to a deeper glance it discloses its inner warmth and fervor. The love of God is the key to this inner treasury.

Spinoza calls this love "the highest good which we can seek for under the guidance of reason; it is common to all men. . . . It cannot be stained by the emotion of envy or by the emotion of jealousy, but it must on the contrary needs be the more fostered in proportion as we conceive a greater number of men to rejoice therein." [40] Here Spinoza abandons the isolated position of the thinker who achieves by the power of his mind and intellect that superior knowledge which the common man can never acquire; he joins all men capable of enjoying the love of God. As Clement wavers between two conceptions of the Christian faith: one, as it were, democratic and open to all believers; the other, aristocratic and granted only to those very few who can climb to the summit of Christian Gnosticism, so Spinoza wavers between a democratic and an aristocratic interpretation of his speculative Gnosticism. [41] In the sentence quoted above he expresses his hope that all men will join the invisible church founded upon the love of God.

As Dante had to go through hell and purgatory before he was at last permitted to meet the saints in heaven, so Spinoza had to go through the hell of his naturalistic determinism and impersonal rationalism in order to arrive finally at the heaven of divine love. As Dante had to look at all the vices of men and their gloomy consequences, so Spinoza had to analyze all the passions and emotions which bring about pain before he was permitted to relish the beatific vision of the highest happiness and to enjoy the perfect union with God. In a solemn conclusion Spinoza expresses this hardship and this supreme joy: "If the way which I have pointed out as leading to this result seems exceedingly hard, it may nevertheless be discovered. Needs it must be hard, since it is so seldom found. How would it be possible, if salvation were ready to our hand, and could without great labor be found, that it should be by almost all men neglected? All things excellent are as difficult, as they are rare."

[40] Part V, prop. 20.
[41] Cf. Kroner, *Speculation and Revelation in the Age of Christian Philosophy,* p. 71.

VII

MAN, THE PATTERN OF THE WORLD

DESCARTES, the initiator of modern epistemology, was a cosmological metaphysician, and Spinoza, the author of the *Ethics,* was a theological metaphysician. Gottfried Wilhelm von Leibniz (1646–1716) was the creator of an anthropocentric speculative system. In this respect Leibniz, more than Descartes and Spinoza, represented the modern spirit. Man to Leibniz is the model of everything, be it organic or inorganic, God or beast, spiritual or physical, material or immaterial. Leibniz was both a scientist and a humanist, but his humanism was dominant. He was a mathematician and a historian, but in his system the historian was in the forefront. He was one of the most universal thinkers that ever lived. He was a man of the world, but he was also a very lonely mind who insisted that the monads have no windows and doors. He was intimately related to statesmen and kings, and he was also interested in religion. He was the founder of a union between Protestant groups, but he wanted also to reconcile Protestantism and Catholicism. He was a politician himself, and also established learned societies in Prussia and in Russia. He corresponded with innumerable scholars in Germany and abroad and wrote innumerable articles, pamphlets, books, and historical records. He was interested in everything human, but also in nature and in things divine. He was a physicist, a biologist, a jurist, and a theologian. In philosophy he contributed to all disciplines: to epistemology and logic, to psychology and ethics, to politics and to metaphysics.

Whereas Descartes was a dualist, and Spinoza a monist, Leibniz was a pluralist. It is a striking fact that the three great possibilities of metaphysical thought were distributed in this way among the three great systematicians of the seventeenth century. In other respects, too, these three thinkers widely differ. Descartes was a nobleman; Spinoza, the son of a Jewish fugitive; Leibniz, a German of the middle class. Man in the Cartesian scheme was divided into two substances; the Spinozistic man was a mode of the divine substance; the monad of Leibniz was a self-dependent unit, as the name indicates. In the long history of the discovery of the self, Leibniz plays an important part. Although his monad is still a substance, it is modeled after the self. Man, more than in the system of Descartes and of Spinoza, is a self endowed with intellect, will, and impressions, directing himself toward a goal, suffering, and acting. In many respects Leibniz is the precursor of Kant, who was lastingly influenced by his system. But on the whole, Descartes, Spinoza, and Leibniz belong to the same group of thinkers who were, at least with respect to their methodical ideal, dependent upon the main current of thought in their century, i.e., upon the primacy of mathematical physics. Although they were naturalists only on the surface, naturalism was still an aspect of their systems. Leibniz was a disciple of Descartes, as Aristotle was a disciple of Plato. But in both cases the disciple outgrew the master and founded his own original system.

Each of the three tried to reconcile revelation and speculation by speculative means without appealing to revelation or adapting thought to it, as the thinkers in the age of Christian philosophy had done. Descartes was relatively indifferent to religion and faith; Spinoza was overtly a severe critic of the revealed conceptions of God, but inwardly he adhered to the Biblical tradition. Leibniz was a theologian and believed that his metaphysics could be easily understood in terms of theology. One of his longest works was dedicated to the purpose of justifying the ways of God. To show that religion and science are compatible with each other and can be united by means of speculation — this was the highest aim of his aspirations. Leibniz' system issued from physical considerations and tried to solve physical problems, but step by step it glided from the physical to the metaphysical sphere. At the end it was the Scholastic polarity of nature and grace which occupied most deeply his thinking mind.

Leibniz was from the outset opposed to the Cartesian definition of the material body as being nothing but an extended substance. He realized early that the physical entities are something more than extended, namely, endowed with force or energy. This difference would have been of little philosophic significance if it had been confined to the realm of physics proper. But Leibniz realized at once that greater questions were at stake. The whole metaphysical duality in the Cartesian system of extended things and thinking things would be overthrown if the corporeal things were endowed with the power of acting. The step from mechanics to dynamics and from dynamics to biology and finally even to psychology and the metaphysical understanding of man would enable the thinker to overcome the original duality and to arrive at a pluralistic conception of being, culminating in an all-embracing unity. Not mechanics, as Descartes thought, but dynamics are at the root of the philosophic interpretation of nature. Leibniz' view always remained dynamic. The ultimate metaphysical entities are power centers, as man himself is such a center.

The solution of the metaphysical problem should be sought in the dynamic nature of intellectual and volitional action. Here we have the prototype of being as such. Not only movement, but development toward an end is the true essence of all change. From the outset Leibniz was impressed by the teleological speculation of Plato and Aristotle, more than by mathematical physics. But the task was to show how these two antagonistic views of nature can be reconciled to each other, since Galileo had defeated the "forms" of Aristotle and had victoriously proved that mathematical necessity, not teleological finality, dominates physical processes.

It is difficult to understand the metaphysical principles of Leibniz because he wrote so many essays and letters in which he propounded them; he never developed a comprehensive system like the *Ethics* of Spinoza or the *Principles* of Descartes. In each essay and in each letter we find another approach to a solution, now starting from merely or mainly physical problems, now sketching the monadology, which gives a more ultimate picture. The themes of most papers and letters are dictated by the questions of various writers; they are therefore more polemical than constructive, and one is often at a loss as to what the ultimate positive answer of Leibniz may be. Even his more explicit book, *New Essays Concerning Human Understanding,* is polemical; Leibniz tried to refute the philosophy of Locke in that book, so that his own views can only indirectly be learned from it. The title itself is an adaptation of the title of Locke's famous essays on the same subject. Besides, this book of Leibniz was never finished, so that his own doctrine is not fully developed.

But there is a more cogent reason for the difficulty of understanding the ultimate intentions of Leibniz. He has, as it were, two versions of his philosophy, the one (called by Kuno Fischer in his *History of Modern Philosophy*) " exoteric," the other " esoteric "; one which is meant for scientists, the other, for metaphysicians. As Parmenides wrote two schemes of thought, one for those who are deceived by the illusion that this world of change truly exists, the other for those who are willing to penetrate into the only true substance of things, so Leibniz too wrote sometimes for those who clung to the physical world of outer things in space and time, and sometimes for those who realized that this is not the true world, but only its outer appearance and that there is an inner aspect of being which alone reveals ultimate truth and reality. These two versions have some similarity to the two aspects of the Spinozistic system: its geometrical appearance and its spiritual and mystical innerness. But while Spinoza did not distinguish the two aspects, but on the contrary denied such a duality, Leibniz saw the duplicity of his own expositions. He knew very well that there are two different or even opposite conceptions of reality, the one taken from physics, the other from metaphysics, and he tried to explain from the metaphysical perspective the possibility and the error of the physical view.

THE CONCEPT OF SUBSTANCE

Spinoza cut the knot of the Cartesian concept of substance, partly applied to finite things, partly to nature or God alone, by choosing this second alternative and denying categorically the substantiality of finite things, even of man. Leibniz went in the opposite direction. He decided that there are finite substances besides the infinite substance. Of course, all depends upon the definition of substance itself. Spinoza eliminated finite substances by defining substance as that being which is absolutely independent and can be conceived by itself alone. Leibniz agreed with Spinoza that substance should be independent of other beings, but he disagreed with his conclusion that therefore God alone is substance or that only the infinite being is absolutely independent. According to Leibniz, finite beings also can be independent and therefore substances in the sense of Spinoza. In that way Leibniz returned to the Cartesian scheme, but he deviated from that scheme in so far as the substances of Descartes were not independent, but, on the contrary, were interrelated, dependent upon one another and upon nature as a whole.

How could Leibniz take such a path between Descartes and Spinoza? How could he assert that finite substances are independent and yet finite? This was the peculiar problem which Leibniz solved or tried to solve by his monadology. The monads are not, as the Cartesian substances, either extended or thinking; they are rather essentially thinking. In this respect Leibniz deviated from Spinoza who had conceived of extension and thought as two equally real attributes of the infinite substance; he also disagreed with Descartes, who had taught that finite substances are either extended (material) or thinking (like man). But how could Leibniz assert that all finite beings are thinking? Is it not evident that this attribute cannot be predicated of beings below the level of man? This cannot be denied, but Leibniz did not apply the term " thinking " to all substances, at least not in the sense of human thinking; what he meant to say was that all beings are souls.

Leibniz took over from Spinozism the thesis of panpsychism. In Spinoza's system the attributes of the divine substance, extension and thought, were also attributes of the modes, so that a perfect parallelism between the two prevailed throughout the universe. Leibniz transferred the second attribute, that of thought, to all beings, though not to all in the same sense or to the same degree. All monads are souls and therefore possess the capacity of producing ideas, although this capacity is not equally strong in all monads. Some can form more adequate ideas than others. The Spinozistic distinction between adequate and inadequate ideas was used by Leibniz in order to distinguish the rank of the monads and also to solve the problem how the monads can be both independent and yet finite. They are independent inasmuch as they produce ideas out of themselves alone, but they are finite inasmuch as these ideas are not absolutely adequate. Adequacy of the produced ideas was the key which Leibniz applied in order to establish a hierarchy of monads according to their rank. The world is a realm of monads each producing ideas independently of one another but the lower monads produce less, the higher ones more adequate ideas.

At first glance such a scheme seems to be very arbitrary and not at all in agreement with the facts of experience. How could Leibniz deny that there are beings which are not souls? How could he reduce the material objects to quasi-thinking souls, thereby making man the pattern of the world? Is not such an anthropomorphic view utterly fantastic? Are the physical atoms or molecules souls? Are the plants souls? Are the lower animals souls? And is not their material existence at least one aspect of all these beings? Are they not at least a mixture of both body and soul?

But we have seen on our journey from Descartes to Spinoza and then to Leibniz why and how the solution of Leibniz grew out of the problem of substance. This problem arose from the duality of matter and mind, or of extension and thought. Descartes solved it by proposing two kinds of substances; Spinoza, by proposing two attributes of the one substance; Leibniz, by denying that the two attributes are of equal metaphysical reality and by asserting that only thought or mind has metaphysical reality, while extension or matter is (as we will see) only appearance. Leibniz thereby did justice to the superiority of thought and mind; indeed, he expressed this epistemological and ethical superiority in terms of metaphysical speculation. In his view the superiority is so great and momentous that only mind and thought can be regarded as metaphysically real. Descartes did not solve at all the problem of the relation between body and soul; hence his disciples created Occasionalism. Spinoza tried to solve it by depriving both body and soul of their metaphysical reality, reducing them to modes of the one divine substance; in other words, he appealed to the oneness of that substance in order to explain the interrelation between body and soul. " By denying the existence of individual substances he (Spinoza) thought it possible to avoid the whole difficulty; but this is to cut the knot instead of dissolving it," Leibniz argues.[1]

To Leibniz, the man of the world, pluralism of substances was the only possible solution; but the substances had to be spiritual in essence. The world is like the society of men, each of whom is essen-

[1] *Philosophische Schriften,* her. v. C. J. Gerhardt, VI, 529 ff. *Considerations About the Doctrine of One All-embracing Spirit* (1702).

tially an individual and therefore independent. Each is confined by his horizon and by the clarity and distinctness of his inner ideas, therefore limited in power and action. But this comparison is not quite correct. The society of men is composed of beings who have bodies and souls. The world that is composed of monads differs from human society, since the monads are solely spiritual. The material world is an appearance that exists in the souls alone, in so far as the souls are not able to penetrate into the metaphysical essence of the monads, or in so far as their ideas of the monads are inadequate so that the monads seem to be material and extended. Leibniz, by stating this somewhat queer doctrine, adopted the Cartesian distinction between objects perceived by the senses and objects conceived by mathematical physics. As Descartes had taught that perception does not see the reality of the objects, but merely their appearance, so Leibniz too asserted that the physical objects as they appear to the senses and to the imagination are not the truly real objects. But whereas Descartes had trusted mathematical physics to such a degree as to believe that science finds the metaphysical truth, Leibniz refused to draw such a conclusion. To him mathematical physics is (as it later was to Kant, who was and remained a Leibnizian in this respect) a science of the appearances of the true substances. These true substances as they are "in themselves" (here Kant abandoned the Leibnizian philosophy) are not merely quantitative relations but spiritual entities. In rejecting the metaphysical relevance of mathematical physics, Leibniz agreed with Galileo, who had denied it.[2]

But in contrast to the scientist Galileo, Leibniz was confident that speculation can comprehend the true essence and substance of things. He was confident that the inward experience of the thinking self can give the clue to the understanding of the "structure of the All" as Galileo had called the metaphysical reality. Leibniz abandoned thereby the naturalism of the seventeenth century and arrived at a complete spiritualism; but he still believed that the physical objects can be understood metaphysically — an opinion that Kant alone abandoned. It is significant that Leibniz belonged to both the seventeenth and the eighteenth centuries, preparing and partly anticipating the epoch of the Enlightenment.

[2] See above, p. 55.

Physical and Metaphysical Energy

Leibniz insisted, along with Galileo, Descartes, and Spinoza, that scientific truth is trustworthy compared to sense perception or imagination. Mathematical physics is definitely superior to the Aristotelian and Scholastic philosophy of nature. However, in a deeper sense, in the sense of metaphysics, it is not trustworthy at all; on the contrary, it must be replaced by speculation. Only speculation sees through the appearance of the material world to the very foundation of being. How can we distinguish two kinds of truth, that of physics and that of metaphysics? What does the term " appearance " mean after all? In what sense are the concepts and propositions of mathematical physics inadequate ideas? Is not " appearance " always connected with sense perception? Can this term be applied to scientific truth? Was not Descartes right in that respect?

It may be questionable whether Leibniz realized clearly in the beginning of his philosophic development that metaphysics must transcend entirely the horizon of scientific investigation and theory. In an autobiographical sketch he relates that he oscillated for a while in his youth between the Aristotelian or Scholastic tradition and the modern science of Galileo. " Finally," he says, " the mechanical theory prevailed in my mind and I was persuaded to study mathematics." However, when he was seventeen years old he chose as the subject of his bachelor's thesis the problem of individuality, which indicated his early metaphysical interest and the leaning toward his later monadology.[3] When he grew more mature he resolutely turned to the " Aristotelian tradition " although in modern fashion. In his *Discourse on Metaphysics* (1686) he says: " I know I am advancing a great paradox in pretending to resuscitate in some sort the ancient philosophy, and to recall *postlimino*[4] the substantial forms almost banished from our modern thought. But perhaps I will not be condemned lightly when it is known that I have long meditated over the modern philosophy and that I have devoted much time to experiments in physics and to demonstrations of geometry and that I,

[3] The thesis had the title: *Disputatio metaphysica de principio individui* (Metaphysical Disputation on the Principle of Individuality), 1663.

[4] A term of international law denoting the right by which things are restored to their former status.

too, for a long time was persuaded of the baselessness of those beings which, however, I was finally obliged to take up again in spite of myself." [5]

Leibniz did not simply return to Aristotelianism; he began by criticizing the Cartesian concept of the extended substance. Descartes, Leibniz argued, did not sufficiently recognize the element of physical power inherent in every material body. By identifying matter and extension he disregarded the difference between the purely mathematical (geometrical) and the physical constitution of the bodies moved and moving. Extension does not exhaust, it does not even truly indicate, the specific reality of those bodies. Physical force or power or energy is involved in the essence of this reality; it is the factor that distinguishes a physical entity from a geometrical figure. Movement itself springs from that factor; it is not only, as Descartes thought, brought into play from outside by a divine mover. This dynamic factor is the very core of physical substances, while figure, size, and relation to other geometrical figures are accidental. This dynamic figure gives to the extended things their substantiality and very corporeality; it is their true " self." This power or energy is not only transferred to the body by outer motion, it is actually inherent in the body; it is an active force, not only " inertia " which resists active interference.[6] It is this inner energy which gives the body a kind of self-dependence or self-existence, and which represents the metaphysical reality behind the physical appearance. " Taken strictly, everything is indefinite with regard to extension, and whatever we attribute to bodies are only phenomena and abstractions. . . . It is as great an error to conceive of extension as a primitive concept without looking into the real concept of substance and action." [7] " Far from the figure being a constitutive element in the body, it is not a quality at all real and determined outside of thought." [8]

" Theological considerations are involved," he wrote to Arnauld. " Each individual substance expresses the resolves which God made in regard to the whole universe." [9] In his *Discourse on Metaphysics*

[5] *Leibniz: Philosophical Classics,* tr. by George R. Montgomery (The Open Court Publishing Company, 1937), p. 17.

[6] See the letter to De Volder (March 24, 1699).

[7] Cf. letter to Arnauld (April 30, 1687), Montgomery, *op. cit.,* pp. 180 ff.

[8] Letter to the same (Oct., 1687), Montgomery, *op. cit.,* p. 222.

[9] Montgomery, *op. cit.,* p. 151.

one section has the title: "That the opinions of the theologians and of the so-called Scholastic philosophers are not to be wholly despised." [10] Whereas Descartes and Spinoza believed that the world should be explained by means of God or nature, Leibniz thought that the world is self-existent and self-dependent, even though created by God. God does not, as the Occasionalists taught, intervene each time the will moves the hand. The world is so instituted that God's plan is perfectly immanent and settled for all times. All things in the world conform to that universal plan, each in its own individual form and according to its own eternal constitution. The Occasionalists allowed contingent and arbitrary actions on the part of God; Leibniz rejected such a view. God has arranged the world in such a way that everything agrees with everything in advance and a universal harmony is therefore the result. The fusion of physical and metaphysical, of scientific and theological, arguments was, of course, a general trend in the seventeenth-century speculation. We find it in Descartes, Spinoza, Hobbes, Malebranche, as well as in Leibniz. But Leibniz deviated from all other thinkers in that he reintroduced Aristotelian concepts into his ontological scheme and thereby surpassed from the outset naturalism and mechanism, which were the fruit of the ascendancy of the mathematical sciences.

MONADOLOGY

The most important step in that direction was his doctrine that physical energy is the outcome or the manifestation of the ultimate substance which he called "monad." Physical energy points to the really real: to that energy which is the very essence of the monad. In so far as it is not merely passive resistance as the Cartesians interpreted it, but rather *vis viva,* a living or actual energy acknowledged as such by the physicists, it is rooted in the activity that is the life of the monad. This activity differs in the different monads according to their rank. Physical energy is on the lowest level, or, rather, energy on the lowest level is perceived as physical. Leibniz resumed the Aristotelian idea of development. All things are in a state of permanent becoming caused by an inner energy. "Matter" is involved in this process, but merely as a subordinate constituent of the substance as a whole in which the "form" or the spiritual soul is domi-

[10] No. XI.

nant. Physics looks at the world only from the perspective of the material energy; the speculative thinker has to look at it from that of the whole. Matter is only the uncreative and relatively passive element within that whole, while the substantial form or the soul is the active element that resembles the creativity of God himself.

Scientifically, we know the organization of the monads only in their external and therefore phenomenal existence, whereas speculation knows them from within, it knows their substantial and intrinsic existence. Introspection is the method by which this inner constitution of the monads must be observed. Leibniz could have said with Augustine, " Look into your own innerness, there you will find the truth." Inward experience of ourselves alone unlocks the secret reality that is the basis of all experience. Man is the archetype, the pattern and model of the understanding of all things. Every monad is essentially a " mirror of the universe." Each embraces the whole, indeed each *is* the whole, as it appears from an individual point of view. The monad is what Aristotle called *entelecheia,* a being that grows according to an inner plan that is in harmony with the universal plan controlling all monads. " I think," Leibniz writes to Arnauld, "I have shown that every substance is indivisible, and that consequently every corporeal substance must have a soul, or at least an entelechy which has an analogy with the soul, because otherwise the body would be only a phenomenon." [11]

The last phrase is an adaptation to the " exoteric " expression of which Leibniz availed himself when speaking to Arnauld. What he really means is that the body is a phenomenon, but a phenomenon that represents a reality, namely, that of the spiritual entelechy, and therefore not " only " a phenomenon. " Extension, matter, and motion are mere phenomena, which have their rational foundation in the concept of energy: they are little real things as an image in mirror." [12] Space itself is a *phenomenon bene fundatum* (a phenomenon that has a real foundation or a foundation in reality).[13] Kant later called space a subjective form of the appearances, closely following Leibniz' idea. But Leibniz still believed that it is possible to know by speculation the " things-in-themselves," i.e., the monads.

[11] (Letter of Oct. 6, 1687), Montgomery, *op. cit.,* p. 225.
[12] Cf. *Schriften,* her. v. Gerhardt, II, p. 269 and *passim.*
[13] Montgomery, *op. cit.,* II, p. 251; III, p. 622.

Space belongs only to the phenomenal aspect of the monads, it is not an internal form of their existence. The monads are not spatial beings, but pure spirits. However, space is not merely an illusion; it is well founded in reality: it mirrors the inner rank order in an external outer way. According to that inner order every monad has its " place " in the hierarchy of things; this place appears to the external eyes of perception as a place in space.

Each monad reflects the whole world, but in a specific, individual perspective. The gradation of the monads is brought about by the degree of clarity and distinctness with which they produce the ideas of the world. The spatial order is only the outer reflection of that inner order. Even the lowest beings, inasmuch as they are not merely the objects of sensation, participate in the inner order. They are not merely material, but they are also spiritual. They are not merely mechanically arranged, but are also dynamic centers of their own life. This order is eternal and cannot be destroyed. " Every substantial form, or indeed, every substance is indestructible and also ingenerate." [14] Only this substantial reality makes a thing indivisible, a genuine unit, a kind of self. " Substantial unity calls for a thoroughly indivisible being. . . . This characteristic cannot be found either in figure or in motion both of which involve something imaginative. . . . It can be found, however, in a soul or a substantial form such as the one called I (ego)." Cautiously he adds in his letter: " I cannot tell exactly whether there are other true corporeal substances besides those which have life. But souls serve to give us a certain knowledge of others at least by analogy." [15] When Leibniz here says that figure " involves something imaginative," he uses the word " imaginative " in a sense different from that in which Descartes used it. Leibniz points to the " intuitive " character of space, to use the term which was later applied by Kant. The monads are " intelligible," as Kant would say; they cannot be grasped by intuition or imagination, but only by " pure reason."

" Every living thing contains a world of diversity in a real unity. . . . Souls have been living from the very creation of the world and they will live to its end." [16] Leibniz believed that the I

[14] Letter to Arnauld (Dec. 8, 1686), Montgomery, *op. cit.,* p. 159.
[15] Montgomery, *op. cit.,* pp. 161 f.
[16] Letter to Arnauld (April 30, 1687), Montgomery, *op. cit.,* pp. 194 f.

or self is the pattern that must guide us when we wish to understand the essence of things: " *Ce Moi, qui dit beaucoup.*" [17] Leibniz was aware that the meaning of the self was deeper than anything else; in that as in many other respects he was the direct forerunner of Kant. He even anticipated in a certain way the speculative metaphysics of Fichte and Hegel. In that sense he belongs to the school of German idealism, although he was not yet able to see the full consequences of his discovery of the self. Not the cosmos of old, not God, as in Christian philosophy, but man assumed the role of the metaphysical principle, man in so far as he is a self. Leibniz aimed at an understanding of world and God in analogy to the self. But he could think of the self only in the biological and psychological terms which underlay his metaphysical vision. The monads have *quelque chose de vital.* He calls them " principles of life " or " formative natures." [18]

The measure of the rank of the monads is the degree to which they are conscious of themselves. According to Leibniz this measure coincides with the degree of adequacy of the ideas which they produce. The lesser monads have only *petites perceptions* (little perceptions), so that the appearances weigh higher in their consciousness than the substantial reality; the sensuous surroundings outshine the true and intrinsic essence of things. This description is not merely psychological, but also epistemological and metaphysical: these three aspects join in the Leibnizian system. Like Descartes and Spinoza, Leibniz was convinced that rational knowledge has the highest position in the entire content of consciousness. Will and desire are subordinated to cognition, and metaphysical cognition is highest in rank and adequacy. The all-important motive of action is directed toward producing true ideas. Inadequate ideas and actions are permeated by error. But even the lowest ideas are produced by the inner activity of the monads.

" Nothing enters into the mind from outside. It is a bad habit we have of thinking as though our minds receive messages from outer things by means of images which enter our soul. The soul has neither doors nor windows." [19] This is an extreme stand indeed. It is the

[17] Gerhardt, *op. cit.,* p. 459. Montgomery, *op. cit.,* p. 58.

[18] Cf. *Reflections About the Principles of Life and the Plastic Natures,* 1705.

[19] Gerhardt, *op. cit.,* IV, 451; *Discourse on Metaphysics,* No. XXVI (Montgomery, *op. cit.,* p. 44).

exact opposite of what Locke and his school taught, namely, that we have no ideas that do not enter the mind from outside. Leibniz was driven to his position in consequence of the Cartesian doubt and the negation of sense perception as a source of truth about the outer world. But a religious reason also was operative: Leibniz believed in the universal and eternal plan of God in creating the souls and in arranging their inner life. It is the idea of predestination which played a part in the doctrine of the inner determination of the souls.[20] Leibniz was aware that his doctrine had a paradoxical tone. He wanted to stress the conviction that the inner individuality of man is the essence of his personality, as Goethe expressed the same view when he said that every man is " a coined form which develops while he lives." The doctrine of Leibniz prepared the way for Kant's theory that the forms of the mind order and determine the materials that the senses receive.

" Every substance possesses a perfect spontaneity (which becomes liberty with intelligent substances). Everything which happens to it is a consequence of its idea or its being and nothing determines it except God alone. It is for this reason that a person of exalted mind and revered saintliness may say that the soul ought often to think as if there were only God and itself in the world. Nothing can make us hold to immortality more firmly than this independence . . . of the soul which protects it completely against external things." [21] Physical and religious considerations thus supported each other.

But if we take Leibniz' statement literally, we must ask: How is knowledge possible if we are completely cut off from the world outside our own individuality? How can we compare our theories with theories of other persons as Leibniz himself did so intensely? How can we verify our hypotheses? Indeed, how is empirical science possible at all under such circumstances? What does observation and experiment mean? Have they any function if we develop our thought from our own inner self alone? How could Leibniz assert such an extreme view when he was so eager to bring about a community of

---

[20] Cf. Hans Schmalenbach, *Leibniz*. Perhaps Schmalenbach goes too far in asserting that the metaphysics of Leibniz represents Calvinism. The idea of predestination akin to that of mechanical determinism, although religiously based, was common to most thinkers in the sixteenth and seventeenth centuries.

[21] *Discourse on Metaphysics*, No. XXXII (Montgomery, *op. cit.*, p. 55). Leibniz points here to the *Soliloquies* of Augustine.

scholars and when he himself was so successful in communicating his own ideas to his friends, thereby eliciting a favorable response, while also learning from them? It is hard to combine these facts with the extremely solitary view of Leibniz' metaphysics. But we must assume that this metaphysics corresponded to his deepest inner sentiment and religious feelings. In the light of his religious conviction his entire external life was insignificant. At bottom he could not learn anything from anyone; he learned from God alone. Seen in this perspective his speculation was determined solely by revelation.

" As the same city regarded from different sides appears entirely different, and is, as it were, multiplied respectively, so, because of the infinite number of single substances, there are a similar infinite number of worlds which are, nevertheless, only aspects of one and the same universe, as seen from the special point of view of each monad." [22] The *Monadology* teaches a perspective view of the worlds alive in the inwardness of the soul. They all agree with one another because they are created by the same God. Therefore, learning is a kind of inner hearing and not an outer instruction. We cannot learn from another man but only from the inner voice by which God reveals himself to every individual in an individual form and yet as the same God. Leibniz anticipated here the existentialist emphasis on the authenticity of individual experience. In the last analysis, the *Monadology* was conceived more from the religious than from the scientific point of view.

One might even say that Leibniz, more than Spinoza, was loyal to the Biblical faith when he upheld that the world is relatively independent and that the individual soul is not only a part of the divine substance but a being that has its own center within itself and is responsible to God alone. The expression that we are ultimately alone with God reminds us of Augustine's stress upon the relation between God and the soul as manifested in the *Soliloquies*. God and the soul are intrinsically and exclusively bound up with each other. We know the world only because of this inner bond between ourselves and God. The higher we stand in the hierarchy of created beings, the more we approach God, while the world, as it were, disappears. Spinoza also let the world disappear in the shadow of God; but together with the world, the soul, man's own self, also disappeared,

[22] *Monadology,* No. 57.

whereas Leibniz insisted that the self has a religious quality that is not absorbed by God but that gives man an existence in the face of God. Individuality has a religious significance after all. " We may say that though every substance expresses the whole universe, yet the other (lower) expresses the world rather than God, while spirits express God rather than the world." [23]

BODY AND SOUL

Every monad is restricted in its ability to reach the truth because its ideas are never absolutely clear and distinct, i.e., adequate. No monad ever transcends the limitation that diminishes the universality of its outlook. No monad reflects the world without a certain degree of opaqueness: the rays of the absolute truth are broken by the medium of its finitude. We call this medium, body. The contrast between body and soul or mind is reduced by Leibniz to that of dimness and lucidity of knowledge. The body signifies the zone of darkness which the soul cannot dispel. It also marks the element of individuality which overshadows and confines the universality of the truth. Individuality has a religious significance in the system of Leibniz.

The body deceives us into assuming that there is an outer world in space and time. This world is only the reflection of the deficiency that hampers the individual mind from knowing the full and unrestricted truth. Without a body we would no longer suffer from this illusion; we would no longer be possessed by the prejudice that sensation is a source of knowledge; we would indeed no longer be finite substances, but " like God." Then the world of appearance would be completely erased in favor of the real inner world — that world which Leibniz' *Monadology* describes. Instead of physical entities we would perceive only the inner activity that produces the images of those entities in our soul; we would comprehend only our own ideas (as the philosopher in fact does). Physics would then be completely absorbed by metaphysics; sensation, by intellectual speculation.

But would we really produce ideas if our inner world were not restricted? Would there be any inner world if its counterfeit, the

[23] *Discourse on Metaphysics*, No. XXXVI (Montgomery, *op. cit.*, p. 61).

world, did not exist? Would there be any individual self if the barrier that separates man and God were abolished? Would there be
any soul without the body? If ultimate truth does not suffer any
limitations, then this truth does not tolerate any individual knowledge at all. The individual ego is then no longer possible. Spinoza,
not Leibniz, would be ultimately right. God alone would exist and
everything else would be reduced to a modification of the divine
being. All this is true. But the Leibnizian philosophy rests upon the
existence of individual beings and the conditions under which they
exist and know. Since we are not God, we cannot understand ourselves by means of God; we must be resigned to understanding ourselves by means of ourselves and of our relation to the revealed God.
This would be the answer to the questions raised above.

The monads are restricted and the body demonstrates sensibly
this restriction. " We have said that everything which happens to a
soul or to any substance is a consequence of its concept; hence the
idea itself or the essence of the soul brings it about that all of its
appearances or perceptions should be born out of its nature in such
a way that they correspond of themselves to that which happens in
the body associated with it, because it is in a particular way and
only for a certain time according to the relation of other bodies to
its own body that the soul expresses the state of the universe. This
last fact enables us to see how our body belongs to us without however, being attached to our essence." [24]

Another question arises from the doctrine of the relation between
body and soul. Since the body pertains to the physical world, must
it not be composed of monads itself? Leibniz does not hesitate to
answer this in the affirmative. Indeed, the body consists of many
lower monads which are held together by their " central monad,"
the self or the soul of the individual monads. The plurality of the
lower monads represents the limitation of the unity which constitutes the individuality in contrast to God who is absolute unity. I
depend upon the body only in the lower levels of my mind where
I am not able to raise the plurality to the oneness of my real essence.
What we call " sensuality " is the dependence upon those lower
levels of perception or thought. This dependence makes me (as

[24] *Discourse on Metaphysics*, No. XXXIII (Montgomery, *op. cit.*, p. 56).

Spinoza also had taught) relatively inactive or passive and susceptible to passions.

But here again Leibniz is a follower of Aristotle. " What is active
in certain respects is passive from another point of view, active in
so far as what we distinctly know in it serves to give a reason for
what occurs in another, and passive in so far as the reason for what
occurs in it is found in what is distinctly known in another." [25] In
this way body and soul are united; they are one entity that is in a
state of continuous development, growth or decay. If it grows, the
activity of the monad increasingly surpasses its passivity and thus in-
tegrates the two aspects of its own self (body and soul); if it decays,
it increasingly disintegrates into its opposite poles, passivity overwhelming activity.

GOD AND WORLD

The ultimate problem of the relation between the monads and
God is not solved and not soluble on the basis of the *Monadology*.
Speculation and revelation join, but they are not completely united;
speculative thought yields to revealed truth. The monads do not disappear in the unity of God as they do in Spinoza's scheme. They retain their relative self-existence and self-dependence. They are not
" modes of God," but created selves. It is God's sovereign and unfathomable will that accounts for their existence. Finitude is not
only an aspect of cognitive deficiency, it is also determined by God's
purpose in creating them. God wants to create beings who, although similar to him, nevertheless are dissimilar in that they are
created. They are endowed with the ability to develop themselves,
but this ability is both restricted by their finitude and individualized
by their degree of activity and their rank in the hierarchy of beings.
They are both bodies and souls. God created a world separated from
himself and conditioned by the finitude that is characteristic of
creatures. It is noteworthy that Leibniz calls himself " Theophilus "
in his *New Essays Concerning Human Understanding*. The last and
the highest ambition of his whole speculation was theological.

" It appears clearly that all other substances depend upon God
just as our thoughts emanate from our own substances; that God is
all in all and that he is intimately united to all created things, in

[25] *Monadology*, No. 52.

proportion, however, to their perfection."[26] Hence Leibniz emphasizes the agreement between his philosophy and his faith. He insists that "far from injuring, [his philosophy] rather serves to confirm religion, to dissipate great difficulties, to inflame souls with a divine love, and to raise the mind to a knowledge of incorporeal substances."[27] All beings are eventually incorporeal, but God alone is absolutely spiritual because his mind is no longer encumbered by a particular point of view, by finitude, by error and ignorance. He alone represents truth in its ultimate purity and completion. In that sense he is the " Central Monad " of the world. He does not belong to the world composed of monads.

Thus the Biblical faith finally triumphed in Leibniz' speculation. He did not try to translate the language of revelation into that of speculation; he simply used it when he speaks about Creation and creatures. The monads are creative, but they are also created. What creation means in terms of speculation, Leibniz never explains. God cannot be creative in the sense of the monads, because their creativity is bound up with their imperfection and their striving after perfection, truth, and knowledge. God, being not a " mirror " but the Creator of the world, is also the supreme author of that harmony which enables man to know and which generates the agreement between different persons. Leibniz called this agreement " pre-established harmony." This harmony is the supreme and indispensable condition of life and knowledge. It is only because the monads agree to a certain extent that social life, the state, culture, and history are possible. God is the highest presupposition of all these human achievements.

The pre-established harmony has a variety of functions; it not only explains the agreement between people, their participation in one and the same world and their collaboration for practical purposes, but it is also the ultimate presupposition of the community of body and soul, of the relation between the world of appearances and that of the really real world of monads. " I trust," Leibniz wrote to a friend, " that I have succeeded in understanding the harmony of opposite realms and of opposite theories . . . , and that I have conceived how everything in nature happens at the same time

[26] *Discourse on Metaphysics,* No. XXXII (Montgomery, *op. cit.,* p. 55).
[27] *Ibid.*

in a mechanical and in a metaphysical way, but that the source of mechanics has to be found in metaphysics. . . . Descartes only entered the antechamber of the truth." [28]

But how did Leibniz arrive at his central principle, the universal harmony? How did he prove its validity? We do not find any definite answer to this question. He might have argued that the supreme principle cannot be demonstrated because it cannot be derived from any higher one. It is an axiom like the axioms in Spinoza's *Ethics*. It is striking that the word "harmony" has an aesthetic character; its origin is in music. Leibniz did not deny that there is an aesthetic meaning in this term. "It is like several bands of musicians or choirs separately taking up their parts and placed in such a way that they neither see nor hear one another although they nevertheless agree perfectly in following their notes, each one his own, in such a way that he who hears the whole finds in it a wonderful harmony"; so Leibniz tries to render intelligible the "pre-established" harmony within each monad and of the monads as a whole.[29] God is, as it were, the composer and the conductor of the world music. There is something Pythagorean in his metaphysics.

"Music," Leibniz says in one of his few German works, "gives a foretaste and a little example of the amazing harmony in nature." [30] And in his *Monadology* he expresses the same idea in the following sentence, "The author of nature has been able to employ this divine and infinitely marvelous artifice." [31] In the last analysis, Leibniz' God is like the cosmic artist of Giordano Bruno and the world is his masterpiece. Here Leibniz harks back to the Renaissance motif, which was still powerful in him and in all modern philosophy. But the Reformation element was even stronger in his speculation. The idea of the pre-established harmony has, as we saw, a close relation to that of predestination. But a third

[28] Letter to Remond (Jan. 10, 1714). Cf. the enthusiastic report Leibniz gives about his own philosophic achievements in his *New Essays Concerning Human Understanding,* tr. by Alfred Gideon Langley, 2d ed. (The Open Court Publishing Company, 1916), pp. 66 ff.

[29] Letter to Arnauld (April 30, 1687).

[30] In the little essay on "Fate." *Leibniz' Philosophische Schriften,* ed. by E. Cassirer, II, p. 132.

[31] No. 65.

element, that of modern science, joined the two others to produce the supreme principle of Leibniz' world concept. Leibniz can even say that the monad is a " divine machine or a natural automaton, infinitely surpassing all artificial automata." [32] By way of an exposition to Arnauld he writes on July 14, 1686, about the pre-established harmony which appeared strange to him: " The individual concept of each person involves once for all, all that will ever happen to him." In utterances like this he denied human freedom, agreeing with Luther and Calvin but also with mathematical mechanics, so that it is difficult to decide which motif was primary and predominant in his mind.

The denial of human freedom, although justifiable with respect to the idea of God's choosing of the elect, was an obstacle in the understanding of man which only Kant surmounted. Kant refused to follow Leibniz in this important point. The critical position which Kant finally took originated in part from his protest against the doctrine of man as being an automaton. Only thus could Kant save moral responsibility and, indeed, the whole sphere of moral life.

The idea of world harmony indicates that Leibniz was moving in the direction of the Enlightenment, which was so optimistically minded about man and his destiny. Leibniz thereby ignored the many dysteleological and disharmonious features of nature and of man as conditioned by nature.

But in Leibniz, optimism was still rooted in religious faith. He wanted, as his *Theodicy* shows, to defend God against the atheistic accusers of the world. The world is created by an infinitely good and wise will. Leibniz interpreted the contrast between reasons a priori and facts a posteriori as pointing to a chasm in the being of the monads which makes room for the will of God. God can choose between the infinite possibilities of empirical, contingent facts because it is not pure reason but the will which determines this choice (Leibniz distinguishes between *véritées de fait* and *véritées éternelles*). No rational necessity prompts the divine will to create just this particular and individual world; his will is completely free. The facts (to which the monads themselves belong), although subordinated to eternal logical laws, are yet contingent in themselves; they are determined solely by the decision of the Creator. In his *Theod-*

[32] *Monadology,* No. 64.

icy, Leibniz infers from this duality and from the free will of God that the world as it is is the best possible; it cannot be better than it is, because certain restrictions are involved in the very idea of Creation, as we have seen; it could, however, be infinitely worse and it is the inherent goodness of the divine will which prevents him from choosing a world worse than the one in which we live. Leibniz goes back in this respect to the Platonic *Timaeus,* in which the cosmic architect built as good a world as the material permitted.

Although God's will is free in choosing the best of all possible worlds, it is not free to emancipate itself from the supreme logical principles which constitute his intellect.[33] The impossibility of a world without imperfection, without ignorance and error, without sufferings and passions, without the differences which we find in the monads, belongs to the a priori conditions dictated by the eternal verities. God is therefore not the author of evil, although he did admit it in creating a world of finite beings.

When Leibniz calls the monads " automata," he uses the " exoteric " language by which he adapted his speculation to the scientific mind. In fact, the monads are not merely automata; they have a creative and productive capacity that presupposes will, action, and striving. It must, however, be conceded that the language of Leibniz here lacks the clarity and precision that distinguish his thought. Leibniz seems to adhere to the idea of predetermination, although creativity can hardly be combined with an idea of necessity. His last thoughts have a strong theological overtone. Man depends upon God's grace and therefore he cannot decide his own development and destiny. The more firmly we believe in God, the more are we at one with his will and enjoy his loving, gracious care. Freedom consists in our ability to refuse the dominion of desires and passions; this freedom is given to us by God through his grace.

The human will in this sense is most free when it is most devoted to the will of God. Leibniz sees the ultimate difficulties in this position, but he despairs of solving them. " Without asking for what you are unable to know and in regard to which you can have no light, act according to your duty and your knowledge. But, someone will object, whence comes it then that this man will assuredly do this sin? The reply is easy. It is that otherwise he would not be a

[33] Cf. Gerhardt, *op. cit.,* VI, p. 115.

man." [34] It is evident that this answer is much too " easy." Can man be a man if he is driven to sin without his own free will?

But Leibniz grants that we are ultimately confronting unanswerable questions. Freedom and sin are shrouded in mystery. " It will be best to say with St. Paul that there are for God's choice certain great reasons of wisdom and congruity which he follows, which reasons, however, are unknown to mortals and are founded upon the general order whose goal is the greatest perfection of the world." [35]

[34] *Discourse on Metaphysics*, No. XXX (Montgomery, *op. cit.*, p. 50).
[35] *Ibid.*, No. XXXI (Montgomery, *op. cit.*, pp. 53 f.).

VIII

HUMAN NATURE

Not man but human nature was the object of that philosophic science which Locke and his successors founded, and which was called the "science of human nature" by the greatest representative of that school: David Hume. Not the self or the soul, not mind or reason were in the foreground of their investigations and theories, but impressions, their relations, their copies, and their associations. Not metaphysical speculation but inner observation was their method. Not ultimate truth or knowledge but psychological laws were the goal and the fruit of their philosophic inquiries.

Already in the Middle Ages the special character and inclination of the British people with respect to philosophic thought began to manifest itself: their scientific interest in the physical world, their empirical and experiential predilection, their psychological concern, their aversion to metaphysical systems, and their nominalistic propensity. Names, such as Robert Grosseteste, Roger Bacon, William Ockham, Jean Buridan, and others, attest these peculiar traits. In modern times Francis Bacon and Thomas Hobbes can be regarded as early examples of the same trend of thought. Hobbes was convinced that mathematics alone is the true science and that both physics and metaphysics should be treated mathematically. He interpreted concepts as terms and thinking as a kind of calculation.

But a new beginning was made with John Locke. He was no longer mathematically orientated, but he aimed at a theory of knowledge which, however, was mainly based on psychological observation and analysis. His school is commonly called "empiricism" because he and his successors believed in empirical knowledge as the only source of knowledge. They understood by empirical knowledge sensation and reflection upon sensation. It is a paradox that the land of Newton and of so many other great physicists and scientists produced a philosophic school that ignored or disparaged the modern method of empirical science. If mathematical physics is regarded as the typical and victorious modern science of nature, then the empiricism of Locke and his successors was outmoded from the beginning; it was not an empiricism at all in the sense of experimental experience. Nevertheless, the British empiricists had the highest philosophic aspirations. They wanted to discover not only the origin of knowledge which they sought in impressions but also the limitation of knowledge, thus criticizing the rational sciences of cosmology, ontology, and theology. It was Kant who rectified these false ambitions and created a philosophy that was indeed able to perform such a criticism.

But in order to understand Kant, it is necessary to study British empiricism, partly because it paved the way Kant was to take, and partly because even today many thinkers mistake the British doctrines for those of Kant, or at least do not recognize the enormous chasm between the two. The term "empiricism" as applied to the movement of the English epistemology is also misleading for another reason. These philosophers did not see the true nature of experience. Instead of looking at experience as it presents itself to experience, they constructed rationally what they regarded as the essence of experience. They abstracted from the concrete and complex structure of full experience one fragmentary element: that of sensuous impressions. Thereby they falsified from the outset the nature of experience. They rationalized it by psychological theories in order to recover what was lost and eliminated. "Impression" is not experience; it is an abstract concept pointing to a certain constituent of a definite kind of experience, leaving out just those constituents which really constitute experience in the full sense. Empiricism, as the English empiricists conceived it, was a rationalistic and constructive doctrine utterly unable to understand the real essence of experience even in the special and narrow sense of the empirical sciences, which deal with physical objects.

Their method frustrated from the start what they wanted to achieve: an understanding of the meaning and validity of knowledge. They never realized that an investigation of the origin and development of knowledge (if we suppose that they really did investigate them) could not lead to an appreciation of the cognitive function and contribution of impressions and ideas; that the genetic approach differs from the epistemological insight. In that respect the English empiricists were as blind as their nominalistic predecessors had been. And they were just as little entitled to judge the validity of metaphysics as that of physics or of any other science. Their whole pretense of giving a theory of knowledge was an illusion. They did enlarge psychological knowledge, but they were totally mistaken when they thought that their analysis could circumscribe the boundaries of possible knowledge in any other field. Utter skepticism was therefore the intrinsically necessary outcome of the whole enterprise.

Of the three chief thinkers in that group — Locke, Berkeley, and Hume — Locke was the least penetrating and the most popular writer; Berkeley, the most speculative and religious; Hume, the most consistent and the boldest. It is interesting to notice that these three figures represent the three British countries: England, Ireland, and Scotland, probably exhibiting the different intellectual and spiritual temper and gift of the three peoples. Locke was strongest and greatest in the field of political philosophy where he founded democratic principles which influenced political events on the Continent and in America; he was weakest in the field of epistemology where he was nevertheless dominant for a certain period, in spite of evident shortcomings in his theories. Berkeley differed from the other two in so far as he did not discard metaphysical ideas, but on the contrary interwove epistemological and theological doctrines to defend a special kind of spiritualism. Hume was most acute and discerning, although extremely antispeculative, so that he did not recognize the real problems with which he dealt, but stubbornly stuck to certain principles and to an analytical and psychological method; however, he discovered thereby some hitherto obscure difficulties in the understanding of cognitive categories which occasioned Kant to mobilize the powerful energy of his logical mind.

Locke was conventionally religious, Berkeley professionally, and Hume only in a practical sense. Locke promoted a conservative attitude toward revelation without allowing any theological tenets to interfere with, or to supplement, his theoretical doctrines. Hume attacked natural theology acutely but was skeptical with respect to revelation. Berkeley believed in the truth of Biblical faith, but he cannot be directly called a Christian philosopher, since he also sternly separated revelation and speculation. All three were empiricists in that they believed in the necessity and efficacy of the religious experience over against pure thought or metaphysical a priori knowledge with respect to theological problems.

The whole movement of an analytical dissection of the human mind and understanding was evidently provoked by the success of a similar method in the physical realm. Although the difference between mathematical physics and the science of human nature was considerable, still the analogy between the two approaches cannot be denied. Hume even says bluntly, " I desired to achieve the same result in the field of the phenomena of human nature as had been attained in astronomy since Copernicus." [1] But this does not mean that the mathematical method was applied by him. On the contrary, his method disparages the validity of mathematical physics and even of mathematics itself (except arithmetic), and his own method is purely psychological and descriptive, though aiming at an epistemological conclusion.

Whereas Continental metaphysics in the seventeenth century tried to expand mathematical physics over the full range of cosmology, the English analysts completely rejected such an attempt in order to inquire exclusively into human nature. Hume might be called the Copernicus or Galileo or Newton of the inner world, but while these scientists never aspired to draw philosophic inferences from their observations and theories, Hume did draw such inferences and presumed to overthrow all traditional speculation. Thereby he admitted indirectly that the inner " stars " had a significance that the physical bodies have not: that the inner world somehow transcends the outer world if only by the pretense to investigate it and to establish truth about the physical facts and their relations. Whereas Locke and Hume asserted that they were only analyzing inner facts, they nevertheless ascribed to those facts a cognitive function or at least laid claim to such a function. But they did not realize that the analogy between their science of human nature and that of " nature " in the sense of the natural sciences thereby broke down, and

[1] *A Treatise of Human Nature,* Book II, Part I, sec. III.

that the divergence between their "empirical" method and the meaning of facts explored by this method ruined their claims from the outset.

"Human nature" is not "nature" after all, since man is the scientist and not the object or like the objects of the natural sciences. The deepest problem involved in the enterprise of the British school was the relation between psychology and epistemology. This is a thorny problem indeed. It is evident that scientific thought is both psychologically rooted and epistemologically directed; or that it consists of a process that goes on in the mind and soul, but that this process at the same time has a logical significance and a cognitive aim concerning the attainment of the truth about the natural phenomena. It is extremely difficult to bring together these two aspects. Neither of the three British thinkers ever realized this difficulty. Kant did. But even Kant never completely succeeded in overcoming it. Proof of this failure is the fact that the first edition of the *Critique of Pure Reason* to a certain degree favored the psychological, while the second favored the logical aspect.

The term "idea" was greatly degraded by the empiricists. Whereas Plato, the designer of the term, meant thereby the most noble, the most divine, the most real reality, eternal, immutable, uncreated, and indestructible, Locke and the other empiricists meant by the term the very opposite. The idea according to their scheme is a shadowy copy of the impression, therefore merely human, transient, mutable, coming and going, without any reality, except that of being present for a certain time in the human consciousness (in so far as they permit of such a thing as consciousness). The Idea could not have been more deprived of its splendor and dignity. It was a long way from Plato to Locke. In the era of Christian philosophy the Platonic Ideas became the thoughts in the mind of God. According to Augustine, God illuminates the human mind by endowing it with the Ideas. The Idea of God still occupies a special place in the thought of Anselm. The downfall of the Ideas set in with Abelard. They then became human concepts although still pointing to their origin in the divine mind. Nominalism debased them even more. They now shrank to the standard of mere names or terms while still keeping a certain logical function. But with Locke they lost even this last honor and sank to the level of a merely psychological entity, which borrowed the remnant of cognitive meaning still granted it from the sensuous original which it reproduced. This was the lowest stage in the degeneration of the lofty Platonic Ideas.

JOHN LOCKE

John Locke (1632–1704) vigorously rejected the " *ideae innatae* " as Descartes had called ideas which do not stem from sensation or any experience, but are inborn in the mind, e.g., the idea of God, of truth, of self, and of others. Descartes had at least preserved a certain reflected glory of Plato's Idea. Locke extirpated this glory as radically as possible. The soul is completely empty before it receives impressions via sensation. It is a *tabula rasa.* Content comes into the soul and the mind only from outside (although Locke did not explain how this " outside " can cause imprints in the soul). Locke called this origin of knowledge " experience." " In that all our knowledge is founded, and from that it ultimately derives itself. Our observation, employed either about external sensible objects, or about the internal operations of our minds, perceived and reflected on by ourselves, is that which supplies our understanding with all the materials of thinking." [2] If Plato had lived again in the time of Locke, and if he had read the *Essay Concerning Human Understanding* (1690), he would have turned away from it with a shudder, and he would have thought that mankind had fallen into a terribly barbarous state of decay, producing such a pseudo philosophy!

Locke at least distinguished sensation, as the passive faculty of receiving impressions, from perception, as an intellectual activity that connects the impressions, so that finally the idea of an outer object results (it is not clear how this wonder can occur; therefore, Hume applied his analysis to the solution of this problem). Locke recognized that perception implies judgment in contrast to mere sensation. Perception cannot be " experienced " in the same way as sensation, but only by way of a reflection upon the operation of the mind. However, Locke did not raise the question how perceptions can be true or false and what it means for them to be so. Since we know the outer objects only by means of impressions and perceptions, how can we

[2] *Essay Concerning Human Understanding,* Book II, ch. I, 2.

compare these with the outer objects? And how can we know whether our perceptions are true or false, if we cannot compare them with the outer objects? This question seems never to have arisen in the mind of Locke.

If Locke had taught that the external objects are themselves bundles of impressions and nothing else, we could better understand his whole procedure, but he left it to his disciple Berkeley to draw this conclusion, while he naïvely assumed that we know the external objects and their miraculous act of imprinting impressions upon the soul before we begin to analyze knowledge. Otherwise he was simply inconsistent, as indeed inconsistency is almost a habit with him as with all his past and present followers. This initial blunder marred, of course, all the following considerations as well as his whole theory. This theory is concerned with the " operations " of the mind. But why these operations help the mind to produce knowledge, Locke nowhere cares to ask, so that one is obliged to state that there is no concept of knowledge at all in his whole theory. The theory is a kind of chemistry of impressions and ideas. Why the fruit of the chemical processes is of any cognitive value, Locke did not inquire.

There is a close relation between Locke and his spiritual ancestor Ockham.[3] Like Ockham, Locke thought that philosophy should not try to raise questions which revelation alone can solve. He separated philosophy as radically from theology as Ockham did. He excluded therefore in principle any " profound " problem from his analysis. But even in this respect he was not more consistent than his nominalist ancestor. He did believe in the possibility of proving the existence of God.[4] He does talk about God's purpose and action in the midst of his philosophic analysis. When he considers the question why we experience many different kinds of pain and pleasure he says: " The infinite wise Author of our being . . . has been pleased to join to several thoughts and sensations a perception of delight." [5] And a little later: " Beyond all this, we may find another reason why God has scattered up and down severest degrees of pleasure and pain in all the things that environ and affect us, . . . that we, finding im-

---

[3] See Kroner, *Speculation and Revelation in the Age of Christian Philosophy,* pp. 236 ff.

[4] Cf. *Essay* IV, ch. XVIII, "Of Faith and Reason in Their Distant Provinces." See ch. X for his proof.

[5] *Essay* II, ch. VII, 3.

perfection, dissatisfaction, and want of complete happiness in all the enjoyments which the creatures can afford us, might be led to seek it in the enjoyment of him with whom there is fullness of joy, and at whose right hand are pleasures for evermore." [6] This may be regarded as a pious observation, but how can Locke, who bases all his philosophic insight upon sensation and who rigorously separates philosophy and theology, justify such a statement that certainly surmounts the competence of his empiricism? The era of the Enlightenment liked to mix up shallow religious reflections with psychological observations in just such a way.

Locke introduced into the theory of knowledge the distinction between primary and secondary qualities, which is, however, identical with the Cartesian distinction between quantitative or mathematical and qualitative or sensuous properties of material objects. Solidity, extension, figure, and mobility — attributes that Descartes reckoned as belonging objectively to bodies — also, according to Locke, belong to outer objects, while the secondary qualities " are nothing in the objects themselves, but powers to produce various sensations in us . . . as colors, sounds, tastes, etc." [7] Such a distinction was well suited to a philosophy which relied upon mathematical physics and which took its point of departure from the duality of extended and thinking things, as did that of Descartes, but it was questionable in a philosophy like that of Locke, which pretended to rely upon inner observation and which reduced all properties to data of sensation alone. That Locke adopted, nevertheless, the Cartesian " bifurcation " shows how inconsistent his reasoning was and how unsure he was when the question was raised, How far are we permitted to accept mathematical physics as an epistemological source?

The same lack of clarity and certainty prompts Locke in some places to adopt almost materialistic theories. When he considers how the primary qualities can generate the secondary ones, he argues: " It is evident that some motion must be thence continued by our nerves, or animal spirits, by some part of our bodies, to the brain or the seat of sensation, there to produce in our minds the particular ideas we have of them. . . . Some imperceptible bodies must come from them to the eyes, and thereby convey to the brain some motion which produces these ideas which we have of them in us." [8] In such

[6] *Essay* II, ch. VII, 5.   [7] *Essay* I, ch. VIII, 10.   [8] *Essay* I, ch. VIII, 11.

a naturalistic way Locke tries to explain the impressions, " gliding," to quote Windelband, " over and away from the eddies which come up out of the dark depths of his historical presuppositions." [9] How can Locke, if we take his principles seriously, know that there are physical objects and that these objects are constituted by " primary qualities " only? How can he, who allegedly follows merely empirical data, know anything about the relation between outer objects and our sensations or impressions? The fact is that Locke simply takes over from common-sense experience and from mathematical physics some bits of knowledge and uses them whenever he faces difficult questions that cannot be solved from his perspective.

The same uncertainty and lack of methodical procedure is omnipresent in his discussions. It is not worth-while to go through them all. One more example will suffice to illustrate this shallow reasoning. When he ponders about the infinity of space, he says: " This, I think, is the way whereby the mind gets the idea of infinite space. It is quite a different consideration whether the mind has the idea of such a boundless space actually existing, since our ideas are not always proofs of the existence of things; but yet, since it comes here in our way, I suppose I may say, that we are apt to think that space in itself is actually boundless." [10] In this cavalier, indeed almost frivolous, way, Locke " glides " over the abysmal problem of spatial infinity and its relation to the actual world. He " supposes " without giving any reason, that the real space also is boundless, although the assumption of an outer world and of the correspondence between our mind's idea and that world is absolutely arbitrary in the scheme of Locke. What does he mean when he says that we are "apt " to assume such a correspondence; does he conclude from this statement that physical space is boundless or not? One is at a loss to answer this question.

When he discusses the concept of substance, he admits that he does not know how to decide whether or not it has an objective meaning. " If anyone will examine himself concerning his notion of pure substance in general, he will find he has no other idea of it at all, but only a supposition (this is the term of Ockham!) of he knows not

---

[9] *History of Philosophy,* tr. by James H. Tufts (The Macmillan Company, 1893 and 1901), p. 469.
[10] *Essay* II, ch. XVII, 4.

what support of such qualities which are capable of producing simple ideas (i.e., sensuous impressions) in us." [11] In contrast to the physiological explanation given above about the generation of secondary qualities by motions outside, here, at least, Locke expresses himself more cautiously and more in line with his general presuppositions. It is noteworthy that he arrives at a skeptical conclusion when he renounces the materialistic theory or hypothesis. He approaches the thesis of Hume when he finally states: " Our specific ideas of substances are nothing else but a collection of a certain number of simple ideas, considered as united in one thing." [12] But whereas Hume was consistent in his method, with Locke we do not know whether he implies that this " collection " corresponds to outer existing substances or not. Does the result of the mind's operation agree with the physical reality? Is there such a reality at all? And if there is, how can our mind agree with it? None of these basic epistemological questions was even raised by Locke as they were by his successors Berkeley and Hume.

George Berkeley

George Berkeley (1685–1753), for many years a bishop, philosophized on the basis of his faith, at least inasmuch as such philosophizing could be combined with the essentially psychological method which he adopted from Locke. Berkeley fused this method with speculation. He wished to " penetrate into the inward essence and constitution of things." [13] He hoped that he could demonstrate the existence and immateriality of God.[14] There is even a speculative cosmology at the bottom of his seemingly psychological and epistemological system, a cosmology resembling that of Leibniz and Malebranche. Not only is God immaterial, but so is the world. Matter and material things do not really exist. The world is composed of finite spirits whereas material things are produced only by our mind. " The ideas imprinted on the senses by the Author of nature are called real things: and those excited in the imagination being less regular, vivid, and constant, are more properly termed ideas. . . . But

[11] *Ibid.,* ch. XXII, 2.
[12] *Ibid.,* 14.
[13] Cf. Berkeley, *Treatise Concerning the Principles of Human Knowledge* (1710), Introduction.
[14] *Ibid.,* Preface.

our sensations . . . are nevertheless ideas, that is, they exist in the mind, or are perceived by it, as truly as the ideas of its own framing." [15]

Berkeley lights up the mist which made the statements of Locke so ambiguous. He definitely teaches that the object of perception is nothing but a collection of impressions and that the impressions are not caused by outer things but by the " author of nature." In that way Berkeley transforms Augustine's doctrine of illumination so that the eternal Idea of Plato is replaced by the idea of Locke, i.e., by the sensuous impression. What we really perceive are not, as common sense and science suppose, things outside the mind: these things do not exist at all. " I see this cherry, I feel it, I taste it and I am sure nothing cannot be seen, or felt, or tasted: it is therefore real. Take away the sensations of softness, moisture, redness, tartness, and you take away the cherry. . . . A cherry is nothing but a congeries of sensible impressions and ideas." [16] The truth of our perception does not consist in the agreement between our impressions and outer things; rather, objects and impressions are one and the same thing.

"To be," Berkeley emphatically states, is nothing, but " to be perceived "; and " to be perceived " is therefore the real meaning of reality.[17] In this fashion Berkeley solves the problem concerning the agreement between the objects of perception and the objects perceived. But how can such an epistemology explain that impressions differ from person to person, and even in the same person from situation to situation? How can we ever trust the evidence of perception in spite of the well-known illusions of perception like the revolution of the sun around the earth which has turned out to be apparent only? Indeed, how can we ever distinguish between appearance and reality, when what appears is itself reality? Truth is objective after all, but the impressions are subjective. How can we jump over that chasm?

Berkeley was aware of these possible objections. He used them in order to demonstrate the existence of God as a kind of master-perceiver who grants the measurement of truth and falsity. It is precisely

[15] Berkeley, *op. cit.,* sec. 33. Compare *Three Dialogues Between Hylas and Philonous* (1713), ed. by Charles W. Eliot (Harvard Classics, 1910), p. 227 and *passim.*

[16] Eliot, *op. cit.,* p. 287 (Third Dialogue).

[17] See esp. Berkeley, *op. cit.,* secs. 3 ff.

the possibility of error and falsity which compels the thinker to appeal to the divine master mind in which there is no falsity. Instead of the nonexisting outer objects God is made the judge of right and wrong in the field of cognition. In this way Berkeley connects his psychological epistemology with a speculative theology. God generates the ideas in our mind, but since we are finite, we may err in combining them. We find the truth only if we see things in God, not distorted by our fallible individuality and relativity of sight. He even asserts that we see God by seeing things in God as we recognize a person by observing his gestures and listening to his words.[18]

To the degree to which Berkeley is more consistent and outspoken than Locke the basic deficiency of the principle and the method which the British analysts follow is magnified. How can we ever know whether we see things in God or not? What is the objective measurement of truth and falsity in the realm of cognition? If our impressions are the objects themselves, no such immanent criterion is possible. Whereas Locke (inconsistently) spoke about judgment in contrast to sensation, such a difference cannot be tolerated if all knowledge is founded upon sensation. According to the Continental thinkers knowledge is not based upon sensation, but upon understanding and reason, whereas the British analysts were obliged to explain objectivity in terms of impressions alone. This, however, could not be done. Thus Berkeley found an asylum in his faith and made God the criterion. But he abandoned thereby the method of his whole undertaking, as Locke abandoned it, when he retained the traditional definition of truth as the agreement between the objects and our knowledge. Locke represented common sense; Berkeley turned theologian. The basic difficulty of epistemology could not be overcome by either evasion.

Although Berkeley's theological speculation reminds one of the Scholastic theories, his psychological approach was utterly opposed to any kind of Platonism or Aristotelianism. He was convinced that the Scholastic theories were based upon the confusion of words and ideas, and that the belief in Platonic Ideas was a psychological misinterpretation. He even abhorred the fact that we think in abstract notions. The Introduction of his *Principles* is mainly dedicated to the destruction of these notions. We are deceived by words which in-

[18] *Ibid.*, sec. 148.

dicate the existence of general concepts. Like Ockham he denied flatly that general concepts exist in any mind. Words only " stand for " common traits in things. To that extent we may retain general ideas, but this generality does not imply abstractness. When we observe by introspection our thoughts, we shall easily discover that every idea which appears in the mind is definite, particular, and concrete. We cannot conceive the idea of a line that is neither rectilinear nor curved; we cannot possess the idea of a triangle that is neither rectangular nor oblique. Each geometrical figure in our mind has a definite size and a definite shape. Abstract ideas exist only in the fictitious doctrines of philosophers. It is easy to see that Berkeley simply mistook concepts or notions for impressions or imaginative ideas. One wonders why he could not realize that he himself, in order to build up his theory, had to use abstract notions like sensation, perception, knowledge, mind, ideas, and so on!

In an unwittingly ironical passage Berkeley mentions that according to Locke " the faculties of brutes can by no means attain to abstraction " and continues, " If this be made the distinguishing property of that sort of animals I fear a great many of those that pass for men must be reckoned into their number." [19] What he really means is that no distinction can be made between man and brute, if Locke is right in asserting that the faculty of abstraction marks their difference, because man also is not possessed of it. Indeed, there is no essential difference between animal and man, if psychology alone is taken into account; there are only different degrees of the same faculties. But if that is true in general, then knowledge in the human sense cannot be explained because it simply does not exist! If natural causality alone governs the life of man, if the sequence of his ideas depends upon this necessity alone, then the same laws bring about knowledge as well as error, the lowest and the highest, right and wrong — all value differences are leveled. The most profound insight is as necessary as the grossest illusion; wisdom and foolishness are no longer to be distinguished. If epistemology is merely founded upon the psychological order of the ideas, truth and falsity disappear; but then no theory of knowledge is possible at all! Psychological investigation can never discover the " principles concerning human knowledge." Berkeley did recognize this impossibility. This was

[19] *Ibid.*, sec. 11.

the reason why he appealed to God. But revelation cannot fill the gap of his psychology of ideas so that a theory of knowledge would be made possible thereby.

DAVID HUME

The fundamentally negative result of the analytical method applied by the English school of thought came to light in the philosophy of David Hume (1711–1776) because he was the most consistent and most methodical of their members. His *Treatise of Human Nature* (1739–1740) disclosed the basic deficiency of the whole school. It really is a treatise not on the human understanding as Locke's *Essay* claimed to be nor a treatise on human knowledge as Berkeley's *Principles* pretended to be, but rather it deals with human nature, which psychologically considered is not essentially different from animal nature. Hume admits this inadvertently, when he says occasionally: "Beasts certainly never perceive any real connection among objects. It is therefore by experience they infer one from another. . . . It is by means of custom alone that experience operates upon them. All this was sufficiently evident with respect to man. But with respect to beasts there cannot be the least suspicion of mistake; which must be owned to be a strong confirmation or rather an invincible proof of my system." [20] Here Hume bluntly admits that his whole theory of knowledge rests upon observations equally valid for man and beast.

It is interesting to read in what mood Hume composed his philosophy. He admits that the skeptical result frightened him because it isolated him from common-sense people and, indeed, from all intellectual commerce with other persons. "I am first affrighted and confounded with that forlorn solitude, in which I am placed in my philosophy, and fancy myself some strange monster, who, not being able to mingle and unite in society, has been expelled from all human commerce, and left utterly abandoned and disconsolate." [21] These touching lines indicate that Hume felt deeply the gap between his destructive thought and his ordinary life. "I dine, I play a game of backgammon, I converse and am merry with my friends; and when after three or four hours' amusement, I would return to these

[20] Hume, *op. cit.,* Book I, Part III, sec. XVI.
[21] Book I, Part IV, sec. VII.

speculations, they appear so cold, and strained, and ridiculous, that I cannot find in my heart to enter into them farther." [22]

It is true that man as man does not figure in Hume's thought, nor does knowledge as knowledge, truth as truth, understanding as understanding, science as science, the self as the self. All these human concepts undergo a curious distortion, so that their original meaning is finally lost. Even what Locke called " operations of the mind " is completely (but in agreement with the principles of such an epistemology) given up. The whole argument is sustained by the presupposition that there are impressions and that there are " ideas," i.e., copies or traces of the impressions preserved by imagination. These are " faint images " of the original impressions, which are themselves distinguished by their vivacity and force missing in the ideas. The understanding can therefore be identified with imagination. [23]

Knowledge, according to Hume, has to be interpreted as a sequence of impressions and ideas and their interconnection. Succession and association are the main principles of his theory. Locke and Berkeley found it difficult to account for the fact that we believe in external objects, their relative constancy, their causal order, their interrelations, in sum, that we believe in the existence of a physical universe that the natural sciences investigate and explore. Hume is infinitely more consistent when he tries to derive this belief from the succession and association of the impressions and ideas and from the effect which originates thereby. His stubborn perseverance in sticking to his principles deserves admiration as it betrays a kind of Stoic apathy. Although he is afraid of the consequences of his own anatomical dissection of the living body of knowledge, he quietly and courageously pursues the path he has entered upon to the bitter end.

Hume penetrated deeper into the world of inner experience than his predecessors. Where they had not seen any riddle, he saw several. Where they had conventionally upheld common prejudices, he discerned real difficulties and tried hard to overcome them by the same method. With great skill he laid bare the hidden mechanism

[22] *Ibid.*

[23] " The understanding or imagination can draw inferences from past experience," Book I, Part III, sec. VIII.

that makes us believe in causality and substance. According to Hume, these categories have no objective validity and reality. Instead they have their origin in a subtle co-operation of sensation, memory, and emotion, or impressions, ideas, and feelings which are interconnected. Hume set out to discover the laws that regulate this co-operation. Berkeley only intimated that the ideas associate themselves; Hume elaborated this hint systematically. He developed a theory designed to explain how, according to rules of association, the consciousness of a causal nexus arises.

As the impressions are never isolated but always connected with each other, so are their images, called " ideas." Three principles or laws control this connection: resemblance, contiguity in time or place, and repetition of their appearance. In the beginning of his inquiry Hume adapts his language to that of common experience, speaking about objects which resemble one another, are adjacent in space or time, and are related to one another by the bond of causality.[24] But in the course of his discussion he abandons this language and replaces it by the results of his fine psychological analysis. Indeed, the question of causality is answered in agreement with the principles of his " subjective idealism " as it has been named.

Berkeley had remarked that the sun does not produce the heat, but that the sight of the sun is accompanied by a sensation of heat: " We do from thence conclude the sun to be the cause of heat." [25] Hume was not satisfied by this observation. He wanted to understand in more detail how this transformation of a connection between impressions into the idea of causality takes place. Causality implies a necessary succession of cause and effect; such a necessity is not implied in the succession of the impressions even if it repeats frequently. The most we could infer is that usually the impression of the sun is accompanied with the impression of heat. What is the origin of the idea of necessity? There is nothing in the so-called cause which entitles us to conclude that the so-called effect is a necessary result of the cause or that the cause necessarily produces the effect. This idea of necessity is added by our mind. But what is the reason why our mind adds this notion? How does the assump-

[24] E.g., *Treatise,* Book I, Part III, sec. II: " The idea of causation must be derived from some relation among objects."
[25] Berkeley, *op. cit.,* sec. 32.

tion arise that there is a kind of tie or bond between cause and effect which produces the appearance of a force or power inherent in the cause to generate the effect? Puzzling questions, indeed, when we start from the presupposition that the cause is nothing but a certain impression or idea and that the effect likewise is such an impression or idea and that the only bond between them is their succession!

Although the way Hume formulated the problem of causality was determined by his empiricist method, and although this formulation was therefore valid only to the degree to which empiricism in general was valid, the problem nevertheless pointed to an intrinsic difficulty. What, indeed, is the origin of causal necessity? How do we come to assume it as valid and as governing the processes of nature? It is evident that this necessity cannot be observed in the same way as the sun or the heat can be perceived. If it does govern nature, then we cannot know it by experience. How do we know it, and how can we prove that it really works within the processes of nature? This was the question which Kant, inspired by Hume's profound analysis, raised and to answer which he wrote his *Critique of Pure Reason.*[26]

But let us first pursue the development of thought in Hume. He divides his discussion into two sections. First, he asks why do we believe that the beginning of something must always have a cause, and second, why do we believe that something in particular must have been produced by a particular cause. Impressions do not indicate such a necessary relation; but impression is the only source of ideas. How then shall we account for the idea of causality?[27] From the experience of single instances we cannot infer the general principle that in all cases the beginning of an event is necessarily occasioned by some other event. Although the idea of an effect does presuppose that of a cause, still this connection of ideas does not explain the connection between two different impressions, even less

[26] Cf. Kant's well-known utterance in the Introduction to his book *Prolegomena to Every Future Metaphysics That May Be Presented as a Science* (1783): "I readily confess that the reminder of David Hume was what first interrupted my dogmatic slumber many years ago and gave my research in the field of speculative philosophy quite a different direction." Edited by Carl J. Friedrich in *The Philosophy of Kant* (Modern Library, Inc., 1949), p. 45.

[27] *Treatise,* Book I, Part III, secs. III ff.

than between two different events. This is just the problem: how do we come to have the ideas of effect and cause and their necessary relation?

Hume is firmly convinced throughout his treatise that the principle of causality can be derived from the association of impressions and the subsequent generation of the belief in causality. What is belief after all? According to Hume's theory it is " a lively idea related to a present impression." He ignores the fact that belief is not an idea at all, but a definite attitude that accompanies the connection of ideas; however, in one place he does say that belief " attends " an idea and in another passage that " belief is somewhat more than a simple idea. It is a particular manner of forming an idea." [28] This uncertainty points to the deficiency of the whole method and its concepts. Hume goes on to argue that we believe in an effect when we have often experienced the connection between two impressions which succeed each other. Since the sensation of a flame is constantly conjoined with that of heat, we come to believe that the two belong to each other or that the flame is the cause and the heat the effect. The constant conjunction thus generates the belief. It first produces the custom or habit of associating one impression or idea with another so that we are urged from within ourselves to produce or reproduce the one when the other appears. It is this urge or pressure which makes us believe that an outer necessity exists in the succession of cause and effect. This theory is akin to what Kant called the " Copernican revolution " in the field of epistemology, which transfers the outer necessity to the inner world of thought. Hume even says in objecting to his own theory: " What! The efficacy of causes lies in the determination of the mind! As if causes did not operate entirely independent of the mind, and would not continue their operation, even though there was no mind existent to contemplate them . . . this is to reverse the order of nature, and make that secondary, which is really primary." [29]

Hume anticipated, at least in part, Kant's " Copernican revolution." He accomplished the same turn from the outer to the inner,

---

[28] *Ibid.*, secs. VII f.

[29] *Ibid.*, sec. XIV. Kant probably did not know this passage, since he read only the version of Hume's theory given in his *An Enquiry Concerning Human Understanding* (1748).

from the objective to the subjective, consideration. However, in his philosophy this turn did not mean what it meant in Kant. Hume inquired only into the origin of belief in causality, not in its validity and objectivity. He indeed denied such a validity and objectivity on the ground of his methodical principles. In other words: Hume's analysis led him to assert that the notion of causality has only subjective reality, but no objective validity; it has a psychological origin and therefore no logical significance for our knowledge of the physical world. One might say that the " malignant demon," whom Descartes feared because he would deceive us when we assume the objective reality of the physical substances, was victorious in Hume. Since his method would not have admitted the idea of God to defeat that demon, Hume was defenseless against the radical doubt which was the point of departure for Descartes's *Meditations.*[30] Our subjective propensity, prompting us to generate the idea of the effect when the idea of the cause emerges, " is the reason why we suppose necessity and power to lie in the objects, not in our mind, that considers them." [31] Our own mind, therefore, is itself the malignant demon which deceives us into the false belief that causality has a cognitive value for the investigation of physical processes! In an analogous fashion Hume also depreciates the notion of substance.

Hume ends in doubt. As we do not know whether there are objects which correspond to our ideas, so we also do not know whether these objects are related to each other by that bond of necessary connection which our mind fancies. It is an ironical fact, however, that Hume, who abrogates the cognitive validity of causation, nevertheless, uses this notion in his own analysis. He does not doubt that he has found the " cause " of the belief in causality and that this belief is the " effect " of the mental determination originated by the constant conjunction of two impressions. He does not doubt that his own method is able to penetrate into the causative connection of the inner realities. Here in the investigation of that inner world, he completely drops his doubts and defies the malignant demon in order to succeed in becoming the Copernicus of the inner world!

---

[30] Hume himself admits this indirectly when he says: " The Cartesian doubt, were it ever possible to be attained, . . . would be entirely incurable." *An Enquiry Concerning Human Understanding,* sec. XII, Part I.

[31] *Ibid.,* sec. XIV.

The skepticism that ensues from Hume's analysis is thus contradicted by the analysis itself. If the analysis is logically valid, then the skeptical conclusion must be wrong. There is obviously a fundamental error in the whole procedure of the science of human nature. After all, no thinker can deny logical validity without defeating himself. Even the often-used word "mind" could not point to a reality, if only impressions and ideas exist. Certainly any logical inference, as Hume cannot help practicing, is impossible if his philosophy is right.

There is another paradoxical presupposition underlying Hume's entire theory. How can he speak about a "constant conjunction" between impressions, if the empiricist method is rigorously applied? The most he could have said would be that a conjunction often occurs. But even such an occurrence cannot be explained by psychological reasons. But the application of the notion of causality to the inner world is vindicated only by this constancy! Why should this notion not also be justified in the case of physical science? After all, Copernicus himself won his victories because he did apply this notion to the movement of the planets around the sun!

The main error of the whole English school of epistemological psychology lies in the identification of the object of perception with the impression or with a collection of impressions. It is simply false to assert that the subjective contents of sensation and perception are identical with the object which we perceive. It contradicts the facts of experience. We do perceive something and not only our own perception. This fundamental datum of experience was denied in advance by the empiricists. They assumed dogmatically that we do not experience anything else than our own impressions. This false hypothesis was bound to lead to false consequences and finally to a complete skepticism which refuted itself, since it was the outcome of an analysis which had to be excluded from that general skepticism. The empiricists, far from making experience alone the source of their doctrines, from the beginning distorted the testimony of experience. They could therefore never truly expound experience itself. It was a wholesome and salutary reaction when the so-called Scottish school turned against the anti common sense of Hume and established a common-sense philosophy which asserted that the usual assumption is right, that outer objects do exist and that there is a world in which order and necessity rule. However, Reid and his friends were not able to demonstrate this assertion. They were completely lost when they had to solve the problems raised by Hume's analysis.

The scholarly world had to wait until Kant devised a new theory of knowledge which would restore common sense not simply by assertion, but by most subtle methods of inquiry and inference. It is another paradox that the most sophisticated method ever applied in the field of epistemology and metaphysics was to confirm and to rehabilitate the common-sense assumption. The famous " Refutation of Idealism " in the second edition of the *Critique of Pure Reason* was directed against the subjective idealism of the English thinkers.[32] Kant defends there the thesis that " the mere, but empirically determined, consciousness of my own existence proves the existence of objects in space outside me." In other words, he returns to the position of Descartes, though on a new level.

Hume was an adversary of speculation, although his own theory itself has a speculative appearance in spite of its pseudoempirical emphasis. He did not believe in any metaphysical doctrine concerning the world or man or God. This opposition led him to deny any natural theology and thereby indirectly to defend the faith which is based upon revelation, as his *Dialogues Concerning Natural Religion* (1779) show. Whereas Locke thought that Christianity is " reasonable " and that it is identical with deism, Hume saw deeper into that matter. He recognized the shallowness of such a " reasonableness." [33] Hume rejected outright all attempts to penetrate into cosmological or theological questions by means of philosophic thought. " Natural religion " does not stand the test either. It is impossible to know how the world was created by God and how it is governed by his will. Religion, therefore, can never be simply rational or natural, it must be *revealed*. He does not deny that the order and direction which we find in nature suggest a supreme being as its author and ruler. But such a suggestion cannot be supported by philosophic reasons. Perhaps mechanical forces suffice to bring about

[32] B (the letter which marks the second edition of the *Critique*), 274–278.

[33] Locke, *The Reasonableness of Christianity* (1695). Cf. John Toland, *Christianity Not Mysterious* (1696) and Matthew Tindal, *Christianity as Old as the Creation* (1730). Deism popularized natural theology by reconciling superficially the Christian faith to the natural sciences.

the same result. If God exists, his nature is entirely unfathomable. No theoretical knowledge whatsoever can fill the gap of ignorance which separates us from the Supreme Being. Here as elsewhere Hume was the predecessor of Kant.

Religion, Hume argues, is the outcome of wish and fear, not of rational reflection. Already in his *Enquiry Concerning Human Understanding* (1748) he says: " Our most holy religion is founded on faith, not on reason; and it is a sure method of exposing it to put it to such a trial as it is by no means fitted to endure." [34] In a strange kind of companionship the skeptic Hume is here in full agreement with Pascal, who was also a skeptic in regard to any speculative theology, but in every other respect the contrary of Hume. Hume was aware of the paradoxical union between his skepticism and the Christian faith. He mentions that the early Christian fathers had applied the principles of ancient skepticism to prove the significance of faith and that the Reformers followed them. " All panegyrics on the excellency of faith were sure to be interlarded with some severe strokes of satire against natural reason." [35]

Throughout the *Dialogues,* Hume severely criticizes and spurns natural religion and extols instead revealed truth. Philo, one of the interlocutors who obviously represents Hume's own opinions, proclaims: " A person, seasoned with a just sense of the imperfections of natural reason, will fly to revealed truth with the greatest avidity, while the haughty dogmatist persuaded that he can erect a complete system of theology by the mere help of philosophy disdains any further aid, and rejects this adventitious instructor. To be a philosophical skeptic is, in a man of letters, the first and most essential step toward being a sound, believing Christian." [36] Almost with the words of Pascal, Hume describes the task of religious faith, " The proper office of religion is to regulate the heart of man, humanize man's conduct, infuse the spirit of temperance, order, and obedience." [37] Of course, Pascal had more to say than this. He would never have identified religion with " the motives of morality and

---

[34] Sec. X, " Of Miracles," Part II.
[35] " Dialogues Concerning Natural Religion," in *The English Philosophers from Bacon to Mill,* ed. by Edwin A. Burtt (Modern Library, Inc., n.d.), p. 698.
[36] *Ibid.,* pp. 763 f.
[37] *Ibid.*

justice," as Philo-Hume does. In this respect Hume was approaching Kant. His most striking argument for the impossibility of any natural religion or theology is the consideration that reason cannot account for evil, physical and moral. In contrast to Leibniz, who tried to vindicate Creation with all its dark aspects, or in spite of these aspects, by defending the wisdom and goodness of the Creator, Hume repudiated all attempts at such a theodicy.

IX

THE PRIMACY OF PRACTICAL REASON

THE PHILOSOPHY of Immanuel Kant (1724–1804) has many aspects and has been interpreted in many ways. Hardly any other philosopher has aroused the interest and the admiration of so many followers and opponents. The literature on Kant and his philosophy is so vast that it fills a library, even though only about one hundred and fifty years have passed since his death. Every European nation as well as America has contributed to Kantian literature. The question whether Kant's philosophy has any peculiar principle that could be called the guiding and dominant one has been answered in various ways. No agreement has been attained about the interpretation of Kant's speculative views. Under these circumstances it is very difficult to write one chapter in this book about Kant's attitude toward the relation between speculation and revelation without adding an appendix that would deal critically with all the interpretations and aspects of this subject. However, such an appendix might soon reach dimensions surpassing the whole length of this three-volume work. This cannot be done. Although I do not claim to represent Kant's main thought in an authoritative fashion, I must avoid any attempt to discuss all the possible aspects of Kant's critical philosophy, and I must concentrate on what I regard as central and as most illuminating for the whole of his thought. Since I have repeatedly exhibited Kant's views in former books, I must ask the reader to turn to them so that my present statement will become more complete.

I believe that "the primacy of pure practical reason in its association with speculative reason," as the title of one chapter in the *Critique of Practical Reason* is called, is the real key to the understanding of Kant's entire work. "Every interest is ultimately practical, even that of speculative reason being only conditional and reaching perfection only in practical use." This is the last sentence of the chapter mentioned. One should ponder this solemn and unmistakable utterance. Here Kant puts forth authoritatively what he himself regards as the supreme principle of his whole thought. The primacy of pure practical reason governs and colors the critical works. Speculation is subordinated. The theory of knowledge is only the entrance door to the castle. And as we will see, even within the theory of knowledge the primacy of pure practical reason is already efficacious. It is foreshadowed by the doctrine of the Ideas and the Ideal of pure reason. It is anticipated by the interpretation of the Ideas as "regulative principles." At the top of these important concepts we find in the "Canon of Pure Reason" at the end of the *Critique of Pure Reason* the following words: "All the interests of my reason, speculative as well as practical, combine in the three following questions: (1) What can I know? (2) What ought I to do? (3) What may I hope? The first question is merely speculative. . . . The second question is purely practical. . . . The third question — If I do what I ought to do, what may I then hope? — is at once practical and theoretical, in such a fashion that the practical serves only as a clue that leads us to the answer of the theoretical question, and when this is followed out, to the speculative question." [1]

Here Kant says most clearly that the practical question is the clue which leads to the highest summit of knowledge. A more illuminating and unequivocal statement about the order which regulates the relation between the critique of theoretical and that of practical reason could not have been given by their author. From all these utterances we can conclude with certainty that Kant did not believe speculation by itself could know ultimate truth; he was convinced that practical reason has to be consulted when we want to climb the summit of knowledge. Speculation unsupported by the interest of practical reason is powerless to furnish us with ultimate knowledge. Kant says in the *Critique of Pure Reason* and in the *Critique of Practical Reason* very little about revelation. It is evident that he was not a Christian philosopher in the sense of those who lived and thought in

----

[1] B. 832–833; A. 804–805.

the age of Christian philosophy. Rather, he was, like Descartes and Spinoza, like Leibniz and Hume, a modern philosopher for whom the separation of secular and sacred thought was a foregone conclusion or an established fact. This does not mean, however, that his philosophy was less Christian than the systems of the Christian philosophers. Instead it was the philosophic result of the Reformation and in some respect more in line with the gospel than the Aristotelian speculation of Thomas Aquinas.

The primacy of pure practical reason in its association with speculative reason can be understood only after Kant's epistemological and ethical views have been expounded. The very term " pure practical reason " has a specific Kantian connotation. Only after this exposition can the relation between Kant's moral philosophy and Christianity be discussed more fully. I will first present Kant's theory of knowledge according to the *Critique of Pure Reason,* since this theory best mediates the philosophy of Hume and that of Kant, and since it shows in what sense Kant corrected the subjective idealism of the science of human nature.

Seen from the perspective of the history of philosophy as a whole the great feat of Kant's theory of knowledge was his resuscitation of Platonism. Although Platonism after its revival in the Renaissance had been pushed into the background, it had never died out completely. In the Cartesian doctrine of the innate ideas and in the Leibnizian doctrine of the eternal verities Platonism had somehow survived. But it had not played the same part which it had in the age of Christian philosophy. Augustine was more Platonic than either Descartes or Leibniz, for whom the mathematical physics of modern times was too much in the focus of attention to permit a real renewal of the Platonic Ideas. The classical English thinkers, of course, had not the slightest understanding of Platonism (apart from the so-called Cambridge Platonists: Ralph Cudworth [1617–1688] and Henry More [1614–1687]). Kant rediscovered that epistemology cannot be psychological, scientific (in the sense of the natural sciences), quasi-chemical, as that of the English school founded by Locke, it has rather to be logical, speculative, metaphysical (in the sense of a " metaphysics of experience " as Paton has called it), or — as the Kantian term is — " transcendental." Kant thereby resurrected the Platonic Ideas though in a completely new and modern fashion.

The a priori concepts of the transcendental understanding correspond in regard to their epistemological function to the Ideas: both make experience of the phenomena possible. The primacy of practical reason is akin to the dominating role of the Good in Plato's idealism. Kant himself was aware of the Platonic trend of his own idealism as we will see later.

Kant's Theory of Knowledge

In Kant the modern principle of an anthropocentric philosophy reached its climax. His theory of knowledge cannot be understood without having this in mind. Kant radically and systematically rooted out rational (natural, metaphysical, or ontological) cosmology and theology. He thereby destroyed not only the cosmocentric scheme of ancient speculation and the theocentric one of medieval speculation, but also that of Descartes, Spinoza, and Leibniz. He destroyed them more thoroughly and completely than Locke and his successors had done, because he used the heavy armor and the penetrating method of his critical logic, and because in contrast to the English thinkers he defended the validity of mathematical physics. The science of human nature was replaced by a new logic, the transcendental logic. Kant was the first thinker in the entire history of philosophy who recognized that the " objective " method, which we apply to the knowledge of the world and of nature, had to be resolutely abandoned when we wish to understand man as the thinking and knowing subject, as the " I " that accompanies all thinking, as the self that acts in the scientist, as the ego that is inseparable from the understanding, the reason, and the mind in general. His philosophy was the first " egological " speculation, to use a newly coined word.

Man is man precisely because he is not an object, but the subject of knowledge. He is man because he distinguishes himself from everything that is not man. He is man because he does not belong entirely to the world, but is " supernatural " by nature! It is a great mistake if this epoch-making discovery is criticized and sometimes even foolishly ridiculed as " egotism," as if Kant had unduly aggrandized man or made the human self the center. The truth is that Kant simply recognized for the first time what indeed is the distinguishing note of humanity, in contrast to all naturalistic falsifications old and modern, which conceive of man as a talented animal or a developed brute. Kant never denied that man also is this, but he maintained that humanity is something *toto genere* different from animal nature. Man is not an object, inasmuch as he is understanding and reason. But he is also not "form" as Aristotle thought, thereby assimilating man to all other things. "Mind" in the human sense is not a specific form distinguished from the "form" of other animals, plants, or inorganic elements. If it were, man could not think of forms and make forms the objects of contemplation and investigation. Man is absolutely unique, inasmuch as he is the one who thinks and investigates and contemplates and understands. In this respect Kant set forth the line that Descartes in his *Meditations* had first proposed but had not pursued.

Kant learned from the skeptical conclusion at which Hume ultimately arrived that the understanding has to be treated not in the manner Copernicus treated the orbits of the planets, but in an entirely peculiar and unique way. The annihilation of the identity of the self by Hume manifested irrefutably that this course led into an impasse. Kant was seeking for a method that would restore this identity and with it the logical validity of the sciences and of thought in general. The effect of his labor was the discovery of the "transcendental" method.

TRANSCENDENTAL ANALYTIC

The *Critique of Pure Reason,* which is at bottom a critique of speculative reason, or of theoretical reason in its speculative use, is divided into two parts: the "Transcendental Aesthetic," dealing with space and time, and the "Transcendental Logic." I shall omit the doctrine of space and time because it has no special reference to our main problem except in so far as it is of importance in the discussion of cosmology, where I shall treat it briefly. The "Transcendental Logic" is again divided into two parts, the first, the "Analytic," which proves the validity of scientific knowledge, and the "Dialectic," which proves the invalidity of speculative metaphysics. The "Analytic" is constructive; the "Dialectic," destructive. The first shows that and why Hume's skepticism is wrong; the second, that and why it is right.

The transcendental method in contrast to the psychogenetic method of the English analysts is not genetic, but strictly analytical, i.e., it analyzes the factors that bring about the logical validity of empirical knowledge. " There can be no doubt that all our knowledge begins with experience. . . . But though all our knowledge begins with experience, it does not follow that it all rises out of experience. For it may well be that even our empirical knowledge is made up of what we receive through impressions and of what our own faculty of knowledge (sensible impressions serving merely as the occasion) supplies from itself." [2] In these words Kant introduces the program of his transcendental theory. Unfortunately, the words are not as unmistakable as one would wish them to be. They may suggest a new psychogenetic analysis and they have often been misunderstood that way. In fact, they exclude such a method, as the subsequent discussions make absolutely certain. Kant distinguishes two different constituents of empirical knowledge, the one empirical, in the narrower sense of impressions or of the data given by sensation, the other nonempirical or a priori, not because they belong to " our own faculty of knowledge," but because they are logically prior to any sense perception and condition it.

The main problem of the " Transcendental Analytic " concerns the question, How can a priori elements in our knowledge, elements not given by the senses, nevertheless constitute the objects of perception, the physical objects existing in space and time? It is true that the " Transcendental Analytic " combines psychological with logical considerations in order to prove the constitutive validity of the nonempirical elements. This combination characterizes the peculiar transcendental method which Kant applies. And it is also true that this combination contains most subtle difficulties which Kant perhaps never perfectly settled. As the difference of the first edition (A) from the second (B) demonstrates, Kant oscillated between two versions of that combination. In the first edition the psychological method was much more in the foreground than it was in the second edition, in which instead the logical method prevails. I cannot enter here into the endless debates about this strange fact and the ensuing interpretation. I will confine myself to saying that in both editions the two elements of the transcendental method are combined and that this combination alone can fulfill the task which Kant set himself.

The main point in Kant's theory is the insight that the object of

---

[2] *Critique of Pure Reason,* tr. by Norman Kemp Smith (Macmillan & Co., Ltd., London, 1933), B. 1.

empirical knowledge (be it that of everyday perception, or that of scientific theory) cannot — as the English thinkers assumed — be reduced to an impression or a collection of impressions or a collection of "ideas," but that common sense is right when it takes the object to exist outside the (individual) mind. The tree which stands in my garden is not the impressions I receive when I look at it; it is not even a compound of impressions, although I do perceive it only when I have these impressions. The tree is more than this. An element has to be added which does not belong to sensation but to the logical understanding, and this element alone makes my perception " objective." Or to put it in another very simple way: the object of my perception is not my perception, but the tree. And I perceive the tree because perception (as Locke had rightly said, but had failed to evaluate in its full significance) contains a logical judgment which can be true or false. If there is no tree but only something that resembles a tree, then my perception of the tree is false, and in that case the tree is really only in my own mind. But when there is a real tree which I perceive, then the judgment enclosed in my perception is true. These are the facts which the transcendental analysis must recognize and understand.

How is objective knowledge possible? This is the fundamental problem of Kant's transcendental analytic. Since the object is not given to us, but only impressions of that object, how is it possible to know whether our judgment is right or wrong? An objectively valid relation between the subject and the predicate of the judgment, Kant argues, " can be adequately distinguished from a relation of the same representations that would have only subjective validity — as when they are connected according to laws of association. In the latter case, all that I could say would be, ' If I support a body, I feel an impression of weight '; I could not say, ' It, the body, *is* heavy.' Thus to say, ' The body is heavy,' is not merely to state that the two representations have always been conjoined in my perception, however often that perception be repeated; what we are asserting is that they are combined *in the object,* no matter what the state of the subject may be." [3] In these momentous words Kant hits the heart of the matter by criticizing Hume's theory of subjective associations.

The logical analysis of the judgment which underlies the percep-

[3] B. 142. Italics are Kant's.

tion or which is the cognitive kernel of the perception finds not only an association of impressions or ideas but a relation between a logical subject and a logical predicate. The question is how can this logical relation which is " in " the thinking understanding reach the object which is " outside " that understanding? How can the understanding ever " transcend " itself so as to judge about the object? Kant answers this question by his doctrine of the understanding as being " transcendental." The " transcendental understanding " has the power to penetrate the objects and to achieve knowledge about them. How does the transcendental understanding perform this seemingly impossible task which according to Hume was not only seemingly, but really impossible?

The task would be impossible, indeed, if the object were essentially cut off from the thinking mind; if there were no inner or intrinsic bond between object and mind or understanding. But then even the term " object " would be meaningless. It has a meaning only if the object has such an intrinsic connection with the understanding, which is transcendental precisely on the ground of this intrinsic connection. The object, although it is not a mere collection or association of impressions, is nevertheless dependent upon the thinking mind: it is *logically* formed by the transcendental understanding or its *logical* form is conditioned by the form of the judgment. If such a logical dependence did not exist, the object could then indeed never be reached by the judging mind; it could then never become its object. This transcendental connection which Kant puts in the place of Hume's merely subjective or psychogenetic connection makes perception or knowledge in general possible; it makes it possible that the mind passes a positive or negative sentence on the relation between subject and predicate and that this logical relation does agree with the corresponding reality of the object.

Kant expresses this dependence of the object upon the logical structure of the thinking and knowing mind in still another way which to a certain extent resembles the subjective idealism of Hume and might therefore easily be mistaken for the same doctrine. The object, Kant teaches, is so intimately and inseparably connected with the transcendental understanding that it might be called an " appearance " or a " phenomenon." Indeed, the object is not a thing-in-itself, a thing which exists without being formed by the mind, or which transcends the horizon of the thinking subject completely. In that case it would indeed be unknowable or unreachable by our judgment; it would be translogical. So far Hume was right, although he never saw this kind of dependence and therefore could never demonstrate the possibility of the knowledge of objects. He could never even attain to the correct concept of an object. Hume was right in saying that there is a subjective foundation of knowledge, but this foundation is logical and therefore as objective as it is subjective. In fact its subjectivity makes its objectivity possible. If we were not able to pass sentence upon the relation between the logical subject and the logical predicate, and if this relation were not at the same time constitutive for the object itself, then indeed objective knowledge would be impossible. The object is therefore in that sense subjectively conditioned; it is within the reach of the judging faculty of the mind. And in that sense the object is " appearance."

" Appearance," of course, does not mean that the object is merely a content of, or in, the mind like hallucinations or impressions which have no foundation in reality. Appearance is real and reality itself is composed of appearances. Hume was unable to distinguish between impressions and hallucinations because he had no concept of reality. This concept is logical in the transcendental sense. Without this concept no theory of knowledge can ever be established. The legitimate relation between knowledge or subjective judgment and objective reality is the pole around which the theory of knowledge has to circle. Kant's subjectivism is logical and transcendental; it is the subjectivism of the transcendental logic. The objects are appearances not in any metaphysical (Plato) or psychological (Hume) sense, but in the new and unique sense of Kant's transcendental philosophy. According to that philosophy reality itself, i.e., that reality which we try to catch by means of empirical perception and theory, is logically subjective and only therefore and under this condition knowable. This is the essence of Kant's epistemology.

On the ground of this transcendental condition the object is itself transcendental, but no longer transcendent. It would be transcendent, and hence unknowable, if it were not conditioned logically, or if it were " in-itself." It is not transcendent in that sense, but transcendental, because it is also " in-the-mind," namely, conditioned by the transcendental understanding. Kant thus resolutely and radically separates " objects " and " things-in-themselves " or metaphysical substances like those of Descartes, Leibniz, or Spinoza. He agrees with Galileo that we can know only the phenomenal world of appearances, but not the world of " inner substances," as Galileo called the things-in-themselves. We can know only that world which is within the reach of logical judgment and which is within that reach because and inasmuch as it is logical and therefore subjective. This doctrine has nothing to do with innate ideas or with subconscious mental forms which are imposed upon the world or anything of that nature. The logical conditionality of the physical world certainly also has a psychological counterpart (which Kant in the first edition of the *Critique of Pure Reason* analyzed carefully), but this does not imply that the transcendental understanding is a psychological concept. Such an interpretation must necessarily destroy the nerve center of Kant's entire theory of knowledge.

The transcendental understanding is the central concept of Kant's transcendental logic. This understanding is definitely not divine, but discursive and human. It takes the place of Berkeley's divine mind and thereby performs the same function which Berkeley's God in his theory of knowledge performed. It also fills the place of Spinoza's God and of the Cartesian God, in so far as he was the guarantee of the truth, and protected the scientist from being deceived by a malignant demon. Kant's transcendental logic, however, keeps within the boundaries of empirical knowledge and inquires into its immanent conditions. The transcendental understanding is not transcendent, but immanent. It is not merely human, if this implies all the restrictions which define man as an animal. Kant was of the opinion that space and time are human forms of perception, but that the forms of the transcendental understanding have validity for all discursive thinking, not only for man's investigation of the spatial and temporal world.

The discursive understanding is compared by Kant with an intuitive intellect which not only would think the objects but produce them. Man has to rely upon empirical perception which receives the data or the material contents from outside itself, while a divine mind " should not represent to itself given objects, but through whose representation the objects should themselves be given or produced." [4]

[4] B. 145.

The difference between a divine and a discursive understanding like that which we as humans possess is generated by the chasm between the self and the objects; we have to experience the objects, to explore them, and to think about them scientifically in order to know them, whereas a divine understanding would see them intuitively within itself. In the *Critique of Judgment,* Kant repeats this speculative concept of a divine understanding and says more about it. In both places he does not assert that such a divine intellect exists; rather, he introduces it as a concept in order to define and to confine the discursive intellect of finite rational beings like ourselves. Such a finite intellect is characterized by the duality of itself and its objects as well as by the duality of itself and the senses through which we receive the stuff of perception and experience, in contrast to the form which pertains to the transcendental understanding. Our understanding is abstract and therefore supplemented by sense materials. A divine understanding would be self-sufficient; it would be intuitive. It would therefore not need completion by experience; it would not need scientific investigation and experiment. God, if we dare to imagine his way of thinking and knowing, is not a scientist or a philosopher. He is not split as we are into intellect and sensation or impression; we must compose the two because we are divided into these two sources of knowledge. Therefore we are subject to error which arises out of that division. We must toil to bring together stuff and form, sensation and understanding. Hence science has a history and progresses slowly by means of hypotheses which are tentative judgments or attempts to synthetize the forms of our understanding with our sense data.

Our mind has to collect and to compare the data of experience in order to control sensation and to subject its contents to the unity of the transcendental understanding which works in and through our finite intellect. In this way we make the relation between the given contents logically compatible and build up the empirical world or a picture of this world through our scientific endeavor. In order to analyze this intellectual activity and to prove that it is possible, Kant wrote the most important but also the most difficult chapter, "Transcendental Deduction," in the *Critique of Pure Reason.*

The pre-Kantian theory of knowledge, ancient as well as medieval, was founded upon the presupposition that to know means to copy the objects of knowledge. Before Kant, modern philosophy had taken over this theory without changing its principle. It is true that Leibniz as well as Hume, the direct predecessors of Kant, had somehow modified the "copy" conception. According to Leibniz, the monads copy the world not by depicting objects which exist outside the mind and are to be reproduced by the mind, but by producing them out of themselves; this conception is akin to Kant's idea of the intuitive divine mind; however, the monads although akin to the divine mind are nevertheless finite because their production of objects depends upon their individual point of view and is therefore imperfect and partly passive. According to Hume, the "ideas" copy the impressions, not the objects; objects originate from the association of the impressions and from the inner necessity of producing the copies of associated impressions. Thus both Leibniz and Hume did break with the ancient tradition, but not entirely. The copy conception was upheld by them.

Kant resolutely and radically abandoned it. Leibniz was right in teaching that the monads know only imperfectly the objects, because they depend upon their individual perspective; however, according to his doctrine, the agreement between their individual perspectives is brought about by an original harmony which in the last analysis is the work of God. How can we understand the possibility of such an agreement without the fictitious metaphysical thesis of an original harmony established by God? Hume was right when he declared that we cannot compare our ideas with outer things-in-themselves; however, he could not explain the validity of our association of ideas, since this association was merely subjective. Kant clearly saw these deficiencies of his two predecessors. He recognized that agreement between our cognitive judgments and the objective truth can be secured only when the transcendental understanding works not only in our subjective intellect, but at the same time conditions the very reality of the objects themselves. We are able to investigate nature successfully by experience and experiment because it is the same understanding which controls our logical activity and the logical structure of the objects in space and time. In his smaller epistemological writing, the *Prolegomena,* Kant expresses this seemingly paradoxical theory by stating that our understanding "prescribes" to nature its laws, i.e., that logical order which enables us to find out the special laws which govern the processes of nature. Science is possible not because there is a pre-established harmony but because the transcendental understanding underlies the objectively real world of physical phenomena. The scientists can agree with one another and their theories can agree with the facts because one and the same transcendental understanding conditions both our intellectual thinking and the physical world.

The "highest principle" of Kant's epistemology therefore is expressed in the sentence, We assert that "the conditions of the *possibility of experience* in general are likewise conditions of the *possibility of the objects of experience.*" [5] The transcendental understanding makes the objects themselves possible, because the objects cannot exist without a logical structure. Kant transformed ontology into epistemology. Reality and logic are bound up with each other. As the ancient thinkers by virtue of their cosmocentric position speculated about a world soul or a world mind, and as the Christian thinkers interpreted this cosmic mind in terms of the revealed God, the Creator of the world, so Kant interprets the agreement between reality and logic in terms of his anthropocentric speculation by the rules which control human thought as well as the objective world in space and time. Knowledge can be achieved only because of this identity of the objective rationality and the subjective theoretical reason. Scientific knowledge is possible, not because the human mind copies the objective world, but because this world is ordered by the same mind. There does exist a pre-established harmony between nature and understanding, but this harmony is not as Leibniz taught, arranged by the divine mind (if it were we could never know it); it is, rather, the consequence of the world's logical constitution which harmonizes with our own logical thinking. "However exaggerated and absurd it may sound, to say that the understanding is itself the source of the laws of nature, and so its formal

---

[5] B. 197; A. 158. Italics are Kant's. The translation is not quite correct. Instead of "likewise" one should read "at the same time." See the German text: "Die Bedingungen der *Möglichkeit der Erfahrung* überhaupt sind zugleich Bedingungen der *Möglichkeit der Gegenstände der Erfahrung.*" In other words: the conditions are in both cases the *same*, not merely *alike*. The principle is Kant's version of the identity thesis which we met first in Parmenides. See Kroner, *Speculation in Pre-Christian Philosophy*, pp. 109 f.

unity, such an assertion is nevertheless correct." [6] It is the Logos of Heraclitus which thus is resuscitated on the level and with the speculative means of modern times.

The objects are themselves "rational," otherwise they could never be made rational by the human scientific mind. This rationality consists not only in their being united in one world and by one experience and one science, but also by their inherent logical structure. This structure corresponds, Kant says, to the structure of the logical judgments themselves. I cannot dwell upon this doctrine; I must confine myself to outlining its main principles. As logical judgments can be regarded under four titles, namely, quantity, quality, relation, and modality, so can the transcendental forms which condition the possibility of objects. There cannot be objects which are not subject to the forms of quantity, i.e., oneness, plurality, and allness or totality. There cannot be objects which are not either real or nonreal or of limited reality. The most important logical conditions are those of relation. Every judgment is categorical or hypothetical or disjunctive, therefore all objects are related to each other either by the form of substantiality (as substance and accident) or by that of causality (as cause and effect) or by mutual dependence (reciprocity of agent and patient). And fourthly, all objects are either possible or impossible, either existent or nonexistent, either necessary or contingent, according to the form of modality.

Kant calls all these forms, which are logical in their origin but ontological on account of the logical structure of the objects themselves, categories. The "Transcendental Deduction" has to show in general that the categories rule the objective phenomena. The categories are both subjective and objective, logical and real. Phenomena can be logically ordered because they are ontologically ordered. The logical and transcendental forms, which are empty if not applied to the given material of sensation, are filled by this material. This is what we call experience. The categories enable us to experience the physical phenomena, their relation, their processes, their laws, and thus to build up the natural sciences, especially mathematical physics. We need sense perception because the categories as such do not deliver empirical knowledge or any theoretical knowledge. So-called

[6] A. 127.

" formal logic " sets forth rules of thinking, especially of inferences, but it cannot grant any concrete knowledge. Those rules are merely formal; we have to obey them if we want to achieve true knowledge, but by itself formal logic is entirely void. It was the chief error of rational metaphysics to believe that we could achieve knowledge of the " things-in-themselves," if we abstract from all material contents and think out the essence of things. Such an undertaking is vain and illusory since the categories as such are mere forms which need the data of sensation to be of cognitive value. This consideration leads from the " Transcendental Analytic " to the " Transcendental Dialectic," or from the constructive to the destructive part of the *Critique of Pure Reason*.

Kant's epistemology is " idealistic "; it holds that the transcendental understanding is the supreme condition of experience and of the objects of experience, but it is not idealistic in the Platonic sense. The categories are not metaphysical or ontological existences or substances, but transcendental forms. Kant's idealism is transcendental, not transcendent. Transcendental idealism is Kant's version of Hume's science of human nature. It is less speculative than Plato's Idealism of the Ideas, but it is more speculative than Hume's subjective idealism of the ideas as residua of the impressions. It is true that without Hume's subtle analysis of causality Kant would not have achieved his transcendental idealism. The transcendental deduction confirmed and at the same time destroyed Hume's analysis and his whole epistemology. Kant fully acknowledged Hume's merits. " David Hume recognized that the pure concepts of the understanding . . . should have an a priori origin. But since he could not explain, how it can be possible that the understanding must think concepts which are not in themselves connected in the understanding, as being necessarily connected in the object " — like the concepts of cause and effect — " and since it never occurred to him that the understanding itself, perhaps, through these concepts, be the author of the experience in which its objects are found, he was constrained to derive them from experience, namely, from a subjective necessity (that is from *custom*), which arises from repeated association in experience. . . . But from these premises he argued quite consistently." [7]

[7] B. 127. Italics are Kant's. See also B. 788; A. 760.

The categories are called rules by Kant.[8] This term has a special significance. A rule is, strictly speaking, not a theoretical but a practical notion. It commands the will first and the intellect only through the will. A practical action is implicit within scientific research and indeed within daily perception. Here we see that not only psychology, logic, and ontology, but also ethics in their theoretical application are involved in Kant's transcendental idealism. The activity which is ascribed to the understanding points to a practical aspect of experience and theoretical knowledge in general. Man has to obey the logical and the transcendental rules if he wants to achieve knowledge. Without obeying these rules he can achieve nothing. That the effect always follows the cause, that there is no change possible if not brought about by causation, this is not a psychological nor a merely logical and ontological necessity, but it is a necessity recognized in concrete experience and by scientific theory, if we obey the rules of the transcendental understanding. Therefore only a conscientious scientist is a good scientist who attains the truth. A certain ethical standard must be maintained for the sake of theoretical purposes if the agreement between our judgment and the objective facts shall be accomplished.

This ethical standard within the epistemological analysis already foreshadows the primacy of the practical reason as compared with the passive reception of sense materials. The necessary connection between cause and effect is based upon the rule that every logically demonstrated statement is the consequence of a conditioning ground. If this rule of consequence is not observed, the causal connection between two events cannot be truly evinced. This rule was called by Leibniz the principle of " sufficient reason." To be consistent is the supreme ethicotheoretical imperative. Only if the intellect conforms to this imperative, can it discover the " consistency of nature " itself, i.e., its physical laws. The coherence of nature corresponds to the unity of the transcendental understanding.

TRANSCENDENTAL DIALECTIC

In the transcendental dialectic the idea of a critique of pure reason comes to the fore. The transcendental analytic, however important is its proof of the possibility of objective knowledge, does not yet reveal the intention of the critique. Only in the second part of the tran-

[8] B. 145 and *passim*.

scendental logic is this intention fulfilled. What Kant wanted to show was the impossibility of a knowledge which is based on pure reason, i.e., on pure theoretical, in contrast to pure practical, reason. Theoretical knowledge in the sense in which it is analyzed in the first part is thwarted when it is applied to a sphere which transcends that of space and time, of sensation and perception, of physical phenomena and processes. The world of appearance is not the Absolute or Ultimate. There is something beyond that world, but this something cannot be known theoretically; it is not given and therefore it cannot be experienced in the way in which the visible universe can be. That such a sphere beyond the confines of space and time nevertheless " exists " (although even this notion cannot be applied here without qualification), is already evinced by the analytics, since the contrariety of object and subject, of nature and self, points to such a " beyond." Nature is not the all-embracing reality, since the self is not embraced by it. We ourselves, inasmuch as we are the subjects of knowledge, do not belong to nature; we are " supernatural." The whole activity of our theoretical faculty transcends the boundaries of the phenomenal world.

But this supernatural sphere itself cannot be known as the all-embracing reality either, because it is opposed by the natural sphere, and there is no possibility of overcoming this opposition. At the bottom of Kant's philosophy we encounter a duality that cannot be abrogated. This duality is exhibited in the character of our discursive intellect which always confronts two elements of a judgment, the logical subject and the logical predicate. Only in the intuitive intellect of God is this duality surmounted. Therefore our speculative thought always confronts contrarieties, as that of sensation and understanding, of material and form, of the given and the activity or spontaneity of thinking, of theoretical and practical reason, and of many others. Our speculation cannot compose these ultimate polarities, as it is also unable to derive them from a higher unity. Indeed, there would not be activity, will, interest, striving, there would not be logical thinking, rules to be obeyed, scientific progress, error and hypothesis, there would not be toiling for discovery of the truth, if this discursive duality did not hamper the ultimate step toward the solution of the ultimate problem: that of the absolute unity which underlies all the dualities.

The transcendental dialectic shows systematically that this absolute unity can never become the object of a science which would correspond to the natural sciences. Antiquity and Christian philosophy believed in the possibility of such a metaphysical science which was regarded as the queen and the consummation of all the sciences. Cosmology and theology were the main branches of this consummate science. There was a third science which dealt with man as inhabiting a special position in the world and as being related in a special sense to God: metaphysical or rational psychology as already developed by Plato and Aristotle and enriched by Clement of Alexandria, Origen, Augustine, and the medieval philosophers. Kant criticizes in the transcendental dialectic these three metaphysical pseudo sciences and discloses the fundamental errors on which they were constructed. The systems of Descartes, Leibniz, and Spinoza also were attacked by this critique, at least in so far as they too tried to set forth the ancient and medieval attempts at a knowledge of absolute or ultimate reality.

The Soul as the " object " of a metaphysical psychology, the World as the " object " of a metaphysical cosmology, and God as the " object " of a metaphysical theology are designed on an illusory presupposition, that is, that of the dealing with these " objects " as if they were objects in the same sense in which the objects of the natural sciences are. The whole transcendental philosophy implicitly denounced such a presupposition from the outset and in principle, inasmuch as it disclosed the transcendental character of the understanding and of the thinking self in general. The duality between the knowledge of mathematical physics and that of the transcendental analytic makes manifest the impossibility of a metaphysical psychology. The thinking self is not an object of such a psychology precisely because it is the knowing subject.

However, in a sense the knowing subject does belong to the world in space and time, otherwise we human beings living in space and time could never actualize the transcendental understanding — we could never become knowing subjects in the sense of the transcendental analytics — we could never become scientists. Science itself would then be impossible. Here we meet a problem not discussed in Kant's epistemology, a problem that has metaphysical implications of a kind not yet envisaged by the *Critique*. The dialectic attacks this problem together with those of a rational cosmology and of theology.

The three pseudo sciences are distinguished in other ways too. The human soul is to a certain extent experienced as neither world nor God is, because it lives in space and time although not entirely. The world cannot be experienced that way, but its parts, the physical phenomena, can. God, on the contrary, is absolutely transcendent; his existence is therefore more questionable than that of soul and world, and speculation cannot withdraw from the task of first proving the existence of God, before saying anything more about him; if it does rely completely on revelation, it would not be in accord with the spirit of modern philosophy.

In this manner Kant sets out to deal with the three pseudo objects of the alleged metaphysical sciences.

The soul is neither merely a temporal sequence of impressions and ideas and of their associative collections nor is it identical with the transcendental self or ego. Rather, it is both and this strange compound makes the character of a rational psychology itself strange. The soul is not so temporary a thing as the impressions are, but it is also not so supertemporal and otherworldly as the transcendental understanding. It neither belongs exclusively to the world of transitory phenomena, because it is also potentially transcendental; nor does it belong exclusively to the supernatural and transcendental sphere, because it also lives in the temporal order. It is this double nature which, on the one hand, caused speculative thinkers to prove the immortality of the human soul, and which prompted Hume, on the other hand, to deny the identity and even the existence of the human self. This duplicity prohibits (and so far Hume was right) a science which would deal with the supernatural destiny of the soul, but it also explains why such a science came to exist. The main blunder of the metaphysical psychology and of all proofs of the immortality of the soul was that they did not distinguish between the empirical and the transcendental nature of the human ego. As some early Christian theologians denied the human nature of Christ and acknowledged only his divine nature, so also the metaphysical psychologists ignored the empirical aspect of the human soul and acknowledged only the a priori aspect, but without truly understanding this second aspect as the transcendental condition of knowledge and of its objects. The result was the fallacious proofs of the soul's immortality. Theoretically such proofs must fail. The transcendental

understanding might be called "immortal" because it is the condition of space and time and therefore not conditioned by them, but
such a designation would be wrong because it suggests that there is
no difference between the transcendental, general understanding and
the empirical, i.e., the individual soul.

An analogous but not exactly identical mistake occurred with respect to the pseudo science of cosmology. The world is never
"given" in the same fashion as physical phenomena are. If we take
the world, i.e., the Whole of all phenomena in space and time, as an
object of knowledge, we are caught in the net of insoluble, but also
unavoidable, contradictions which Kant calls "antinomies." We can
demonstrate equally that the world has and that it has not a beginning in time, or that it is and that it is not limited in space. We can
demonstrate that the physical substances are composed and are not
composed of indivisible particles; that causality is and is not the only
form which controls all changes in the world, and finally that there
is a cause of the world itself and that such a cause does not exist.
These "antinomies of pure reason" spring from the basic error that
we are speculating about an object that defies the categories of objective knowledge. The world cannot be subjected to these categories
because space and time condition only finite appearances. The world
which embraces all phenomena is itself no longer a phenomenon.
When we nevertheless treat it as a phenomenon we must necessarily
contradict ourselves. The basic contradiction underlying all the special ones is that which arises between the All of phenomena and a
definite phenomenon. The world is no longer the world if treated in
that way; if not treated so, however, it is no longer in space and
time and therefore contradicts all temporal and spatial possibilities.

The transcendental dialectic confirms what Kant in the transcendental aesthetic, the first part of the *Critique of Pure Reason,* teaches,
namely, that space and time are forms of human perception only.
They are in one respect like the categories, forms, i.e., they condition
our experience and the objects of our experience; but they condition
them not logically, but only in so far as our experience is sensuous
and its data therefore adapted to forms of our sensibility. Space and
time are such forms. Not the transcendental understanding, but
"pure aesthetic intuition" frames the materials of sensation and
thereby restricts the categories themselves to their spatial and tem-

poral application. In the transcendental dialectic this doctrine turns out to be true, since the world cannot be understood as restricted by space and time and yet it must be thought so restricted if it is to be understood at all as an object of knowledge. Thus the contradictions ensue with inner consistency. If space and time were conditions not only of appearances but of things-in-themselves, independent of our forms of perception, then it should be possible to answer the questions of cosmology without contradiction. The Greeks answered the questions concerning the boundaries of the world in the affirmative without feeling any difficulty. The world was a sphere to them, a closed cosmos, therefore beautifully formed. As to time, Aristotle answered that it is potentially infinite, but actually finite; the world is therefore as eternal as the forms of things. The Christian thinkers agreed with the Greeks about the finiteness of the cosmic space; and they agreed with the actual finiteness of cosmic time, since they assumed the world to be created by God. Modern times, as we have seen in the section on Giordano Bruno, got into trouble, because it thought of space and time no longer in an aesthetically cosmic fashion, nor in a religiously created manner, but instead in a mathematically rational fashion. Thus the infinity of space and time had to be accepted and the antinomies arose which marred the conception of Bruno's cosmology.

The same difficulty plagued the concept of ultimate particles. Bruno and Leibniz found their refuge in their idea of monads, ultimate units which are not spatial and temporal, but intellectual or intelligible. Spinoza escaped the difficulty by eliminating finite substances altogether.

But the most important antinomies are those concerning causality as a principle that demands the assumption of a first cause of the world, although such a cause, if the world is really the sum total of causes, must belong to the world itself, so that the contradiction is inescapable. Even more aggravating than the plight of pure reason dealing with the world is the question whether causality has to be accepted as the principle of all changes in nature or whether a causality of freedom, i.e., a causality that marks an absolutely new beginning, can be admitted. Both can be proved either on the basis of the view that the world is composed of appearances only, or according to the other view that some appearances, as for instance we ourselves, are not merely objects and therefore are not totally subject to physical causality.

The transcendental dialectic culminates in the refutation of the proofs of God. The existence of a supreme being in whom all reality is concentrated or in whom reality is absolutely perfect cannot be demonstrated. Kant examines three traditional modes of demonstrating God's existence: the cosmological, the physicotheological, and the ontological. The first two pass from the existence of the world or of certain facts in the world, which betray a special excellence and fitness to the existence of a supreme intelligence, which has created the world. These proofs have been already refuted in essence by the cosmological antinomies. A first cause of the world cannot be irrefutably demonstrated. Kant argues that these proofs have validity only if the third proof — the ontological one — is valid. Only if it can be shown that the very concept of God assures his existence, as Anselm held, can God be acknowledged as the Author of the world and the Designer of those facts or things which manifest an intelligent purpose. The whole question concentrates therefore upon the ontological argument.

The most we could attain by the physicotheological proof which Kant respects as " the oldest, the clearest, and the most accordant with the common reason of mankind " would be the certainty that a skillful architect, such as Plato's Demiurge, has arranged the visible universe, but not that the world is created by an almighty, omniscient, and holy God.[9] The ontological proof is the only one that does not advance by " the empirical road," but is based on pure thought alone and therefore deserves a special attention and examination. Kant's refutation of this proof is based upon the assumption that it is purely rational or conceptual. He leaves the religious root of Anselm's argument entirely out.

The existence of a being cannot be founded upon rational reasons alone. Existence, as we know, is a category that applies only to empirical objects which are connected with other empirical objects in the unity of experience. God is not such an object. Kant illustrates the impossibility of a purely conceptual proof of God by a comparison with one hundred dollars. One hundred dollars are one hundred dollars whether they exist in fact or not; existence is never a possible predicate that could be contained in the concept of

---

[9] Cf. B. 651; A. 623; B. 655 f.; A. 627 f.

the existing thing. Whether I think of the hundred dollars or whether I really own them makes indeed a considerable difference to the possible owner, but it does not affect in the least the concept.[10]

This argument is both very convincing and very crude. After all, there is a tremendous difference betwen the concept of one hundred dollars and that of God. Not only the defenders of the ancient argument, but also metaphysicians of the rank of Hegel, declined Kant's refutation on the ground that God cannot and should not be compared with one hundred dollars. If God were an empirical entity, then his existence could not be demonstrated. Indeed, Kant is right in this respect. But God is not such an entity. However we may define the Supreme Being, it is ridiculous and disgusting to think of him as an empirical reality. If we define the concept of God (as Kant does in some places) as that of the most real entity (*ens realissimum*), or as that of the All of reality (*omnitudo realitatis*) as he does in other places, or as the primordial being (*ens originarium*) or as the highest of all beings (*ens summum*), or as the being of all beings (*ens entium*), in any case this concept is incomparable, unique, and of a special excellence. Kant explicitly says in one passage that the idea of God is not that of a sum total of all things, but that of their ground. He calls this idea the "Ideal of Pure Reason."[11] How can we assert that this Ideal should be on the same level as one hundred dollars? What is certainly true with respect to one hundred dollars is certainly wrong with respect to the Ideal of Pure Reason!

God is not an object of theoretical experience; he does not exist as empirical things do. But this consideration does not solve the problem suggested by the ontological argument. The idea of God theoretically regarded might indeed demand that Being and Thought be inseparably connected with each other in the Supreme Being. In one section of the dialectical discussion of rational or speculative theology Kant speaks of God as "the absolutely necessary being," in distinction from all empirical beings which may be at the most conditionally or relatively necessary.[12] Does not the idea of such a necessary being imply that this being is necessarily real? Kant states that "theoretical knowledge is speculative, if it concerns an object, or those concepts of an object, which cannot be reached in any experience. It is so named to distinguish it from the knowledge of na-

[10] B. 626 f.; A. 508 f.   [11] B. 608; A. 580.   [12] Cf. B. 620; A. 592.

ture, which concerns only those objects or predicates of objects which can be given in possible experience." [13] Such a speculative knowledge, Kant concludes, is impossible. But is it not absurd to demand that God, in order to become an object of speculative knowledge, should first be " given " in theoretical experience? In other words, is not perhaps the whole Kantian concept of a speculative knowledge of God preposterous?

If there is an object which by its nature cannot be known by means of that knowledge which is concerned with empirical objects, should we then not infer that the conditions of such a knowledge cannot be the conditions of speculative knowledge? To be sure, most historical examples of speculative knowledge did commit the blunder of dealing with such an object as if it were conditioned in the same way as the objects of empirical knowledge, and thus failed to comprehend it in the proper way. But is not another way possible by which this " object " can be known in accordance with its unique nature, and would not then such knowledge be the truly speculative knowledge of God? Here opens a path which Kant has not seen, but along which Kant's successors, especially Hegel, moved. Kant was certainly right in asserting that " in order to have knowledge of a supreme being we should have to put them " — the principles of reason — " to a transcendent use for which our understanding is in no way fitted." [14] Nevertheless, we might be able to realize that our understanding cannot grasp the concept of a supreme being as analogous to empirical knowledge precisely because being and thought are inseparable in him! Such an insight would indirectly confirm the ontological argument.

Thomas Aquinas rejected the ontological argument, because he thought that we must infer from the existence of the world to that of God. In this way he became guilty of the fault with which Kant upbraids the defenders of a cosmological proof who reject the ontological argument. But Aquinas inadvertently went back to that argument by saying that in God essence and existence coincide, and that this coincidence characterizes the uniqueness of God's existence. [15]

[13] B. 663 f. A. 634 f.
[14] B. 664; A. 636.
[15] Cf. Kroner, *Speculation and Revelation in the Age of Christian Philosophy*, pp. 200 f.

Does not the term *ens realissimum* point to this unique excellence of the Supreme Being? Kant was right in distinguishing this Being from all empirical objects, and in showing that God cannot be known as these objects can; he also was right in laying bare the deficiency of the cosmological argument. But was he right in denying any speculative knowledge of God? Did he not himself contribute to that knowledge by defining the idea of God as the Ideal of Pure Reason?

This Ideal at least circumscribes a necessary concept. It is the Ideal of Pure Reason because it denotes the solution to an indispensable problem. Since the finite understanding implies its separation from the data of experience, the problem of how this separation is overcome by an infinite understanding cannot be ignored. Kant himself outlined for this purpose the idea of an intuitive divine understanding which would not receive the materials of experience, but would produce them out of itself. Such an intuitive understanding is not a chimera; it is a necessary requisite of Kant's entire epistemology. Only if an ultimate unity of empirical data and the forms of our consciousness is assured, are experience and knowledge possible. Kant emphasized in his transcendental deduction that the forms are the necessary presuppositions of experience and that experience is therefore possible only if the forms condition the objects. But do they *really* condition them? Do the sensuous data *really* obey the rules of the transcendental understanding? This question was not explicitly discussed in the transcendental deduction or anywhere else in the *Critique of Pure Reason*. The only place where Kant intimates the necessity of this question is in the transcendental dialectic and in the discussion of the transcendental Ideal of Reason. Kant's successors have pointed to this lack and have tried to furnish a solution to this supreme problem.

In the Introduction to the *Critique of Judgment* (which is most illuminating in many respects) Kant admits that the applicability of the forms to the sense material must in the last analysis be regarded as "a happy chance," thereby confessing that this applicability is by no means secured through the transcendental understanding and the categories, but rests upon an ultimate "harmony" (to use the word of Leibniz) between the forms and the stuff of experience. If this harmony is not an incomprehensible and irrational incident, but is conceived from the perspective of Kant's own theory, then it must be understood as granted by the Ideal of Reason, i.e., by the ultimate unity of all the dualities distinguished by the transcendental analytics and characteristic of finite knowledge. The transcendental dialectic is concerned with the highest condition under which finite knowledge is possible. This knowledge can materialize only if the split between sensation and understanding, between the " given " and the thinking ego, between physical reality and scientific thought, is gradually surmountable and is really surmounted by the Ideal of Reason.

Of course, such a consideration is not a proof of God if we think of God as the Creator and the Lawgiver, the Judge and the Savior. This God cannot be proved at all by speculative thought; only revelation can make us believe in him. But speculation can point to the concept of an infinite understanding which is necessary even for the possibility of a finite understanding because only by it is the duality of reality and thought overcome. According to its idea, such an infinite understanding is therefore not only a concept or an idea, but the idea guarantees its existence or its reality, as the ontological argument suggests.

The transcendental dialectic looks at the Ideal of Reason only from the perspective of empirical knowledge and therefore denies the possibility of realizing it; but Kant does offer a more constructive and positive interpretation of the Ideas of Pure Reason, when he defines them as necessary tasks or as " regulative principles." These principles direct our finite knowledge toward a goal that, although it can never be attained, nevertheless must not be dismissed because it does give unity to the manifold of our finite knowledge. The transcendental Ideas are therefore of positive value. They not only mark the boundary of empirical experience but they also indicate how this experience can be and should be completed, if it could be pursued to its very end. Soul, World, and God are not simply fallacious notions, they are also real, although our understanding cannot comprehend their reality. The term " regulative " points to the fact that our understanding is not stable and can never be completely satisfied by its own results, but tends toward the Infinite. It also stresses the epistemo-ethical character of our cognition. The regulative principles command our intellect to progress toward an infinitely remote, but nevertheless indispensable, end. They " have an excellent, and indeed necessary, regulative employment, namely, that of directing the understanding toward a certain goal upon which the routes marked out by all its rules converge, as upon their point of intersection." [16] In that remote point all our experience is gathered together and fully completed in its infinite focus. This ethical trend within the theoretical activity foreshadows the primacy of pure practical reason and its postulates.

ETHICS

The *Critique of Pure Reason* is only the entrance door to the *Critique of Practical Reason*. It is noteworthy that in the field of theoretical cognition pure reason is criticized because it cannot produce a science like those sciences based upon empirical knowledge, whereas in the field of practical action not pure, but rather empirical, practical, reason is criticized. Pure practical reason is in this field not fallacious, as pure theoretical reason is, but on the contrary it is productive and corresponds therefore to empirical knowledge. Kant deals in the *Critique of Practical Reason* with man as an empirical individual being endowed with desire and inclination, pursuing practical interests and purposes, making decisions and carrying them into effect. All this is done by empirical practical reason, whereas pure practical reason disciplines the will morally, sets up moral standards of doing and of judging motives and actions. Practical reason is empirical and hence can be criticized; pure practical reason, on the contrary, commands the empirical will and makes moral character and moral life possible. Practical reason falsifies morality, if it pretends to be the source of ethical principles.

The transcendental significance of man is not confined to his ability to investigate nature and to establish sciences which discover the laws governing the world of physical phenomena; rather, he is in the first place a willing and doing being, a being that aims at the fulfillment of his desire and his wishes. Theoretical knowledge has to be restricted and finite in order to allow room for practical volition and action, and eventually for practical faith and hope. [17] What is truth in the realm of the understanding, is goodness in that of the will. But whereas the understanding is interested in knowing the

[16] B. 672; A. 644.

[17] Cf. Richard Kroner, *Kant's Weltanschauung* (University of Chicago Press, 1956), esp. ch. IV.

truth about objects, the will is interested in forming itself, in making itself a good will. Theoretical understanding is extroverted; the will is introverted. In the practical field, man is ultimately concerned about himself, whereas in the theoretical field he is concerned with outer objects, with nature, with the phenomenal world. Inasmuch as man is superior to the objects, the will is superior to the intellect, as Clement of Alexandria had insisted. The objects are the objects of the thinking ego, but the subject aims at itself. The objects appear to the human consciousness, but as will man is no longer an appearance, he is rather a "thing-in-itself," he is what he is for himself.

Section 6 of the chapter that discusses the "Antinomy of Pure Reason" in the *Critique of Pure Reason* has the title "Transcendental Idealism as the Key to the Solution of the Cosmological Dialectic."[18] Here Kant expounds perhaps more clearly than anywhere else the concept of things-in-themselves. This section precedes the "Critical Solution of the Cosmological Conflict of Reason with Itself."[19] The solution consists in the thesis that one set of the contradictory propositions in the cosmological antinomies has to be applied to the appearances, the other to things-in-themselves. The appearances are generally subject to space and time, to causality and contingency, but if we understand the world as the totality of all appearances, it is itself no longer an appearance but exists "in-itself." Then the opposite is true: the world in this sense has a beginning in time and boundaries in space; the principle of causality in accordance with laws of nature is then no longer the only principle from which the appearances are to be derived. There is then another kind of causality, that of the free will.[20]

The transcendental dialectic thereby paved the way for the *Critique of Practical Reason*. It effected the transition from the theoretical to the practical realm. That man does not merely belong to nature or to the phenomenal world, that he is essentially supernatural and metaphenomenal (or, as Kant says, noumenal), this can already be learned from the transcendental analytic. It is the presupposition and the consequence of the entire epistemology, in

18 B. 519; A. 491.
19 B. 525; A. 497.
20 Cf. B. 454; A. 426; B. 473; A. 445.

so far as it teaches that the objects depend upon the subject. But only in the *Critique of Practical Reason* does this motif unfold. Here the "dignity" of man, his autonomy, his freedom, his responsibility, his very selfhood, are the themes discussed. Here alone is scrutinized the spontaneity and activity of man, his speculative as well as his moral interests. Here alone is an answer given to the question as to the sense in which man is a thing-in-itself, transcending the limits of space and time, of substance and causality, not only in so far as the transcendental, abstract understanding is at work within him, but also in so far as he is an individual person. Here alone are the ultimate issues of immortality and God positively and affirmatively treated. Kant's speculation culminates in the *Critique of Practical Reason*.

Man is the only empirical being which is also noumenal. The problem of man is therefore unique. To the degree that the problem is solvable, speculation is able to reach its goal. But man is fundamentally a willing and acting being; speculation has to take its stand therefore in ethics. In a way Kant's ethics is his metaphysics. Only on the ground of ethics can thought enter the otherwise closed gateway to the Absolute. But this way is no longer theoretical, in the sense of empirical and scientific knowledge. It is a way that can be taken only for practical purposes. How is the relation between such a practical use of reason and the Ideal of Pure (speculative) Reason to be comprehended? This is the formidable question that looms at the horizon of Kant's ethical system.

As Kant in his theory of knowledge separated the empirical and the rational, the a posteriori and the a priori, so in his ethics he distinguishes empirical and rational, "pathological" and moral, motives. The moral law takes the place of the pure concepts of the transcendental understanding. Practical reason has to be criticized in order to ward off its claim to explain morality. Neither hedonistic nor utilitarian motives are moral. If ethics adopts them as moral principles, then it is as much mistaken as theoretical reason, when the latter pretends to solve the problems of speculation. Hedonism and utilitarianism borrow the moral principle from empirical impulses and desire; but the moral principle is a law that commands the will. Morality is characterized by an imperative which tells the will what it ought to do. Man is acting as a moral *inclination + duty)*

person when he is motivated not by inclination, but by duty; not by his nature, but by his reason. To be sure, inclination and duty, man's nature and his reason, must not necessarily clash, as is thought to be the case by some interpreters of Kant's ethics who exaggerate the contrast. They may both be present; but the point is that only the motive of moral reason makes man's decision and action moral. This is particularly illuminated by the fact that the two motives can indeed clash. Moreover, the moral character of a decision is especially evident when a person does not yield to inclination or desire, and is not swayed by passions or interest, but by the moral law alone. Whereas in the theoretical field the impressions have to be formed by the transcendental understanding which is empty, if it is not applied for this purpose, in the moral field, on the contrary, reason can move the will even against the impulse of nature.

The moral law is a law precisely because it does not necessarily agree with the natural inclinations. The moral law is the law of pure practical reason, while interests and selfish purposes are dictated by an impure practical reason, which has to submit to pure practical reason in order to act morally. Principles of prudence, conventional norms, and worldly wisdom are not truly moral. The moral law does not depend upon considerations about happiness, which the Greeks made the foundation of their ethical systems, nor does it take into account the possible effect of action. Even if a man's life is at stake the moral law does not take this into account. Its command is absolute and does not allow any condition. The so-called goods are not the objects of moral action, but the goodness of the will alone. What makes an action morally good is the inner goodness of the intention, not the goodness of its end. In contrast to the ethics of Christian philosophy, Kant abrogates the distinction between good and bad ends. Nothing objective can ever be good or evil in the moral sense, but only the subjective motive, the disposition of the heart (if the heart is identified with the will). "Nothing in the world — indeed nothing even beyond the world — can possibly be conceived which could be called good without qualification except a *good* will." [21]

[21] *Foundations of the Metaphysics of Morals* (1785), sec. I. Translated by Lewis White Beck in Immanuel Kant's *Critique of Practical Reason and Other Writings in Moral Philosophy* (University of Chicago Press, 1949).

Kant's ethical principle is in accordance with the gospel which emphasizes throughout that not the effect of our doings, but only the purity of our heart matters in the sight of God. " Blessed are the pure in heart: for they shall see God." (Matt. 5:8.) "From within, out of the heart of men, proceed evil thoughts . . ." (Mark 7:21.) " The word of God . . . is a discerner of the thoughts and intents of the heart." (Heb. 4:12.)

Morality alone makes the person a person, the self a self. Kant breaks resolutely with the pre-Christian notion of man as a substance, a notion which Christian thinkers still held. Man is a subject because he is will; he is a person precisely because he is able to obey the moral law. Even Descartes and Leibniz had still clung to the Greek notion. Only Kant made a sharp cleavage between the world and the self and thereby recognized that similarity between man and God spoken of in the Bible. Thinkers had extolled the dignity of man beginning with the Renaissance; Kant alone gave a speculative justification for this predication. His ethics aroused the enthusiastic applause of the German poets and thinkers; and more than his theory of knowledge, it was his ethics that made him popular and eventually famous in the world.

The moral law is called " holy " by Kant, although he rejects any religious foundation or sanction which would make the law valid. It is valid by virtue of its own unconditional sovereignty. It is " categorical " precisely because its validity is not based upon any qualifying or restricting legislation. Reason itself is the only legislator. Therefore the law is not connected with any purpose outside itself. It has no empirical content. Like the categories of the transcendental understanding it is a pure form that conditions every act of the will. As pure form it is the principle of all particular rules, norms, prescriptions, regulations, etc., but it is itself no particular rule or norm. All particular moral codes are historically contingent, but the moral law as such is not; rather, it gives historical codes their moral character, in so far as they agree with its pure form.

The moral law differs, however, in one important respect from the theoretical forms of knowledge: it is not objectively obeyed; it does not constitute objective reality; it does not belong to the order of nature. Rather, the individual person decides to obey it or not. The moral law commands, but it does not bring about what it commands. The person is free to act in accordance with the law or

— respy'

— f'dom

against the law. Responsibility rests upon this freedom. Man is in no way coerced to comply with the command of the law, either by the causality of nature or by any mechanism or determination from within himself. In this respect man is unique in the universe. He alone is to be blamed if the law is ineffective. Wickedness or depravity as well as virtue and righteousness are possible only among men. The dignity of man is based upon this freedom. Empirical psychology, biography, and history generally ascribe the decisions and actions of men to previous causes or conditions, either to circumstances and situations under which they were born, educated, or influenced, or to morals and habits of the epoch in which they live, or to an individual nature that was theirs from their birth. But Kant insists that responsibility would be an empty word, if it were so restricted. For here is a transcendent character of every individual for which the person alone is responsible.

We know from the cosmological antinomies that the "causality of freedom" cannot be proved by theoretical reason, that it cannot be upheld without contradictions. But here a higher court operates: morality is superior to any theoretical demonstration. It rules with sovereignty. From the perspective of the empirical sciences, such as sociology, psychology, biology, history, anthropology, this sovereignty is impossible. But, as we know, the whole range of the empirical sciences is restricted, because they are concerned solely with finite reality, with the world in space and time. Morality transcends this world. Its legislation, its judgment, its freedom point to another world, a world in which we as subjects, as selves, as persons live and will and act. This world, although it is also subject to empirical laws, is not yet subjugated by them. On the contrary, in so far as it is the world of free persons who act of their own accord and are accountable for what they do, it surmounts the boundaries of nature and of the whole empirical horizon. Something greater is here at stake: the moral worth of the person.

That which is called "character" in the strictly moral sense is not identical with the "nature" of an individual, but it depends upon the free decisions and actions of the person. I am responsible for my character; I myself am its author. There is something in me which absolutely surmounts all objective causation; this something is my real self. Kant sees that our understanding meets here an insoluble riddle; he admits that moral freedom is an unfathomable concept. The " existence " of this freedom cannot be demonstrated. Any attempt to prove it leads into a circle, " because freedom and self-legislation of the will are both autonomy and thus reciprocal concepts, and for that reason one of them cannot be used to explain the other and to furnish a ground for it." [22] Moral freedom is not an empirical property of the will, it is rather a moral *Idea;* without freedom morality is not morality. Freedom is, as Kant says, a " postulate of pure practical reason."

The term " postulate " needs an explanation since it plays a great part in the *Critique of Practical Reason.* The postulate is not a command. I am not morally obliged to assume freedom, since obligations concern only what I ought to do. But in so far as I am under the moral law, I am interested in the question whether or not I am free and therefore responsible. Indeed, ethical or psychological theories which deny moral freedom are not simply false, since freedom cannot be demonstrated; they are outright immoral because they violate the interest of the moral person, an interest that is not individually founded, but based upon pure practical reason itself. Those theories are therefore irrational; they offend reason and thereby mankind. The ethical interest is not arbitrary, rather, it is reason in its moral prerogative which is interested in freedom. " Reason, as the faculty of principles, determines the interest of all the powers of mind and its own." [23] My moral freedom is as certain as my ability to judge myself and other persons morally, to condemn or acquit myself or them. Philosophy has no right and no authority to deny my moral freedom. On the contrary it is morally obliged to defend it and to justify its legitimacy as best it can.

Freedom of the will to obey or to disobey the moral law is an Idea of pure practical reason. It has the same or an even higher rank than the Ideas of pure theoretical reason which Kant treated in the *Critique of Pure Reason.* But this freedom is not the only Idea in the practical realm. Later on we will learn that there are other Ideas as important as freedom. All of them are connected with the Ideas of pure theoretical reason. Freedom points back to the cosmological antinomies. The distinction between the phenomenal and the noumenal spheres here assumes practical reality.[24] Man

[22] Beck, *op. cit.,* p. 105.   [23] *Ibid.,* p. 223.   [24] *Ibid.,* p. 247.

as a noumenal being is not subject to natural causality, but to the moral law. The moral will is a "noumenal cause." [25] Speculation cannot explain how such a cause operates, but it can understand it as a postulate of moral reason. In the realm of ethics such a cause attains a reality that it cannot attain on merely theoretical ground.

This subtle relation between speculation and morality is elaborated by Kant in the most meticulous manner. He strongly emphasizes that the "enlargement" of speculation gained in the ethical realm has only an ethical and practical, not a theoretical, validity. We are not entitled and not enabled by the ethical postulate of freedom to speculate about the origin of human selfhood as Origen and others did. Kant mocked at the ghost-seeing of men like Swedenborg. "Only the concept of freedom enables us to find the unconditioned for the conditioned and the intelligible (noumenal) for the sensuous without going outside ourselves. For it is our reason itself which through the supreme and unconditioned practical law recognizes itself, and the being which knows this law (our own person) as belonging to the pure world of the understanding and indeed defines the way in which it can be active as such a being. Thus it can be seen why in the entire faculty of reason only the practical can lift us above the world of sense and furnish cognitions of a supersensuous order and connection, though these cognitions can be extended only as far as is needed for pure practical purposes." [26]

I have quoted this passage in full because it is the *locus classicus* for Kant's conception of the relation between theoretical and practical reason; it also illuminates his doctrine of the primacy of practical reason. Only the moral consciousness and will makes man competent to soar above the world of sense. In that sense practical reason is the root of reason in general, as Kant says, and the root of the whole transcendental idealism. Only for the moral intention is the negative outlook of the transcendental dialectic surpassed and the cosmological Idea positively completed. Kant is eager and careful to restrict the Idea of freedom to the moral use and realm in order to prevent a relapse of thought into the Leibnizian monadology, which pretended to know metaphysically, i.e., theoretically, something about the transcendent nature of man and the world,

[25] *Ibid.*, p. 159.   [26] *Ibid.*, p. 211. Cf. pp. 223 ff.

and which thereby falsified the true significance and meaning of moral freedom.]

It must be admitted that the concept of speculation for the sake of practical reason is beset with inner difficulties. It seems to hover between speculation and will, between the theoretical and the practical realm without belonging to either. Indeed, it is not easy to conceive of a speculation that serves the practical purpose and fulfills a practical need. Out of the difficulties inherent in such a doctrine Fichte's ethical speculation arose. But did not Socrates also hover in an analogous fashion between speculation and ethics? It is true that the outcome of the Socratic conversation was also analogous to that of the Kantian "postulate": the Platonic idealism resembles the Fichtean speculation in that the Good was placed above the theoretical and ontological doctrine of the Ideas. Kant admits in the *Critique of Pure Reason* that his theory of the transcendental Ideas resembles the Platonic doctrine. He sought to recover the noble term "Idea" and to re-establish the teachings of its initiator.[27]

RATIONAL FAITH [28]

The Idea of moral freedom does not transcend the horizon of man's own existence and of his moral experience, although it does enlarge speculative thought beyond the confines of theoretical knowledge. The Ideas of immortality and of God are no longer rooted in our immediate consciousness in the same way; they are therefore even more speculative than the Idea of freedom. We can not grope for them without a special kind of faith. Kant calls this faith "rational" because it is rooted in reason alone according to his opinion. This doctrine of rational faith is even more subtle and open to doubt than the combination of speculation and practical reason. Every man, if he is not misguided and does not misunderstand himself, "believes" in the moral freedom of his will, whereas the belief in God and immortality is more questionable and controversial. It is even difficult to decide whether Kant wanted to give a moral or ethical "proof" of the existence of God.

However, Kant was indeed convinced that the Idea of God can

[27] B. 370; A. 313.

[28] Cf. Richard Kroner, *The Primacy of Faith* (The Macmillan Company, 1943), ch. III.

be defended on ethical grounds and that the existence of God can be " postulated " in a way analogous to the demonstration of freedom. It is not easy to define exactly what Kant meant by " postulate." In some way it is a kind of assumption,[29] not a proof; but it is neither a theoretical hypothesis nor a willful supposition, but one for which irrefutable reasons can be given, although solely on the ground of practical reason. Although the Idea of God is not so necessary a presupposition of moral action and judgment as that of freedom, still man as a moral being needs faith in God. Without such faith morality itself would be ineffective and incomplete. The argument leading to the postulate is not objectively conclusive, but it is subjectively binding upon us as moral beings.[30] In this respect Kant can be regarded as a precursor of Kierkegaard. Indeed, the primacy of practical reason has an " existential " flavor. It might be called the principle of an ethical existentialism.

Kant has given some suggestions why a moral being should be induced to believe in God as " the moral author " of nature. The basic reason is the moral need to bring together nature and ourselves as moral beings. If the moral law had no roots in the world apart from our moral consciousness, or if we as moral beings were living in a morally indifferent world, our moral striving would be an entirely subjective activity. But then such an activity would be a questionable undertaking; we could never be sure that it had a meaning beyond that which we gave to it. Our duties are not merely subjective, they are related to the surrounding world and they have an effect upon the institutions for which we work. But this effect is not in our hands. Although Kant's ethics exclude all consideration of the effect of our decisions and action, nevertheless, we cannot help wishing that out of the fulfillment of our duties, moral consequences may flow.

Although Kant does not carry out these implications of the moral law, he demonstrates in a definite way the need of moral beings to believe that there is a connection between moral effort and its effect. We may call the end which we pursue " happiness," not in so far as we are subject to the moral law, but in so far as we depend upon the world and other beings. The ancients were right when they insisted that happiness is the sum total of all our desire and longing; they

---

[29] *Für wahr halten* in German.   [30] Cf. Beck, *op. cit.,* pp. 228 f.

were wrong only when they made happiness the motive of moral striving. How can we combine the need of happiness and the inexorable and sometimes even cruel austerity of the law? Only by faith in God as the Creator of the world. Only if we can believe that we as moral beings are, as it were, not lonely in the world, that we do not live in a world completely insensible to the moral law. If we can feel an echo from beyond ourselves, the austerity of the law and the hardship of our trials can be mitigated. Only then can a certain equation between our own efforts and its consequences be hoped for. Only then can the claim of a righteous man to be happy and his inability to create happiness by his very righteousness be reconciled to each other. Kant believed that his doctrine was in complete agreement with the Christian religion, although he insists that the faith which he deduces a priori from his ethical principles is purely rational.[31]

The agreement between the moral demands and happiness is called by Kant the "Highest Good." In this way he reaffirmed, on the basis of his own principles, the ethical doctrines of the ancients and of the Christian thinkers. Faith alone assures us that this good, which we ourselves cannot generate by our own resources, will be realized by the Creator of the world. Kant tries to solve the dialectic of practical reason which springs from the impossibility to unite worth and happiness by our empirical knowledge or by philosophic speculation. Neither can be done. Experience does not confirm the postulate that the righteous man should also be happy nor can the ethical imperative assure us that the postulate is fulfilled. Faith alone can satisfy the need which pure practical reason sanctions.

Kant's language in this section of his ethics may today appear obsolete and therefore not very convincing. But there cannot be the slightest doubt that Kant was in earnest when he developed this theory, nor can it be denied that there is a profound wisdom in his considerations. He tries to achieve a delicate balance between speculation and the practical requirements, between the moral imperative and the longing for happiness. As in the case of freedom, here too the theoretical reach is enlarged but solely "for practical purposes." Kant rejects natural theology as vigorously as Hume had rejected it.[32] He even says that the word "natural theology" is

---

[31] Cf. *ibid.*, pp. 229 ff.   [32] Cf. above, p. 189.

" curious since a theologian in the proper sense can be only the teacher of revealed theology " and then he should be called a " divine " (*Gottesgelehrter*).[33] However, in the *Critique of Judgment* he speaks about an " ethicotheology " that consummates the whole philosophic enterprise.

An ethicotheology has to take the place which speculative theology occupied in Aristotle. But it does not grant " a transcendent knowledge of supersensuous objects." " There remains a knowledge of God, but only within a practical context." The Idea of God " can never support speculative knowledge " ; its use is " restricted solely to the practice of the moral law." [34] In spite of this restriction it cannot be denied that the Idea of a moral author of nature does transcend the strictly theoretical Idea of a most real entity or that of an absolutely necessary being, and approaches the Biblical God by means of an ethical speculation. The transcendental Ideal of Pure Reason is definitely surpassed. One can hardly deny that the Idea of a " moral author of nature " is modeled after the concept of the Old Testament Creator of the world. Even so the doctrine of an ethical postulate was original with Kant and has stirred theological thought ever since. It was an attempt on the part of philosophic speculation to vie with religious revelation. God was thereby more than ever before conceived as a personal being whom man as a moral will encounters and whom he urgently needs for his own moral life. Ethical theology is deeper and more adequate than any cosmological or ontological theory of a supreme cause or of a being greater than any that can be conceived. Whereas Aquinas defined God as the highest intellect and as an immaterial form, Kant's ethical idea definitely surmounted all Platonic and Aristotelian concepts of God. The Kantian God is no longer essence or substance, but " the head of a moral kingdom."

Whether Kant succeeded in his ethicotheology in supplanting the Biblical Creator, Judge, and Redeemer by philosophic means is another question. Apart from the difficulty of thinking of an idea of pure practical reason which enlarges the horizon of theoretical knowledge, rational faith is not acceptable for anyone convinced that faith is real only when given by God himself and that reason should not pretend to " postulate " the existence of the Highest.

[33] Beck, *op. cit.*, p. 240.   [34] *Ibid.*, p. 239.

Such a postulated God remains, after all, a kind of concept, whereas the God of revelation is a living God, Father and Lord who " postulates " *us* by commanding us to be as perfect as he is, instead of being himself postulated by our reason. Furthermore, the term " moral author " is incorrect, if morality is thought of in terms of a moral law that has to be obeyed and in terms of the freedom to obey or to disobey, as Kant in fact does think of morality.

There are other difficulties involved in the rational faith as proposed by Kant. Can the harmony between the merit which makes a person worthy to be happy and actual happiness, or the harmony between nature and morality in general, be achieved only by faith in a moral author of the world, or is it possible to think of such a harmony in other terms? Fichte later suggested that a moral order which would manifest itself not only in moral legislation, but also in controlling the world, an *ordo ordinans,* as he defined it, would also fulfill the function of Kant's moral author.

It is obvious that Kant still shared the optimism of the Enlightenment in believing that the equation between merit and happiness is a postulate that the righteous are entitled to set up. He did not seem to agree with the gospel which depicts the Son of God as suffering and which announces that the disciples will be martyred. Kant had to add another postulate in order to make the equation credible, namely, that of immortality. Only if we can believe in a life beyond the grave, could this equation become effective. Faith in the harmony between merit and reward can be established only if in another life God would recompense the morally good man for the sufferings which he has to endure on earth. Kant had another reason for postulating immortality. Since man is called upon to obey the law, but since the time in which he may learn to discipline himself is restricted, moral reason requires another opportunity for achieving this end. But this postulate is even less easily reconciled to Kant's theoretical speculation than faith in God. If time is only a form of human intuition and perception, how can we assume or demand that it also has a transcendent significance and permits the idea of a continuation of moral striving and improvement?

SPECULATION AND REVELATION

These and other considerations finally led Kant to a philosophical analysis of the Christian faith. The basic problem that underlies Kant's doctrine of the primacy of practical reason is the relation between speculation and revelation. This relation had to be clarified in order to consummate Kant's transcendental idealism in general. He undertook to accomplish this clarification in his last great work, *Religion Within the Limits of Mere Reason* (1793). Here Kant rediscovered and reinterpreted his own faith as it was taught him in his youth by his pietistic mother and his pietistic teachers. At the instigation of Prof. F. A. Schultz, who ardently cherished pietistic views, Kant entered the Collegium Fredericianum, in which classic antiquity was joined to pietistic religiosity. " This training," Windelband says, " gave to his mind that purity and austerity, that sublime power of self-control, which imprinted upon it the antique features of simple and noble greatness." The pietism of the Collegium Fredericianum was, as Windelband goes on to state, " a gentle reminiscence of German mysticism and sought the essentials of religious life in the inwardness and moral activity of faith." [35]

The main problem with which Kant was concerned was the Christian dogma of original sin. This dogma was at odds with the ethical doctrine that Kant held. If the moral law is the law of man's practical reason, and if man is free and responsible for obeying or disobeying that law, how can original sin be admitted, which inescapably condemns man to disobey habitually? Can the principle of moral autonomy be combined with the Christian dogma? If the individual is the only author of his decisions, if he is even the only source of his character, how can we assume that he is at the same time subject to a sinfulness which is " original," i.e., inherited from the first man's fall? Nevertheless, Kant felt the weight and truth of that dogma. By turning to a philosophic examination of the meaning of sin, Kant, in fact, deserted the principle and basis of the age of the Enlightenment and initiated that movement which again recognized the irreplaceable value and profound meaning of traditional religion, in contrast to a rational faith. Kant was, however, too deeply imbued with the spirit of rationalism to be able to develop

[35] *Geschichte der neueren Philosophie*, Vol. II (Leipzig, 1898), p. 5.

fully this new insight. It was enough that he did envisage the necessity of examining the concept of sin from his own point of view.

Sin in its religious sense could not, of course, be adapted without an ethical transplantation. Original sin had to be understood as an irrecoverable moral evil or, as Kant styles it, as a " radical evil," i.e., a moral defect so ineradicably rooted in man's will or heart that even the "righteous" man cannot correct it. If such an evil exists, what of the freedom of the will? Is man perhaps free to disobey but not free to obey the law strictly? In the *Critique of Practical Reason,* Kant comprehended moral freedom as the ability to resist desire, if it is in disagreement with the demand of duty or of obligation. Is this ability perhaps restricted? Is man, although ideally free, perhaps in fact not able to comply always and entirely with the law? Man is free in so far as he is not simply driven by impulses or instincts, as the irrational brute is driven; he can control himself, discipline himself, determine himself in accordance with his moral vocation. If he does control himself in such a way, then he acts not by nature, but by his will; not as a phenomenal, but as a noumenal, being. Such freedom exalts man above the level of "blind" nature and makes him a person who arouses respect. Man thereby not only gains moral recognition but acquires a metaphysically higher rank. He acts as a self in contrast to all other things which always act and react as objects and which are determined by their natural essence and the general laws of nature. Man belongs to an " intelligible " world that is totally different from the world in space and time. But what about the morally bad person? What about wickedness and depravity? Is the person who does not resist the temptations of his own nature or of the surrounding world also free? Does he also belong to the noumenal or intelligible world?

Is man driven by his passions or by his self-interest as free as the one who acts out of respect of the moral command? Is the freedom to disobey really freedom after all? In his ethics Kant did not raise this question, although it seems to suggest itself. He concentrated so exclusively on his ethical analysis that he disregarded this deeper problem. Only when he came to see the significance of the religious aspect of morality did he realize the enormous force of these questions. Man can indeed forfeit his dignity, and he does forfeit it when he commits dishonest acts. But there is no man who would never be

tempted to act dishonestly and who would always reject such temptation. Although man as a moral being is exalted above the level of the
brute, he is also degraded by his own failure to comply with the high
call that reason imposes upon him. He enslaves himself when he
habitually disobeys that call. He voluntarily abandons the privilege
that is given him. He misuses that freedom which distinguishes him
from all other beings. How can we derive such misuse, such self-
degradation from the ethical principles which Kant developed in
the *Critique of Practical Reason?*

Within the *Critique,* moral evil seemed to be due to the " pathological " inclinations which are opposed to the categorical imperative.
Such failure seemed to be a relapse into the state of nature. Man
simply acts not as man, but as an animal, when he refuses to obey
the imperative. But if this were really true, then man would not be
responsible for his faults and moral defects, as the animal is not
responsible for the ferocity and violence of his actions. But we must
not allow man to dispense with his human rank and privilege. Man
is also the author of his decisions and actions when he degrades himself and forgets his high calling. He acts as a responsible being when
he acts irresponsibly. He remains metaphysically the noumenal
being he essentially is, although he permits himself to deny this
ethical dignity.

At the beginning of the *Critique of Practical Reason,* when Kant
introduces the concept of freedom, he defines it in the following
way. If " the mere legislative form of maxims is the sole sufficient
determining ground of a will," in other words: if the moral law
alone determines the will, then such a will " must be conceived as
wholly independent of the natural law of appearances in their mutual
relations, i.e., the law of causality. Such independence is called freedom in the strictest, i.e., transcendental sense." [36] Here Kant unmistakably defines freedom only in the sense of the good will, i.e.,
when man makes the moral law " the sole ground " of his decisions.
He does not at all reflect on the problem of the will which does not
determine itself in this way, although the whole context of Kant's
ethics does not leave any doubt that man in this case is also accountable and therefore is not subject only to the principle of natural
causality. Only in his book on religion did Kant fully realize the

[36] Beck, *op. cit.,* pp. 139 f.

gravity and difficulty of the question.

Here he became aware that he would violate his own ethical principles if he restricted freedom to the good will alone. He now came to see that it is not abstract reason but the concrete individual man that has to be regarded as free. Freedom, therefore, cannot be confined to man as a noumenal or transcendent being. It must be applied to the totality of the empirical person, whether good or bad, for man is never completely good, although he is also never completely bad. Kant now fully recognized the abysmal riddle of man as a moral being under the obligation of obeying the moral law, but unable ever to obey it wholly. This discovery forced him to extend his philosophic inquiry from the ethical to the religious realm.

The Christian religion, long regarded only as an illustration of his ethical views, now claimed rights of its own which the philosopher could not afford to refuse or to neglect. This new situation compelled him to revise the relation between speculation and revelation and to correct the concept of freedom which dominated the *Critique of Practical Reason*. When man disobeys the moral imperative is it his reason that disobeys? If so, how can reason ever disavow itself? If reason is the power that sets him free and puts him on a level above nature, then it must come into play whenever he acts as a moral agent whether in the positive or in the negative sense. Therefore neither natural nor noumenal causality can explain the enigma of the immoral will and of moral evil in general.

Kant, when he realized this situation, could no longer uphold the separation of the two worlds, the phenomenal and the noumenal, the empirical and the intellectual, the world in space and time and the world beyond these boundaries. He had reached the point where this fundamental disjunction, which was the cornerstone of his whole philosophy, had to be abandoned, or at least amended to the extent of understanding man as a totality, as a being in whom both the universal and the individual aspect are united, in whom both reason and his irrational nature are integrated, as a self that is not entirely a self, as a person that is only on the way to becoming a person. Kant had to admit that in the act of the evil will (and there is no act which is absolutely good) man is both free and not free. He faced a new kind of dialectic more difficult than any he had previously met.

This problem was particularly hard for Kant to solve because he had reconciled the contradictions of theoretical reason by introducing the concept of the duality of the two spheres; now he encountered a contradiction that could not be treated that way, but could only be solved by uniting the separated spheres. This was the new situation created by the recognition of the religious reality. The antinomies of cosmology are here surmounted. Kant confronted the same wonder of man which prompted Pascal to exclaim: " What a chimera is man! What a monster, what a chaos, what a prodigy! " Kant had to admit that in doing wrong man contradicts himself, his reason perverts itself, his freedom negates itself, his very selfhood willingly destroys itself. Kant was honest enough not to shun the impasse which opened before him. Courageously and boldly he tried to settle the problem. Transcendental idealism had to yield to this new realism. The spirit of the enlightened century, so proud of reason, so supercilious when dealing with the wondrous and the mysterious, now breaks down. It was a memorable moment in the history of philosophy when we look at it from the perspective of the relation between speculation and revelation.

Kant's contemporaries regarded his new book as a "relapse " into the obscurity and superstition of religion and could not pardon the great thinker for " betraying " philosophy and reason, for offending the dignity of man and his own ethical position. They believed that only senility could have persuaded the author of the Critique of Reason to yield to religious scruples and intricacies. Goethe, the indefatigable defender of humanism, the hard-boiled " pagan," was indignant about Kant's apparent recantation. We today must change this verdict. We no longer believe in the optimistic and moralistic views of the Enlightenment, and we also no longer share in the " paganism " of classical German culture. We have lost confidence in man's ability to overcome moral evil, and we have seen events so horrible that we cannot ignore man's fundamental sinfulness. Many minds and works have convinced us that the dogma of original sin defines indeed the " foul spot " in mankind, as Kant called it. Kant's book on religion is therefore more modern and actual today than it was when it appeared; at least Kant's recognition of sin can be better appreciated by us than it could by Kant's contemporaries. Whether we accept or reject Kant's interpretation of original sin as the " radical evil" in man, we must admire the energy of Kant in dealing with this new problem, for he was nearly seventy years old when he embarked upon the stormy sea of religious thought.

Moral evil, Kant teaches, is not merely accidental; it is inherent in man's finite will and due to a chronic defect in his moral disposition. Since man is both a beast and the likeness of God he cannot help perverting the moral maxims in his heart. His divine element does not casually succumb to the animal; " the source of evil cannot lie in an object determining the will through inclination, nor yet in a natural impulse; it can lie only in a rule made by the will for the use of its freedom, that is in a maxim." [37] A maxim is not an incentive or motive, rather, it is a principle of reason that concerns the whole personality of the moral agent. But it is a " perverted maxim." [38] Freedom corrupts itself when it assents to this maxim which permits occasional deviation from the moral law.[39] " Man is evil in that he reverses the moral order of the incentives when he adopts them into his maxim." [40] Under certain circumstances he is ready to subordinate the moral to the selfish incentive and thereby to deprave himself radically.

" When incentives other than the law itself (such as ambition, self-love in general, even a kindly instinct such as sympathy [41]) are necessary to determine the will to conduct conformably to the law, it is merely accidental that these causes coincide with the law, for they could equally well incite its violation." " The peace of conscience of so many men (conscientious in their own esteem) who . . . merely elude evil consequences by good fortune " is based on a " dishonesty which extends outwardly also to falsehood and deception of others." [42] This is " the foul taint in our race." [43] Kant thus agrees now with the verdict of the gospel, " Men are all under sin — there is no one righteous, no not one."

This radical corruption of man's heart is incomprehensible be-

---

[37] *Religion Within the Limits of Reason Alone,* tr. by Theodore M. Greene and Hoyt H. Hudson (The Open Court Publishing Company, 1934), p. 17.

[38] *Ibid.,* p. 51.

[39] Cf. *ibid.,* p. 27.

[40] *Ibid.,* p. 31.

[41] Hume's principle of ethical conduct.

[42] Greene and Hudson, *op. cit.,* p. 26.

[43] *Ibid.,* p. 34.

cause it extends to reason and to freedom. It contaminates freedom itself. It cannot be an inheritance from our first parents, because then man would not be accountable. Adam is the symbol of man as such. " If we wish to address ourselves to the explanation of evil in terms of beginning in time, we must search for the causes of each deliberate transgression in a previous period." [44] But this can never explain the perversion of the maxim. The inscrutability of radical evil is depicted by the representation of Satan as a fallen angel. But men, although they are radically depraved, are not satanic; they do not do evil for evil's sake. Therefore " there remains hope of a return to the good from which men have strayed." But " how it is possible for a naturally evil man to make himself a good man wholly surpasses our comprehension," [45] even if we concede that " the respect for the moral law we have never been able to lose." [46] Kant considers in genuinely pietistic terms such a return to goodness as a gradual self-improvement. He stresses the Protestant conviction that all endeavor aiming at such a goal is not meritorious, although " there is one thing in our soul which we cannot cease from regarding with the highest wonder . . . and that is the original moral predisposition which announces a divine origin." [47] In this he fully agrees with Augustine against all sorts of Pelagianism. We cannot perform what grace alone can, " hence we can admit a work of grace as something incomprehensible, but we cannot adopt it into our maxims either for theoretical or for practical use." [48]

The first (and most important) part of his book on religion ends with this religious " observation." The following books deal with the idea of Christ and of the church. Kant tries to understand them from his moral perspective; we cannot be surprised, therefore, that he runs into trouble and that his reflections here are less satisfying than any other part of his philosophy. Kant seems to fall back into the age of the Enlightenment. Ethics seems to triumph over religion once more. It is excruciatingly painful to pursue Kant's tortuous and self-defeating attempt to do justice to the Christian faith and at the same time preserve his fundamentally rationalistic tenets. He insists that the idea of Christ is not " man-made "; it is thus

[44] *Ibid.*, p. 38.   [47] *Ibid.*, p. 45.
[45] *Ibid.*, pp. 39 f.   [48] *Ibid.*, p. 49. Compare p. 70.
[46] *Ibid.*, p. 42.

" more appropriate to say that this archetype has come down to us from heaven and has assumed our humanity. . . . Such union with us may therefore be regarded as a state of humiliation of the Son of God."[49] Nowhere else did Kant approach so obvious a reconciliation between his ethical speculation and religious revelation. But, he continues, the idea of incarnation surpasses our comprehension, and we must understand it as a kind of " schematism " by which the rationally unfathomable is imaged. Such picture-thinking is necessary, but has a merely practical (moral) value and function.[50]

Although the idea of Christ surmounts our understanding, Kant insists that "we need . . . no empirical example to make the idea of a person, morally pleasing to God, our pattern; this idea is as a pattern already present in our reason." Moreover, no example is possible, for what we see, does not suffice. Miracles are not only not a normal requisite, but rather " he who demands this, thereby confesses to his own moral disbelief." " If it were a fact that such a truly godly minded man at some particular time had descended, as it were, from heaven . . . , even then we should have no cause for supposing him other than a man naturally begotten."[51] Kant concedes, however, that the portrait of such a divine being " in actual possession of this eminence and this bliss from all eternity . . . must attune our hearts to admiration, love, and gratitude."[52] The cross achieved the task of defeating the evil principle and establishing " a moral dominion . . . as an asylum where men can find protection for their morality, if they wish to forsake the former sovereignty of Satan "; but " the evil principle is still designated the prince of this world where those who adhere to the good principle should always be prepared for physical sufferings, sacrifices, and mortifications of self-love." " There exists absolutely no salvation for man apart from the sincerest adoption of genuinely moral principles into his disposition."[53] Here Kant seems to denounce the reasons he gave for the postulate of the existence of the Highest Good.

The church is defined as an ethical commonwealth, i.e., a people under ethical laws whose supreme lawgiver and head is God. It is not a historical theocracy based on a government of priests, but an institution where laws are purely inward.[54] This reminds us of the

---

[49] *Ibid.*, p. 55.
[50] Cf. *Ibid.*, p. 59.
[51] *Ibid.*, pp. 56 f.
[52] *Ibid.*, p. 59.
[53] *Ibid.*, p. 78.
[54] Cf. *ibid.*, p. 91.

language of Jeremiah. The true church is thus sharply distinguished from the historical churches, its " pure " faith as a solely ethical faith is separated from all historical events. All that God requires from man is " steadfast diligence in morally good life conduct." " Statutory " laws can never reach the height of purely moral laws. They can " merely comprise the means to its furtherance and spread." [55] The moral end remains the only content of religious revelation, of worship and devotion. The churches are meeting places for the instruction and quickening of moral dispositions. A moral religion takes the place of revelation. " The pure religion of reason is a continually occurring divine . . . revelation. . . . It is carried into effect . . . through gradually advancing reform." [56] " When the religion of reason has advanced so far that it takes over all ecclesiastical faith, then we can say: ' the kingdom of God is come unto us.' "

Ethical reason thus retains ascendancy over all historical revelation. In spite of Kant's sincere and frantic effort to acknowledge the need for a religious faith surpassing that of moral reason, in the end the spirit of the Enlightenment remains victorious in the final creed of its greatest representative. The " universal moral church " is, like the Ideas of speculative reason, a regulative principle of practical reason.[57] Kant even writes a eulogy of his own age at the conclusion of his book. " If now one asks what period in the entire known history of the church up to now is the best, I have no scruple in answering, the present. And this because the seed of the true religious faith, as it is now being publicly sown in Christendom. . . is allowed more and more to grow unhindered." [58]

Words like these ring tragically today when we think of the fruit which the " pure religion of reason " has brought in the nineteenth and twentieth centuries, especially in the country of Kant himself. What would he think of the " rational faith " of the Communists who have now taken possession of his native town of Königsberg?

[55] *Ibid.*, pp. 94 f.   [57] *Ibid.*, p. 114.
[56] *Ibid.*, p. 113.   [58] *Ibid.*, p. 122.

X

THE ABSOLUTE EGO

KANT's philosophy was bound to provoke a reaction when the literary revolt of *Sturm und Drang* (Storm and Stress) began penetrating into the core of philosophic thought as it did in the person of Johann Gottlieb Fichte (1762–1814). But Fichte was a disciple of Kant and for a time he was convinced that he was only continuing the movement initiated by his teacher. There were some obscure points in the scheme of the transcendental idealism. The problem of the thing-in-itself was raised but not solved by Kant. It is evident that the meaning of that term is not the same throughout the works of Kant; it is subject to change even in various parts of the *Critique of Pure Reason*. It was also dubious whether Kant had intended the *Critique* to be the final and conclusive result of his thinking, or merely to serve as an introduction to a system that he would expound on the basis of the *Critique*. Kant himself was inconsistent in that respect. He never gave a systematic account of all his views, although he promised it in some places. Furthermore, the whole impression made by his critical works was incomplete. They seemed to form one whole, but what kind of whole was not quite clear. In particular, the guiding idea of the positive and constructive aspect of the transcendental idealism, the primacy of pure practical reason, was not made the principle of one system.

Some predecessors of Fichte had pointed to these inconsistencies. But it was Fichte himself who resolutely and boldly determined to mend Kant's critical philosophy by means of one encompassing plan. After appointment as professor at the University of Jena, he began to lecture on his own system which was the realization of that plan. He called it *Wissenschaftslehre,* a " doctrine of science," because he,

239

like Kant, intended to speak about the theoretical conditions of scientific knowledge, and also because he wanted to emphasize that this new undertaking was to serve the sciences and was itself scientific. However, the salient point was not epistemological, but ethical. The system was to be united by the primacy of ethical thinking, in fact, it was a system only by uniting epistemology and ethics under the supremacy of ethics. Although Fichte apparently retained the fundamental principles of Kant, he changed them considerably. The very notion of uniting epistemology and ethics under one head was novel. Although a certain parallelism of problems and solutions exists in the *Critique of Pure Reason* and in the *Critique of Practical Reason,* the unification of the two philosophic sciences would hardly have met with the approval of the old master.

By unifying the theoretical and the practical perspectives under one guiding principle, Fichte necessarily had to abandon the analytical and discerning method of Kant: the critical method. In its place a more constructive, synthetic, and speculative way of thinking began to dominate philosophy. Instead of the abstract concepts and theories of Kant, a much more concrete and intuitive method of thinking prevailed.[1] In Kant, ethics took the place of metaphysics in the traditional sense, or more correctly, rational faith as the postulate of pure practical reason was substituted for metaphysics; in Fichte this transformation was carried to the extreme. He transformed rational faith into a speculative metaphysics, or in other words, he replaced rational faith by an ethical speculative system. From the outset such an enterprise was not only uncritical; it was also awkward. How can ethics, which concerns man's moral will and moral goal, dare to solve the age-old problems of World, Soul, and God? A certain discrepancy between the aspirations and the tools for satisfying them was inherent in such an adventure. Ethics cannot transcend the finite ego; speculation aims at transcending it. How did Fichte overcome this chasm between end and means?

He recognized the unfortunate nature of rational faith which was neither truly rational nor truly faith. He also wished to eliminate the ambiguities involved in the concept of a thing-in-itself which

[1] Cf. Richard Kroner's essay "The Year 1800 in the Development of German Idealism," originally delivered as the Powell Lectures at Indiana University, Bloomington, Indiana. Later published in *The Review of Metaphysics,* Vol. I, No. 4, June, 1948, pp. 1–31.

was supposed to be incomprehensible, but nevertheless comprehended in various ways by Kant. Friedrich Heinrich Jacobi, a friend of young Goethe, had already protested against that concept, saying that it is impossible to enter the *Critique of Pure Reason* without it, but that it is also impossible to stay in the *Critique* with it. A third reason for Fichte's system was the incomplete nature of Kant's philosophy. With one stroke Fichte intended to improve these deficiencies. Fichte had been most impressed by the *Critique of Practical Reason,* which he read with enthusiasm as a student. Up to that time he had been something of a Leibnizian. Kant taught him that it was not theoretical, but only practical, reason which could penetrate the core of ultimate truth; that practical reason is the " root " of reason in general. Fichte wished to prove this thesis by uniting the theory of knowledge with the theory of moral volition. Kant, he said, had done only three quarters of the task; he himself had the ambition to do the whole.

THE ABSOLUTE EGO

His system started from the concept or the idea of the Ego, of that ego which underlies both knowing and willing, thinking and acting. The supreme principle, from which everything else can be derived methodically, is that ego which is not yet divided into the two directions marked by the duality of epistemology and ethics. It is the ego as such which thinks as well as acts, which acts by thinking and thinks by acting. Fichte called that ego " absolute," a fateful term as it developed later on. The absolute ego is neither one-sidedly theoretical nor one-sidedly practical; it cannot be conceived in a merely logical fashion. Instead, it has to be activated, since it is itself an acting ego. One can grasp it by activity alone. Only in such a way can its own spontaneity and productivity be maintained. Indeed, when we grasp it, it activates itself. We can understand it only as pure activity, and therefore we must be active ourselves in order to catch its nature. Thinking and the " object " of thinking are here the same. The absolute ego is not an object at all, it is pure subject, as Kant's transcendental ego was, and as the pure moral will was supposed to be. Fichte's absolute ego is the root of both; it unites them before they separate.

This first act by which the absolute ego brings itself into existence is therefore itself absolute. It does not depend upon any earlier or higher presupposition; it is itself the highest principle of thought as well as of action; it is its own cause and basis. Fichte was encouraged to this bold step by Kant's own ethical speculation. According to this speculation the moral will as such is absolutely free, without any precondition; it is its own supreme cause, *causa noumenon*. Fichte transfers this postulate from the strictly and specifically ethical realm to a system that unites ethics and speculation. Whereas Kant had carefully circumscribed the speculative postulates of pure practical reason as being valid only for practical purposes, Fichte, for whom the system itself was both speculative and practical, removed this restriction and made the postulates the supreme ground of his system. Whereas Kant had spoken about the Ideal of Pure Reason as an Ideal, which man can never think out because it is merely formal and without the material stuff which makes objective knowledge possible, Fichte consistently denies this restriction. The Ideal is not an object of empirical knowledge and should not be treated as such. We should not demand any material element, except the actions of the thinking mind itself. Thus considered, the Ideal does not remain an ideal but can be carried out by speculative thinking. The absolute ego itself carries out the task implied in it by realizing itself in a speculative way.

The absolute ego solves the task of theoretical reason and at the same time fulfills the postulate of practical reason. From the ethical point of view we must think of ourselves as being absolutely free and autonomous; we can think of ourselves in that fashion only if we think as we ought to think. Fichte interpreted the categorical imperative not only as an imperative for moral action in the ethical realm but as an imperative for speculative thinking itself. If we want to conceive of the supreme principle, we have to act according to the supreme imperative that concerns both thinking and acting; we have to think of the ego as absolute. The first principle is ethically commanded. It is philosophically imperative to conceive of the act by which the ego creates itself as absolutely free. The philosophy that we adopt is the philosophy that we as moral beings ought to adopt. The famous dictum of Fichte, that everyone adopts the philosophy which conforms to the kind of man he is, should not be subjected to the interpretation of relativists who would agree with it; on the contrary, its meaning in Fichte's mind is rather that there is only one true philosophy and that this is the one that we ought to think out. Fichte's whole system is ethically commanded as it is ethically postulated. The difference between command and postulate disappears when we deal with the supreme principle on which the whole content and spirit of our philosophy depends.

Fichte scholars disagree in their interpretation of the absolute ego as the fundamental thesis of the *Wissenschaftslehre* on which Fichte lectured in 1794.[2] In my work *Von Kant bis Hegel* (1921-1924), I tried to show that the absolute ego is, and yet is not, the divine self. This ambiguity is not casual; it is not an accidental, logical defect or a slip on the part of Fichte. It is not due to vagueness in his thinking. It was, instead, necessary in view of his whole plan. On the one hand, Fichte did not intend to discard Kant's analytical and critical method; yet his very problem forced him to discard it. It is this basic character of Fichte's entire system which brought about other fundamental contradictions. Fichte's system implies the presumption of being absolutely true and final, while at the same time it abhors such a presumption. Therefore, as we will see, the action by which the absolute ego creates and thinks itself is counteracted by another action which opposes this thesis and asserts that an absolute nonego is set against the absolute ego. Fichte thus deliberately and intentionally made a contradiction the point of issue.

In some respect it is the divine ego which underlies and holds the system together. Without the divine ego neither empirical knowledge nor the empirical world are possible; and similarly without the divine ego neither moral volition nor the realization of the supreme moral goal is meaningful. Fichte had, therefore, to postulate and to activate the divine being as the absolute thesis. But out of the absolute being alone no system could be constructed; neither empirical knowledge nor moral life could be understood in terms of the system. Hence Fichte had to counter the first thesis by an antithesis that sets the movement of thinking in motion. Speculative thought is bottomless, if God does not direct it, but God cannot direct it, if something besides him does not cause a contradiction and thereby occasion the rise of that finite sphere in which science and

---

[2] See Richard Kroner's article on Fichte in the *Encyclopædia Britannica*, Vol. IX, 1958, pp. 214–217.

morality move. It is the perennial contrast between the Infinite and the Finite which here unfolds as the basis of Fichte's ethical speculation. This initial contradiction is, as it were, the salt that savors the thinking mind. Fichte uses the antinomies in a systematic way; he makes them universal and uses them as the foundation of his *Wissenschaftslehre*. To deny this methodical principle is to misunderstand the whole intention and procedure of Fichte's speculation. Therefore, one cannot either assert or reject the identity of the divine and the absolute ego. The ambiguity is not an ambiguity according to Fichte's thought; it is rather the exact expression of his method; it is the very soul of the system.

The character of man's mind and of all its manifestations is to be both finite and infinite, human and divine. Man must live within this tension. And his philosophy must methodically develop from this tension all other categories and concepts, first of all the duality of knowing and acting. What makes the system of Fichte modern and post-Kantian is the definition of the divine being as pure activity, in contrast to Aristotle's definition as substance or form. God is Subject, an Ego, a Self, he is not substance or form. It is true that Aristotle had said that the divine form is pure energy, but energy in his vocabulary did not mean ego or subject, but form, as power. And the same is true with respect to all his followers, including Christian Aristotelians.

According to Fichte the thing-in-itself is no " thing " at all, but the ego which alone is " in-itself," because it alone is a self. In this respect there cannot be greater variance than that between Fichte and Spinoza. Spinoza denied the very existence of an ego, whereas Fichte made it the absolute. The self alone is in and for itself what it is, while all substances are what they are only in and for the self. Man resembles God in that he is a self or an ego; inasmuch as he is an ego he too is absolute.[3] There is, however, a momentous difference between the divine and the human ego. Man never acts without being hampered and hemmed in by the opposite of the ego, the non-ego, as Fichte generally calls this opposite. Man is composed of the

---

[3] In our time Berdyaev has asserted that freedom precedes being and therefore characterizes both God and man. Cf. his *The Beginning and the End* (Harper & Brothers, Torchbook, 1951), pp. 104 ff. This thesis has a certain similarity to Fichte's concept of the absolute ego.

ego and the nonego; therefore, he is a finite ego called upon to become or to make itself absolute.

The human mind is prevented from attaining an uncontradicted knowledge of the absolute ego, because this ego is opposed by the nonego. The first principle would not be a principle without the system. But the very duality of principle and system contradicts the nature of the absolute, which is the absolute precisely because it is absolutely independent and does not need the system to be conceived. We have already met this supreme contradiction which makes Fichte's system thoroughly dialectical. Although the absolute ego is sovereign and independent, still as the supreme principle of a system it depends upon the system just as the system depends upon it. One might therefore say: inasmuch as the absolute ego is the supreme principle, it is also nonabsolute or restricted; it is the function of the nonego to restrict the first principle by contradicting it. The first principle, however, holds the primacy. The absolute ego is contradicted only, in so far as it contradicts itself by positing its own counterpart, the nonego. The sovereignty of the absolute ego extends also to the second principle in that it is the absolute ego itself which postulates its own contrary. Just as morality could not exist without the tension between impulse or desire and pure practical reason, since in that case the law would no longer be a law and the " ought " no longer an " ought," so also in the universal foundation of all things, a supreme tension must be assumed in order to make possible moral life and empirical experience. The absolute ego itself demands such supreme tension which in its logical version appears as a supreme contradiction: that of ego and nonego. It is a dialectical contradiction because the ego is absolute and thus does not tolerate anything that restricts its activity. And yet activity has to overcome such a restriction in order to be activity. There must be a supreme barrier that can be surmounted. Only thus does the activity of the ego unfold and make itself absolute.

Religiously speaking, it is the mystery of Creation which Fichte attacks in his adventurous and audacious speculation. If God is absolute and sovereign, if he is perfect and all in all, why does he create? This was the question of Jacob Boehme too. If one answers that it is because he wants to glorify himself, we might then ask why God needs to be glorified if he is self-sufficient and self-exist-

246 Speculation and Revelation in Modern Philosophy

ent? If the answer is that he creates because he wants to be loved and to love, we might say: if he needs love, then he is not without want and in that sense not perfect. Whatever we may answer, the question would remain essentially unanswerable because the human understanding is unable to conceive of the Infinite without the contrast of the Finite. It was this religious mystery which Fichte tried to penetrate by his two supreme principles or theses.

We may cut the knot by saying: Fichte could only comprehend how we think of God, but not how God thinks of himself. Since, however, he pretended to think of the absolute ego as separated from all finiteness or all restriction, he was compelled to start from a contradiction. This indeed is a possible exposition of the dialectical antagonism that underlies the system. But it does not precisely convey Fichte's meaning. He certainly did not reflect upon this intrinsic restriction of the absolute ego. He did not say that the self-actualization of the absolute ego is only our human thought. On the contrary, he wanted to think out the absolute as such; this is the reason why he united thought and action in the supreme thesis. It is true that though Fichte aimed at the understanding of man's morality, he wanted to derive its possibility from its highest presupposition which, as Kant had shown, is God. Here the turn toward Hegel set in.

The system of Fichte stands exactly between the "finite," "human," and "critical" philosophy of Kant and the "infinite," "absolute," and "speculative" systems of Schelling and Hegel. It is this intermediary position of Fichte which makes it so difficult to interpret the *Wissenschaftslehre*. One can say that Fichte occupies a position on the way from Kant to Schelling and Hegel. Therefore one cannot stand where he stands because he himself does not stand but moves. He has no point to stand in, but only a point of departure. His system is the living image of action and life. It resembles man's own fluid position, his own striving toward a goal that cannot be reached. The absolute principle veils a task that can never be discharged. The moral tension, the tension between ignorance and knowledge, between error and truth is found in the Fichtean system; it is its soul and its grandeur. But it is also the reason why we cannot adopt it, why Fichte never founded a school, why German idealism went beyond it almost the moment it was born, why even Fichte himself was never content with any of the concrete versions he gave of the *Wissenschaftslehre,* and why he was always driven to compose ever new ones.

When we compare Fichte's system with Neoplatonism, we can say that it was a new attempt to derive from the One (called by him the Ego) the whole content of the world and bring the world back to the divine origin. But this Neoplatonic interpretation was not, at any case in the beginning, in the foreground of Fichte's mind. He first attempted to understand man as that being in whom the absolute ego of God meets the negation of the nonego and tries to master it. Thereby the absolute ego becomes itself finite, restricted, imperfect, but also titanic, striving toward the infinite, breaking all barriers, and defying all obstacles. There is a definite similarity between Fichte's system and Goethe's *Faust.*

The chasm between the finite and the infinite can be gradually filled by scientific investigation and theory as well as by moral striving and action, but it is a task never finished. The absolute ego also can never be absolutely comprehended, the contradiction never absolutely dissolved. Speculation has to be content with an imperfect, always incomplete, always humanly finite solution, which, however, is absolute within the confines of finitude. There is indeed a certain infinity in our comprehension; but this infinity is itself finite, i.e., it is an unbounded acting, producing, working, longing, and planning. Our infinity implies an infinite approach to the Absolute from which it proceeds. In that respect Fichte was still a Kantian. The Absolute for all its speculative activity remains in the end an "Ideal of Reason," a regulative principle, a thesis that is never fully united with its antithesis. There remains to the end a contradiction and a tension.

This finite infinity or infinite finitude characterizes Fichte's system from the beginning. This method or mode was later denounced by Schelling and Hegel as a "finite" idealism, a "reflective" subjectivism, a "relative" speculation. It cannot be denied that Fichte himself, although he never arrived at the "absolute idealism" of his successors, nevertheless, approached them in his own development; he widened the horizon of the *Wissenschaftslehre* in the direction of a speculation that tended to divorce itself from ethical restrictions and to become ontological and outright theological. But the fact

that he kept the name *Wissenschaftslehre* for his philosophy demonstrates clearly enough that he did not intend to change its fundamental nature.

The *Wissenschaftslehre* of 1801, 1804, and 1812 were published
only after his death. Hence they had no immediate historical effect.
The version of 1794 should be regarded as the classical one that released a wave of speculative systems among which those of Schelling
and Hegel are the most original and the most outstanding. For the
first time it applied that speculative dialectical method which
reached its climax in the system of Hegel. As I pointed out, the
dialectic of Fichte was set in motion by two supreme theses, one
that posits the absolute ego and the second that negates this position
or pro-position. The second thesis or antithesis is, as Fichte expresses
it, absolute only with respect to its form (negation), but dependent
upon the first thesis with respect to its content (the ego). Since even
negation is an act of the ego, however, one can say that the ego
negates itself by the negative proposition which establishes the nonego. After the initial affirmation and negation are posited, their
unification is demanded.

The first solution of this problem is a mutual restriction of the
ego by the nonego, and of the nonego by the ego. Since it is the ego
that acts in both the affirmation and the negation, the solution must
propose a synthesis in which the ego prevails. It is the same " I "
which asserts itself in the thesis and which reasserts itself in the
synthesis. The synthesis is already prefigured in the absolute posi-
tiveness of the ego. I unite myself with the opposite by affirming
that, although divided against myself, I am still the unity of both
the thesis and the antithesis, inasmuch as I am the absolute ego that
affirms as well as negates itself. Although negation is opposed to
affirmation, there is a unity that links both together so that the nonego can become a constituent in the synthesis. I partly affirm and
partly deny myself, so that the absolute ego now turns into the
finite ego which is the subject of empirical experience and of moral
decision and action. Of course, this synthesis is only the first step
toward the unification of ego and nonego, since I, as the finite ego,
remain divided against myself; only the theoretical conquest of the
nonego and the activity of moral discipline can gradually diminish
this division.

Out of the first synthesis springs the duality of two attitudes toward the divided ego and nonego. Either I recognize myself as restricted by the nonego, which is the basic relation between the knowing subject and the objects to be known; or I recognize myself as restricting the nonego within myself, which is the basic relation of the moral will and the desires, impulses, inclinations, interests, in so far as they resist the moral imperative. In the first case, a plurality of new steps is necessary in order to dissolve the remaining theoretical tension between ego and nonego; a plurality of intellectual acts ensues by which the knowing subject increasingly masters the barrier of the nonego. Fichte believes that in such a way a deduction of the categories is possible which condition the objective world and make it knowable: even the origin of the impressions or the material within the objects is demonstrated as necessary. In the second case, the moral will and the moral law are deduced as the consequence of the original tension in the synthesis: the ego makes the nonego the occasion for moral action and thereby diminishes step by step the inner impediment that hinders the realization of full unity and the removal of the tension.

I can only hint at the very subtle and difficult dialectic which leads through the tissue of Fichte's thought.[4] With a kind of visionary imagination he finds his way through the complicated arguments and counterarguments that generate the concepts dominating the relations between the objects of experience and those between the will and its purposes. The theoretical part of the *Wissenschaftslehre* concludes with the proof that only the productive imagination can finally give the key to the synthesis of thinking and impressions. The practical series of dialectical propositions shows that theoretical activity is ultimately to be understood as subordinated to the goal of striving and longing for the absolute self-unification of the divided ego. The whole system offers a grandiose but somehow forcible attempt to demonstrate that the primacy of practical reason permits us to understand the necessity of causality and substance, of space and time, of perception and imagination as the means for the knowledge of the objects, and similarly the necessity of feelings and desires, of urges and drives, of longing and intending as the con-

[4] For details, turn to Richard Kroner, *Von Kant bis Hegel* (J. C. B. Mohr, Tübingen, 1921 and 1924), Vol. I, pp. 397 ff.

ditions for the possibility of the absolute incentive which aims at the perfect satisfaction of the finite but also infinite practical ego.

" The world," Fichte says in one of his most telling phrases, " is nothing but the material of my duty." In this sentence the primacy of morality as the origin and the end of all that exists is expressed. Action as such is therefore the highest virtue according to Fichte; laziness, the most severe moral defect. Fichte pursued his ethical ideas in the *System der Sittenlehre* (1798) and in the *Naturrecht* (1796). Both realms, that of morality in the precise sense and that of original and inalienable rights, are intrinsically connected although they belong to different spheres. The Kantian separation of morality and legality was taken over by Fichte; he contended that the state should be so arranged as to exist even if no citizen acts out of moral motives, even if all citizens are devils! Although the final end of the state is moral, nevertheless, the state as such cannot enforce morality, but merely the conformity of acts to the laws which are valid.

In his ethical writings Fichte tried to penetrate more deeply into the concrete life and into the complexities of modern culture than Kant had done. As he climbed higher in the realm of abstract thought, so he also descended lower in that of application. He wanted to comprehend the intricacies of man's various vocations and professions. He had been an enthusiastic observer and friend of the ideas of the French Revolution and although he was an ethical idealist, he never ceased to acclaim some of the social purposes of that revolution.

In all these aspects he was a typical representative of the period of Storm and Stress. Of course, his main interest lay in the field of that profession which he himself practiced with such an enormous vigor and eloquence, the profession of the learned teacher. His booklet on the vocation of the scholar (*Bestimmung des Gelehrten*) is one of the most beautiful and most impressive of his writings. But he also expressed profound views about the essence of marriage, about the special duties and rights of the industrialist and of the labor class, and about other special vocations. Man confronts the task of unifying the divided spheres of his personality not only as an abstract individual but also as a member of the family, of society, and of the state. Fichte thus approached the romantic predilection for the historically real, in spite of his revolutionary and socialistic tendencies. More than Kant, Fichte emphasized the particular vocation that every person has to follow, although he did not go so far as Friedrich Schlegel or Schleiermacher later went in this direction. He exalted the national community in contrast to an abstract cosmopolitanism, especially after Prussia had been defeated by Napoleon.

Pestalozzi, the great Swiss educator, one of the leading literary figures of Storm and Stress, kindled a flame of enthusiasm in Fichte's soul. When Fichte addressed himself to the German nation in his famous *Speeches* (1808), he recommended the methods of Pestalozzi for the moral awakening of his country. In arousing the feelings of shame and repentance he became one of the most eloquent orators the German nation has ever heard. He preached spiritual resistance in the very face of the victorious enemy and thereby aroused the people, so that the later war of liberation was possible.

SPECULATIVE RELIGION

At bottom Fichte had a religious, even a prophetic, mind. He came into his own when the occasion prompted him to apply his rhetorical gifts and his speculative power not only for the national but also for the religious education of his nation. His religion itself grew more and more speculative. Although he had been a student of theology, he was dissatisfied with the then dominant theology which was affected by the Enlightenment. He desired a more imaginative and philosophic approach toward the divine. His very first publication, *Critique of All Revelation* (1791), was critical of the traditional Christian sources. It was a bold undertaking when Kant set out to criticize pure reason, but it was infinitely bolder when Fichte dared to criticize revelation. Kant at least could assume that pure reason is able to criticize itself, but how was it possible to criticize " all revelation " by means of reason? And what else could be the instrument with which Fichte was to criticize revelation? Fichte made it a rule that it was only what moral reason found within itself that was worthy of recognition as revelation. He thereby anticipated Kant's writing on religion. Since the academic world expected the work of Kant to be published, and since Fichte's book appeared without the name of the author, it was believed to be Kant's philosophy of religion.

Fichte later wrote the article about God as *ordo ordinans* which I previously mentioned. The article was supposed to be understood by everyone — it was the first popular version of Fichte's philosophy — and here Fichte seemed to ignore his speculation about the absolute ego. The moral world order which realizes itself seemed to be an impersonal principle. In fact, Fichte now began to reform his speculative scheme. Windelband calls his views in that period an "ethical pantheism."[5] This word somehow sounds preposterous, since the ethical order, whatever its origin and its reign, cannot be ethical at all if it is entirely impersonal, quasi-cosmic, an order that makes itself real. Kant was certainly more consistent when he concluded that ethics must postulate a moral author of nature, although this conception was not free of difficulties. Kant's postulate and Fichte's idea of a self-efficient moral order both disclose and conceal the abysmal incomprehensibility of an ultimate entity that is simultaneously cosmic and moral uniting the contrasting poles of necessity and freedom, nature and will. The Idea of God, if it can be postulated at all, must transcend this duality as did Fichte's absolute ego.

But Fichte moved away from this concept, perhaps because he realized that it too was beset with insurmountable difficulties, in so far as it did not truly transcend the duality of nature and ego. The dismal experience that ensued from the publication of the popular article and brought about the accusation of atheism had a tremendous effect upon Fichte's inner life and his entire speculation, as well as upon his external circumstances. Fichte was forced to leave the University of Jena, where he had enjoyed an enormous success. His inner life was driven toward religion even more intensely than before. The need arose to conceive of God in terms more objective than in his first *Wissenschaftslehre*. The farther he went in the new direction, the more the concept of Being came to the fore, as a more adequate way of comprehending the mystery of God. He was perhaps influenced by the German mystics, although he was surely subject also to the influence of Schelling, who had turned to nature as one aspect of the Absolute itself. In the little book *The Vocation*

---

[5] *Geschichte der neueren Philosophie*, Vol. II, p. 299.

of Man (*Die Bestimmung des Menschen,* 1800), Fichte followed Schelling to a certain degree and philosophized about the Absolute as a power that governs nature as well as our moral life.

In any case, the later versions of the *Wissenschaftslehre* avoided any one-sided subjectivistic speculation about the Absolute and made *Sein* (Being) the unity of both nature and freedom. Fichte remained, however, true to his earlier version, in so far as he insisted that speculation cannot grasp Being itself, but only its image. He began to teach that only mystical union can reach what is unattainable by rational comprehension. Philosophy can only direct our mind toward the supreme One, but it can never adequately understand it. In public lectures he now presumed to show how man can arrive at that beatific vision which is the highest goal of all speculation. His philosophy became an *Instruction on How to Gain a Blessed Life,* as the title of these lectures runs (1806).

Fichte did not have by nature a poetical mind or a deep appreciation for art in general, as did Schelling. Nevertheless, there was a kind of poetical vein which manifested itself in his popular speeches and lectures. Already in the *Bestimmung des Menschen* he had struck this chord. According to this book, faith attains to the certainty that there is " One Eternal Infinite Will." In language that reminds one of The Book of Job he exclaims: " I hide my face before Thee and lay my hand upon my mouth. How thou art and seemest to thine own being, I can never know, any more than I can assume thy nature." [6] Then he seems to be transported by ecstasy when he adds: " Now that my heart is closed against all desire for earthly things . . . the universe appears before my eyes clothed in a more glorious form. The dead heavy mass . . . has vanished, and in its place there flows onward, with the rushing music of mighty waves an eternal stream of life and power and action, which issues from the original Source of all life — from Thy life, O Infinite One; for all life is thy life, and only the religious eye penetrates to the realm of True Beauty." [7] Here one might think that Schelling, not Fichte, speaks although there are nuances of meaning which are distinctly not Schelling's.

[6] *The Vocation of Man,* tr. by William Smith, 3d ed. (The Open Court Publishing Company, 1916), p. 151.
[7] *Ibid.,* p. 172.

These and similar sentences betray that Fichte had undergone a remarkable metamorphosis. The religious temper formerly suppressed now prevailed, so that his voice burst into a psalmlike praise of God, although one does not know in speculative terms what God. Did Fichte return to the faith of his childhood? Did revelation triumph over speculation? Or was this only a romantic mood, brought on by the example of his romantic friends? It is conspicuous that he involuntarily uses the word " revelation " when he tries to describe the source of his religious rapture and joy.

In any case this new mood was to transform his system profoundly. The word " life " emerged from his thought as a cardinal concept and was accompanied by the words " light " and " love," so that one could speak of a Johannine period in his philosophy. No doubt a saintlike prophet was hidden behind the brazen cuirass of the rigorous moralist and the subtle dialectician. This is probably one of the reasons why Fichte did not publish the new versions of his *Wissenschaftslehre,* publishing instead the more or less religious lectures that he delivered orally. One of these has the title *Characteristics of the Present Age* (1806); here he severely censured and derogated the age of the Enlightenment, scourging its spirit as that of " consummate sinfulness." He delineated in these lectures the historical development of mankind in a speculatively religious manner.

In the beginning, reason was unconsciously at work in primitive man as a sort of instinct, so that individuals and the community lived in perfect peace as in a paradise. Then a break occurred, so that individual separated from individual and anarchy was near; therefore reason assumed the character of an external authority: this was the age of " initial sinfulness." Later, man revolted against the authority and the law, the individual followed his own caprice, and sinfulness reached its climax. In the final future stage man will acknowledge the law as that of his own reason. Authority will pass over into autonomy. Fichte calls this last stage that of Reason as an Art. The individual will then of his own accord subject himself to the universal will of the community. In a strange combination Kantian, romantic, Biblical, and historical ideas mingle with those of Rousseau and Schiller. It was the first philosophy of history in that concrete sense in which Hegel was soon to excel.

XI

SPECULATIVE ROMANTICISM

Fichte's *Wissenschaftslehre* had some romantic traits, but the full power of romanticism in the field of philosophic speculation came only with Friedrich Wilhelm Joseph von Schelling (1775–1854). Whereas Fichte relied heavily on Kant's *Critique of Practical Reason,* Schelling, who was for a time Fichte's disciple although he soon departed from Fichte's principle and chose his own way, was most impressed by the third main work of Kant, the *Critique of Judgment.* It is therefore appropriate to say something about this work here, since I did not refer to it in Chapter IX. Although Kant did not alter his critical position in his third critique in which the primacy of moral reason still remained the cornerstone of his system, he did enlarge considerably the horizon of his thought and thereby prepared for the novelties that the romantics and Hegel finally introduced.

The special subject that Kant discussed was of a double nature: the Beautiful and the Organic Life. Why did he join these seemingly disparate realms in the same book and under the same title? According to Kant's terminology " judgment " in general conjoins the separate spheres of sensation and reason. As subject and predicate are coupled in a logical fashion by judgments, so it is a cognate relation that binds together the data of the senses and the forms of the understanding in the supreme transcendental propositions; the forms are predicated of the material and thus the experience of the objects is made possible. The " Transcendental Analytic " in the *Critique of Pure Reason,* after the exposition of the categories and their transcendental deduction, dealt with axioms that contain the highest theses about the experience of the objects, the first premises of all scientific knowledge of nature.

In the *Critique of Judgment* the realms of sensation and reason are mediated on a new level. The aesthetic judgments which reflect upon the beauty of certain objects rest upon an agreement between them and the Ideal of Reason. What is beautiful is perceived as a complete Whole in which all parts are totally united, not as particular things are joined under general laws, but in a concrete harmony, so that the senses and the reason are no longer separated but work together. Because of this harmony which unites our own subjective faculties of apprehension, we judge things to be beautiful. Beauty is not an objective quality, property, or attribute, but the reflex of that subjective balance which enables us to enjoy them. A similar synthesis of the whole and the parts, of means and ends, takes place in the realm of organism. Here too the material is ordered according to a concrete harmony from which life results. This inner fitness and adaptation also pleases us because our own faculties of sensation and understanding are working together. Therefore we judge organs as harmonizing with the existence and the processes of the organic whole. It is as if an unconscious purpose had composed this whole, as in the realm of artistic creation a conscious purpose is at work in composing the beautiful.

In a way both the beautiful and the organic correspond to the Ideal of Reason and thereby satisfy the highest need of the thinking mind. The fine arts and biology seem thus to meet in offering the tools to speculation which can perform what neither theoretical nor practical reason was able to attain. They can lead the philosopher to the zenith of all his ambition and aspiration. They can fulfill the postulate that remains a matter of rational faith in the sphere of practical reason. These great ideas attracted the romantic mind to enter upon the most daring adventure of speculation, discarding entirely the support of religious revelation. What is always in the future of scientific endeavor and of moral striving seems to be immediately presented to him who perceives the beautiful and who thinks the organic harmony in nature.

Both the work of art and the organism are themselves united intrinsically from within. There is nothing in the work that does not contribute to the beautiful form, as there is nothing in the living being that does not serve the purpose of life. They are not like machines, constructed in order to work for an outer purpose; they are ends in themselves. They themselves integrate the manifold which is united in them. In so far as they are considered in themselves, they can be regarded as self-sufficient. Form and content, means and end, are completely interwoven, so that every part of the work can be enjoyed as the end of the whole, as every organ in the organism can be conceived as the end of life as well as its means. Here we perceive not only theoretical objects or practical duties but something that seems to be the image of the absolute. What could more strongly invite the romantic mind to raise its wings for the flight to the highest height?

Kant had insisted that both the beautiful and the organic are merely human reflections, and that speculation cannot build upon them. It is human understanding and human perception that are in harmony, not any objective state or relation. The romantics paid no heed to these warnings. On the contrary, they believed themselves permitted to transcend the Kantian circumscription because they no longer maintained the contrast between the objective and the subjective in the Kantian sense. They were convinced that Kant was mistaken when he denied an objective reality for the beautiful and the organic. Such a fictitious objectivity was not at stake, but rather the absolute reality, the reality of the Absolute. The contrast between the objective and the subjective must be surpassed by the Absolute which is the Absolute precisely because it unites these contrasting aspects and is itself neither completely subjective nor completely objective. It must be admitted that the Kantian position could not effectively refute such an argument, since Kant's concept of the thing-in-itself or of things-in-themselves (this alternative already shows a certain vagueness in Kant's concept) was indeed untenable.

Kant had hinted at another very significant idea concerning the ego of the artist and its relation to nature as the author of life and living beings. This idea aroused even greater enthusiasm in the romantics and inspired them even more ardently to pursue their goal of an absolute idealism. In the form of the artistic creator the human ego reaches a higher stage than it can reach in the sphere of theoretical knowledge or moral activity, because it joins together what is forever separated on these stages: nature and mind, necessity and freedom, the objective and the subjective. In so far as it accomplishes this momentous synthesis, we call the ego "genius." The man of genius creates as nature does, with the same necessity and objectivity, but he creates as a conscious, willing being and in perfect freedom. He thus works as an ego, but in a way similar to nature. The two poles of existence are intimately one in the creative mind of the artist. He acts out of purpose, not by sheer rational reflection, not as the engineer or as one does who deliberately chooses the means to achieve a certain end. He creates in a state of inspiration, driven by his own mind and guided by a definite vision or intuition. Kant described and carefully circumscribed this mysterious phenomenon and tried to understand it by means of his transcendental philosophy. He did thereby enlarge and expand the frame of his critical philosophy, but he did not abandon the chief lines of his thought. The *Critique of Judgment* culminates in the doctrine of an "ethicotheology" which upholds the fundamental ethical ideas and the rational faith of the *Critique of Practical Reason*. Man is the end of nature — but not man as the artist, rather, man as the moral being. God remains separated from man. There is the gulf between human and divine apprehension and comprehension, between intellectual demonstration and intellectual intuition, which cannot be bridged.

The poet Schiller, an ardent disciple of Kant, in his philosophical writings, had already tried to apply the principles and insight of the *Critique of Judgment* to an appreciation of art and poetry, in a manner that somehow transgressed the ethical verdict of Kant's *Weltanschauung*. Schiller emphasized more strongly than Kant had done the synthesis which the artist can and does achieve. But only Schelling dared to give up the Kantian restriction and the Kantian ethical emphasis. Schelling opened a new field to speculation in his philosophy of nature.

PHILOSOPHY OF NATURE

Fichte had utterly reduced the significance and function of nature. The material universe was nothing but the occasion for man to cultivate it and to use it as material for his moral aims and ends. Whereas Kant respected nature as the object of science and even thought of God as the author of nature though only from the point of view of an ethical faith, Fichte utterly disregarded this idea and made nature only a steppingstone toward the absolute moral goal of the ego. Schelling revolted against this degradation. In sympathetic admiration with the great poet Goethe, Schelling looked at nature through the eyes of this nature worshiper. Whereas to Kant nature was that huge mechanism which it had also been to Descartes, the realm of objective laws, the order of causality, to Goethe and Schelling nature was in the first place the author of life and beauty. In his philosophy of nature, Schelling conceived of nature as a living entity, a mysterious unity in which the organic was cosmic, as it had been to Plato and Aristotle, to the Stoics, to the Neoplatonists, to Giordano Bruno, and to Shaftesbury.

Disdaining Kant's warnings, Schelling designed a huge system of nature in which all the various phenomena of physics and chemistry, of astronomy and biology were to be investigated, not in agreement with the principles of Galileo and Newton nor in a mathematical fashion (which finally was victorious in the nineteenth and twentieth centuries), but rather from his speculative point of view. He organized a large school of adherents, founded journals, and experimented in order to demonstrate that behind the mathematical and mechanical order disclosed by the scientists, there was another higher and more real order of nature, which intellectual intuition had to discover in union with empirical observation and experience. As Goethe had maintained in his own natural studies and essays, it was only in this way that Living Nature, which is divine and creative, can be grasped and understood. There was, of course, a chasm between Goethe's careful and unmetaphysical descriptions and Schelling's presumptuous and haughty attitude, which claimed to know the secret of nature in terms of conceptual construction. Goethe never forgot that nature is mysterious and that only fragmentary and forever tentative ideas can be learned from it. Schelling, on the contrary, pretended to possess the magic wand that can decipher the riddles by deriving them from one highest principle.

At bottom, Nature is itself an ego, though unconscious and not yet knowing itself, an intelligence working instinctively and without a purpose set by a will, ever growing and approaching the goal. And what is the goal? To awake from its slumber, to become conscious in man, to acquire intelligence and will, and to live the life that is ours. Nature and Man are one in their innermost essence and being. Their difference is relative, while their true and absolute reality is the same. Sometimes ingeniously, sometimes arbitrarily, Schelling interpreted the phenomena of the natural sciences as known in his own time according to this basic program. Nature develops from the inorganic through the organic to conscious life. An original duality corresponding to that of subject and object or to that of intuition and understanding, is ever more closely knit together as we climb higher on the ladder of that development. Schelling thus prepared for the evolutionary theories of the nineteenth century. He did not, however, think of a development in time, but rather in terms of rank, as Aristotle had done.

Aesthetic Idealism

The philosophy of nature underwent some alterations in the course of the years. But it was never isolated entirely from the philosophy of the ego as propounded by Fichte. On the contrary, it was planned from the outset as complementary to that philosophy or as another branch on the tree of transcendental idealism, as founded by Kant. Schelling was aware that the ego does not belong to nature, although it is at bottom one with nature. Both nature and ego are different stages in the development of an underlying something that was not named before the system of 1801. In the year 1800, Schelling published his version of the whole philosophy, comprising both the philosophy of nature and that of the ego or the mind. This system had the title " System of Transcendental Idealism." Here for the first time Schelling tried to understand both nature and mind in terms of the same original principle or rather in terms of the duality of two principles, the finite and the infinite, the restricting and the unrestricted, as Fichte had developed his system out of the antagonism of ego and nonego. But in contrast to Fichte, nature was conceived as the peer of the human ego and consciousness, though on a lower level. And also in contrast to Fichte the ego did not culminate in morality, but in artistic creation. Man as genius is the zenith and the final consummation of the development of the mind.

Schelling's system of 1800 is probably the most perfect and most satisfying representation of transcendental idealism. It is less intricate than Fichte's *Wissenschaftslehre,* more lucid and enjoyable, and written in a readable style. Many aspects of transcendental thought that are common to Kant, Fichte, and Schelling were better demonstrated and more convincingly exhibited here than anywhere else. It is as though the artistic spirit that infuses the whole had cast a radiant light upon the form of deduction or construction, so that the system has almost the effect of a work of art; in a sense, it is the product of the aesthetic imagination according to the ultimate principle of intuition which prevails over discursive intellection. What Kant had attributed to God alone — intellectual intuition or intuitive intellect — Schelling claimed for the philosophic mind. This mind is guided by intuition. The philosopher himself should be a genius in order to be equal to his task: the apprehension and penetration of the ultimate essence of nature and mind. If he is not endowed with intellectual intuition, he can never analyze and synthesize the fundamental elements of existence. The philosopher needs, therefore, the same imaginative creativity which characterizes the poet and the artist in general.

Art is, as Schelling expresses it, the " organon " of speculation. Poetry is the model and pattern of thought. In the work of art the process of production which underlies the development of both nature and mind reaches its climax and comes to perfection. " The whole impetus of producing attains its perfection and rests in the artistic product: all contradictions are resolved, all riddles are answered." [1] Art is " therefore to the philosopher the Highest, because it opens, as it were, for him the Holy of Holies; there is eternally and originally united, burning with One Flame, that which is severed in nature and history, and which must flee each other eternally in life and action as well as in thought." [2] This quotation shows that Schelling in 1800 did not yet assert that speculation can solve all problems. It solves them only by analyzing art and its achievement.

Whereas the philosophy of nature is the correlate of Kant's philosophy of the organic, the philosophy of art is the correlate of Kant's analysis of the beautiful and the genius. Schelling fuses the two

---

[1] *Schelling's Werke,* ed. by K. F. A. von Schelling, 1856 ff., Vol. III, p. 615.
[2] *Ibid.,* p. 628. (Translation by Richard Kroner.)

doctrines as they were fused in the *Critique of Judgment*. But in his version the critical frame is abandoned and both parts are integral organs of the transcendental philosophy as a whole. Inasmuch as Schelling in the system of 1800 still hesitates to speak about the Absolute as the One that unites the two parts, and inasmuch as he still admits that thought can only point to art as the Highest without ever overcoming the contradictions as art itself does, the author of that system may still be called a Kantian of a sort. But as compared with Fichte he had made a further step on the road that led eventually to the philosophy of the Absolute.

Schelling preserved in his transcendental idealism the primacy of the subject or of mind in so far as it is the artist who brings about the work which reflects the ultimate synthesis. Nature too is a kind of artist, but not in the proper sense, because she works unconsciously and because her work does not yet reconcile ultimately the contrary elements. But in another sense the aspect of objectivity defeats that of subjectivity, not only because nature has the dignity of the ego and is essentially one with the mind but also because it is the *work* of art and not artistic productivity that exhibits that final rest which characterizes the fulfillment of all striving and longing. Here in the work of art, if anywhere, the Absolute is present. Productivity only generates the work of art: the objective and aesthetically real is the work, while the act of creation is the subjective aspect. It is significant that according to Schelling the work triumphs over the worker. The ego reaches out to the summit of perfection not by its own labor and toil (the moral aspect), but by achieving the Beautiful which is an attribute not of the subject's will or the power by which the artist achieves his purpose, but of the objective work in which it is achieved. Fichte's *Wissenschaftslehre* is thus surpassed by Schelling's transcendental idealism, ethical by aesthetic speculation. This was the victory of romanticism in the realm of philosophic thought. Aesthetic idealism is the philosophy of nature transferred to the philosophy of ego or mind.

The dialectical difference between Fichte's and Schelling's method and result is therefore remarkable. While Fichte, according to his ethical principle, ended in the idea of an infinite approximation to the ultimate goal, Schelling evolved the idea of final attainment. The step represented by the system of 1800 was therefore momentous; it was succeeded by another the very next year, which Schelling thought was final and ultimate. Absolute philosophy claims to bring about the final reconciliation by means of conceptual speculation. In this new system, which bears the proud and romantic title *My System of Philosophy,* Schelling was no longer content with the aesthetic solution. Neither art nor poetry, but speculation itself, must start from and end with the Absolute. The whole system is no longer a movement toward the Absolute, but its adequate and perfect display.[3]

Why did Schelling in the course of only one year fundamentally change the basis of his philosophy? How could he abandon after so short a time the great achievement of his *System of Transcendental Idealism?* I believe that two motives are responsible for this surprising shift: one internal, the other external. Schelling might have realized that, after all, the very multiplicity of works of art discloses that none can be as absolute as he had proclaimed it to be. There is never One work that could take the place of the Absolute, as he asserted in his aesthetic idealism. The Absolute must be absolutely One. If artistic production is therefore unable to produce the Absolute, is perhaps speculation itself capable of doing it? If there is a conflict between artistic creativity and speculative thought, is the second one perhaps victorious in the end? This argument must finally lead the thinker to build a system that is thoroughly autonomous, thoroughly rational, thoroughly self-sufficient even though it might include a metaphysical aesthetics. Such a conclusion was eventually drawn by Hegel.

The second, more external reason that might have persuaded Schelling to alter his scheme and to write a new system so shortly after the publication of that of 1800, was probably the arrival of Hegel in Jena, where he was soon to become a teacher in the same university as Schelling. The two men had become friends when they had studied together at the theological seminary of Tübingen. We shall never know what they discussed with each other after their reunion in Jena. But one thing is sure: Hegel had already taken a position essentially superior to that of his friend. Although he joined Schelling not only as a colleague but also as a collaborator

[3] Cf. Richard Kroner's article in *The Review of Metaphysics,* " The Year 1800 in the Development of German Idealism." Vol. I, No. 4, June 1948, pp. 1–31.

in his journal, and although he seemed to agree basically with the philosophy of nature (which indeed he always maintained), he had seen that aesthetic idealism was not ultimately tenable and that Fichte's ethical idealism had some advantages in the competition between the two schemes. One cannot help assuming that Hegel influenced Schelling's change of mind. He probably formulated some argument that convinced Schelling that a new step had to be taken, that a new approach toward the goal of an absolute philosophy of the Absolute had to be taken. We know from Hegel's first publication, an essay on *The Difference Between the Systems of Fichte and Schelling* (1801), that he did not fully agree with Schelling's position and that he regarded Fichte's ethical and subjective idealism as in some respects even superior to Schelling's philosophy of nature and to his aesthetic idealism.

SYSTEM OF IDENTITY

The system of 1801 is usually called the system of Identity, because Schelling now asserted that he was able to conceive of the Absolute by speculative means, and that absolute identity or indifference is the key to this. He now philosophized in a bluntly dogmatic way reminiscent of Spinoza's *Ethics*. Definitions, axioms, and propositions derived from the axioms indicate this relapse into a mathematical method. The Fichtean dynamic movement toward an infinite goal no longer determines the character of that method, but rather the stability of geometry. Since the Absolute is supposed to be conceived in the beginning, it cannot be reached by a tortuous tension; instead, a perfect equipoise reflects the presence of the absolute solution. Like Spinoza's Substance the absolute identity is self-sufficient and self-existent. And as Spinoza assumed that attributes divide the original unity of the divine nature, so Schelling too declared that there are opposites which, however, are not absolute but eternally reconciled to each other. In order to symbolize this identity of the opposites, he introduced mathematical signs, such as plus and minus which check each other, so that the sum each time is zero or the negation of the contradicting elements. Oneness and plurality, infinity and finiteness, subject and object, etc., are in this quasi-quantitative manner neutralized; the dialectical contrast is settled. The absolute identity thus keeps its perfect balance in spite of the opposites which tear it asunder.

One can say that this system performed what the work of art alone was supposed to perform in the system of 1800; it is itself the perfect work of art, the One which does not exist in the realm of art. In that sense Schelling retained his aesthetic idealism in a modified fashion. Whereas the system of 1800 can be compared with an epic (Schelling himself did compare the development of nature to mind with the *Odyssey*), the system of 1801 resembled a statue or a building in which opposite weights are completely harmonized with each other. The trouble was that a conceptual system never can have such an aesthetic effect, for the simple reason that it is necessarily abstract and not sensuous, so that aesthetic beauty is missing. The system of Identity was especially formalistic and rationalistic because it was pseudo-mathematical. The whole attempt of Schelling to create a system that was probably suggested by Hegel (hence the title *My System* does not lack a certain irony) was a failure. Perhaps Schelling himself was aware of this: he never finished the fragment which he had published. As the system was the product of a hastily conceived idea, so it also was only a transient stage in the fugitive development of his thought.

If Schelling did work out this new system at the suggestion of Hegel, or in order to anticipate what Hegel was about to write, he became the victim of such a precocious undertaking. He was not able to do what Hegel alone could do. He had not even truly understood what Hegel had in mind, as Hegel's essay of 1801 clearly shows. In any case the solution offered by Schelling was utterly unsatisfactory and even superficial. It must be said that Schelling was never so original as Kant, Fichte, and Hegel were. He always imitated someone, whether Spinoza, Giordano Bruno, Plato, or Aristotle. In spite of his brilliant mind and his lucid demonstrations he was never so deeply rooted as was Hegel. The Identity system shows a dangerous relapse into thought bygone. Schelling approached a cosmological speculation at the cost of losing the insight gained by Kant. A pagan feature is clearly manifest in the *Philosophy of Nature* and in the aesthetic idealism.

The subsequent development of Schelling's philosophic genius only confirms this impression. Although he turned back eventually to the theosophic speculation of Jacob Boehme, the philosophy of nature was never entirely effaced from his thought. In the years following the fragment of 1801 he published several new versions of his philosophy of nature. Step by step he began to talk about Ideas like a Platonist although he meant thereby the different stages in the development of nature; he also called these stages potencies or powers (*Potenzen*). Finally in 1804 he published a book with the title *Philosophy and Religion,* in which for the first time he seriously considered the idea of God. The theological student of the seminary at Tübingen began to remember his past after some years of juvenile adventures.

PHILOSOPHY AND RELIGION

Schelling now discovered that it was impossible to deal effectively with the problem of the Absolute without reflecting upon the idea of God as revealed in the Christian religion. The year 1804 was in this respect the most momentous in the development of his speculation. In his Identity system Schelling had already admitted that the concept of absolute identity cannot be reached by argument, but has to be accepted on intuitive ground. He also had admitted that the step from absolute identity to the opposites and to their neutralization in an absolute indifference posed an unsoluble problem. Schelling did not disclose how the absolute identity divides itself or is split so that the realm of the finite world can ensue. He hinted at the possibility that this world is merely our appearance, while the absolute identity alone is " in-itself." However, this relation was itself mysterious and never clarified.

In the treatise of 1804 Schelling admits that he had neglected the most weighty and urgent problem of speculation: how the finite emanates from the Absolute. This question never let him rest until he had found the final solution in his *Philosophy of Mythology and Revelation*. It was the God of Biblical revelation who did not permit him to rest until he had deliberately turned his eyes to revelation. None of the many changes which his speculation underwent from 1804 up to his last philosophical position could truly satisfy his mind and quiet his conscience. With ever-increasing intensity he endeavored to tackle the hardest and toughest mystery the human mind confronts — the mystery of Creation. For more than fifty years, from 1804 to the end of his life in 1854, he was fascinated by this mystery and mobilized all the energy of his dynamic speculative thinking in order to find the right attitude toward this greatest of all riddles.

Schelling realized that all his thought before 1804 was superficial compared with the effort necessary to master this riddle. In a retrospective mood he called the movement he had sponsored in Jena till 1803 (when he left this university and town) an " impure fire." [4] In his treatise on *Philosophy and Religion,* Schelling made speculative use of the dogma of the original Fall as Origen had done before. But he thought the fall was to be understood as an event in the mind of God himself in order to derive from it the creation of the finite world. Schelling turned back to Jacob Boehme to find the clue to the mystery. There is something in God which makes him a living God, apart from which he would be only an Aristotelian world mind thinking his own thinking, eternally blessed and at rest. Such a God would never create the world, as the Aristotelian unmoved Mover in fact did not do. God is not such an unmoved Mover; he is himself moved although by himself and out of himself.

Schelling asserted that we must think of this original movement as a kind of apostasy from an original rest. The apostasy occurs or can occur because there are Ideas in the divine mind. These Ideas are originally united in One primordial Idea as Philo had said.[5] Schelling pointed thereby to the Logos-speculation of the early Christian Platonists. It is the Logos-God who defects from God who originally is One. Through this defection the finite world comes into existence. Schelling agreed that there is a leap (a word later used by Kierkegaard) between the original unity and the subsequent disunity, but he thought that the idea of a revolt against the One God by the Ideas which are a multiplicity can explain it. Here he followed the scheme of Plotinus. It is remarkable that Schelling's return from a pagan cosmology to Christian thinking was achieved by the mediation of Neoplatonism which itself was influenced by Christianity.[6] One can say Schelling projected his own impetuous desire to know, into God. He also projected into the Ideas the abso-

---

[4] Cf. Kuno Fischer, *Geschichte der neueren Philosophie,* Vol. VII, 1923, p. 173. (Letter to his brother of Jan., 1816.)

[5] *Schelling's Werke,* Vol. VI, pp. 34 f.

[6] Cf. Kroner, *Speculation and Revelation in the Age of Christian Philosophy,* pp. 87 ff.

lute freedom which characterized the absolute ego of Fichte and thereby paid a high tribute to his former teacher.[7]

In 1809 Schelling composed another treatise, *Philosophical Inquiry Into the Nature of Human Freedom*.[8] This was the last version of his philosophical thought which he himself published. Here Schelling attached himself even closer to the mysticism of Jacob Boehme. He now proclaimed that the Absolute or God does not only harbor the Ideas, he is not only Mind, but he is in the first place Will. The will is not self-sufficient, since it aims at something which it does not yet possess; it has a purpose. To be a will presupposes, therefore, a certain lack in the very essence of God; he cannot be such a perfect One as the Neoplatonists thought him to be. An original duality must be present in him, a tension between desire and the object of desire. In an earlier essay Schelling had already insisted that we must distinguish between essence and existence in God, otherwise he would be lifeless, a pure notion or form, but not Will.[9] The divine essence is only one aspect of the divine being, the other is his existence through which he is actual and active. Whereas Aquinas taught that the will of God does not differ from his intellect, that in God the will at bottom is intellect, Schelling (and in this he manifested himself as a " Protestant ") emphasized the will (as Duns Scotus had done before).

In his essay Schelling stressed two opposite elements or constituents in God, the one rational, bright, and cognitive, the other dark, impulsive, and volitional. Like Boehme he calls the second element *" Ungrund "* and *" Abgrund "* (abyss). God generates out of the unconscious will his thinking mind or the Ideas in which the will contemplates its own being. But this duality generates a contradiction that God tries to dissolve. Therefore he creates the world in which he reveals himself and he creates man through whom he heals the break between the two elements of his own being, impulsive nature and reason or mind. In this way the new religious version of Schelling's system leads back to the old scheme of his transcend-

---

[7] See the Introduction to the translation of Schelling's posthumous work *The Ages of the World* (only the first part was actually written), by Frederick de Wolfe Bolman (Columbia University Press, 1942).

[8] Translated by James Gutmann. The Open Court Publishing Company, 1936.

[9] *Darlegung des wahren Verhaeltnisses der Naturphilosophie zu der verbesserten Fichteschen Lehre*, 1806.

ental idealism, so that it can be interpreted as a supplementary enlargement of this earlier system.

Whereas in the transcendental idealism, the human ego finally reaches its goal by creating the work of art, now God reaches his goal by creating man and thereby finally reconciles himself as will to himself as reason. Not Art but Religion is now the ultimate means of uniting what was divided in God and in his creation. But man must be endowed with free will so that this reconciliation can take place. This is the " nature of human freedom." Man's fall is instrumental in this process, since it is only through the redemption of man that the last step toward God's own self-reconciliation can be taken. Thus man's redemption is in the last analysis God's own self-redemption. As God bears within himself the two antagonistic aspects of his dark will and his bright reason, so does man. Man is like God but he is not God, since he is created and finite. Therefore, freedom of the will means that man can either subject his reason to nature or nature to his reason. (Here Schelling was influenced by Kant's doctrine of Radical Evil.) [10] In man's evil will the primordial blind desire in God, his unconscious nature, comes again to the fore. Only through this self-manifestation of the divine darkness can God actually overcome the division in his own nature.

It is obvious that the treatise on freedom has a Christian tinge. Although Schelling did not yet mention revelation, it is evident that he philosophized with the purpose of making Christian dogma speculatively acceptable. Of course, since he was still under the spell of the philosophy of nature, his speculation was still very unchristian or un-Biblical. Nevertheless, the original duplicity in God as being both Will and Reason has a certain affinity to the dogma of God as Father and Son. But he still had to go a long way, until he eventually arrived at the position that he exhibited in his lectures at the University of Berlin in the years 1841 and 1842. These lectures were published after his death under the title *Philosophy of Mythology and Revelation*. They are also known as *Positive Philosophy,* because Schelling now confronted a negative philosophy, which was merely speculative, with a positive philosophy, which was based on the

---

[10] Schelling himself mentions Kant in his essay. But he might also have been stimulated by the writings of the Catholic mystic Franz von Baader, who was an enthusiastic reader and disciple of Jacob Boehme.

history of the world religions, pagan as well as Christian.

In spite of Schelling's intense and extensive speculative creativity he also was, since his student days, most interested in the historical religions. In his earliest period he wrote a treatise on the oldest mythical stories. He also sketched the outlines of a system in which he wanted to deal with mythology.[11] At the end of his life Schelling actually formulated that system, so that one can rightly speak of one consistent line in his development. It also cannot be denied that Schelling, although his speculation was romantic and often bordered on the fantastic, always had a strong inclination to include empirical facts and theories in his philosophical schemes. He tried to understand the great works of art in his speculation about the nature of art. He studied the experiments and results of the empirical natural sciences in his speculation about nature, although he often interpreted them in an arbitrary or willful way. The whole trend toward an absolute idealism was from the beginning also a trend toward an understanding of the concrete historical reality, as romanticism in general was historically minded, and, in fact, inclined to historicism, i.e., to an idolization of history.

In the period of his philosophy of nature (which, in fact, can be traced through his thoughts at all times), Schelling called his system an "absolute empiricism," and he strove to include all empirical facts known in his day. He believed like Leibniz in a "pre-established harmony" between the a priori and the a posteriori, the speculative principles and the empirical detail. The great systematic power of his thinking rested largely on this firm belief, as did also the power of Hegel's speculation. Schelling's most fervent ambition was to avoid a merely conceptual or rational metaphysics and to catch the actually real, so that one can even assert that he was one of the fathers of existentialism — a thesis that is true only in a very restricted sense. No wonder that he finally turned to the existing religions and inquired into their speculative meaning. His "positive" philosophy (which has also a certain affinity with the positivism flourishing in the nineteenth century) was indeed a kind of religious

[11] Cf. Franz Rosenzweig, *Das älteste Systemprogramm des deutschen Idealismus* (The Oldest Program of a System in the School of German Idealism) (Sitzungsberichte der Heidelberger Akademie der Wissenschaften, Phil.—Histor. Klasse, 1917, 5te Abhandlung).

positivism; it aspired to understand the positive myths and creeds by means of speculation and to "construe" the religious development of mankind out of a priori principles, as he had always tried to understand the positive facts of nature in a philosophical fashion.

The basic idea guiding the positive philosophy was closely akin to the trend of thought which he had first followed in his essay on *Human Freedom*. He had further developed those ideas in his lectures and fragmentary systems between 1808 and 1841. In 1815 he published a paper on *The Deities of Samothrake*. This was his first attempt at a theogonic interpretation of mythology. The underlying presupposition was that the religions of the past are not only historical documents of man's own imaginative views, but they also point to a metaphysical process in which the divine being itself developed. There is an inner growth, not only in the consciousness of man concerning the nature of the divine but in God's own consciousness. Both the human history of religion and the divine history of God himself culminate in the Christian revelation. This was the final and definitive stage in Schelling's own speculative growth. Speculation and revelation permeated each other and mutually illuminated each other. This insight found its most mature expression in the *Positive Philosophy*.

Negative or purely rational and conceptual thought can never accomplish this task. The superempirical has to penetrate the empirical, and the empirical has to illustrate the superempirical so that the highest degree of insight and knowledge can be reached. Speculation alone cannot produce the vast variety of mythical stories and legends; the history of religion can never fully understand the significance and deepest meaning of its own subject. History and philosophy must join in order to attain that understanding. The deities of pagan religions are not merely fictions, or allegoric images of nature and natural forces, they are also not merely deifications of the heroes of the nations and their heroic deeds; it is the divine mystery itself that gradually reveals itself in these stories and creeds. Rational thought is negative, because it can only think out the idea of God, but never grasp the living God himself as revelation does. The existing God is forever excluded from this negative speculation. He has to reveal himself in order to be known. But if we read the Bible with the eyes of a speculative thinker, then we are able to comprehend the mystery.

In every religion a certain aspect of religious truth can be found since it is the same God who speaks in all religions, although in different stages of his self-disclosure. The more primitive forms are surpassed by the higher forms in which the lower ones survive only as subordinate elements. Such an interpretation is certainly more profound than psychological, sociological, or aesthetic explanations and expositions of the historic religions. After all, the religions of the past were religions and not only tales; they displayed some aspect of the mysteries inherent in the revealed religion. And to speak religiously, it was God himself who appeared to the eyes of primitive nations in the clouds of their mythical images. In every religion there is something that transcends the horizon of merely human imagination, experience, memory, or fiction — something transcendent — something divine. It was this something which Schelling desired to comprehend.

Christianity alone is true religion because it declares itself as revealed by God, thereby emphasizing the presence of that something which transcends the human mind. Schelling interprets from this point of view the dogmas of the Trinity, of incarnation, and of atonement. He distinguishes three stages of revelation: that of the Father (Old Testament), that of the Son (New Testament), and that of the Spirit which lies in the future. He follows closely the intimations given in former centuries, and more recently by the poet and critic Lessing in his essay *Die Erziehung des Menschengeschlechts* (The Education of Man). The three stages correspond to the spiritual events of Creation, redemption, and consummation. Schelling throughout construes these phases of revelation by means of his speculative theology according to which God gradually reconciles himself to himself. The consummation will be accomplished when man is actually won back by God and united with him. Schelling compares the Roman period, as the Petrine church, with the Protestant period, in which Paul was victorious; but he insists that the final church will be that of the Holy Spirit.

Although such a speculative exposition is certainly attractive and suggestive, especially if one can be persuaded that Schelling's theogonic and theosophic thought achieves ultimate truth, it nevertheless suffers from one great mistake. Is not the religious truth revealed in Scripture more adequate than Schelling's attempt to surpass it?

Is not the half-mythical and half-legendary form in which God appears in the Bible more true to his mysterious and forever incomprehensible reality than the half-rational form in which he appears in the ideas of the speculative thinker? Is not therefore dogmatic or systematic theology better adapted to revelation than theogony and theosophy ever can be? And was not the attempt of Hegel, who was convinced that the mystery of God can be conceived by philosophic thought, more consistent than the account of the romantic Schelling, who hovered between the two possibilities of a theological and a metaphysical understanding? Is not, moreover, the juxtaposition of a negative and a positive philosophy the symptom of a basic rift in Schelling's thought? In any case the positive philosophy did not gain adherents. Schelling never published it. It was a compromise that satisfied neither the historian and the systematic theologian nor the metaphysician and the philosopher of religion.

XII

SPECULATIVE DIALECTIC

SCHELLING never reflected on thought as such. He never raised the question whether reason can penetrate the mystery of Being and of God. He presupposed, rather, that this is possible as all his systems show. Even his last system, in which he denied that such a penetration can be complete without religious experience, was based upon the assumption that in principle God can be comprehended by thought, although only in his essence, not in his existence. But the main problem as to whether the essence of God and indeed of all things can be known by means of speculation was never considered by Schelling. He was simply convinced that it could, although only to a certain degree or up to a certain limit. This neglect was the more striking since the time had not long passed when Kant had made it his main concern to inquire into the possibility of knowledge and when he had come to the conclusion that only empirical and transcendental, but not speculative and transcendent, knowledge is possible.

It is true that Fichte had already violated this verdict; he had dared to begin from a thesis about the absolute ego. Schelling went a step farther in the same direction, and he finally indulged in theosophic and theogonic speculation. Hegel went back to Kant — in a certain sense.

Hegel regarded the question of logic as the most central of all questions. What is the relation between logic and Being? Between Being and thought? Only when this question can be answered in a methodical way and only after this question has been answered satisfactorily can thought dare to think about the essence of all things. Only then can the relation between essence and existence, which was the background of Schelling's distinction between his negative and his positive philosophy, be studied and understood really and in a reliable way. After all, Hegel's philosophy was not less " positive," " empirical," or " existential " than Schelling's; it was only more methodically and logically anchored. How a priori thought and experience a posteriori, how reason and Being can be united by means of thought was the primary and the most fundamental of Hegel's problems. Schelling had united them without any consideration of this problem. Schelling never really understood the weight and the depth of this consideration, and he never paid any attention to the relation between logic and reality. Even after Hegel's death he accused the system of his former friend of being " rationalistic "; he never saw that this rationalism was the condition also of his own positive philosophy, since he could dare to interpret the data of religious life by means of his speculative theosophy only if he was sure that such an interpretation was legitimate. But this legitimacy was never called in question by him. This lack was the reason why he could fall victim to a theosophic mysticism; it was the reason why he could indulge in his speculative romanticism and uncritical aestheticism.

Hegel early recognized all these weaknesses of his friend, although for a time he was himself drawn into the current of romanticism and never entirely freed himself from this bondage, as we will see. Although Hegel exalted the absolute tendency more than any successor of Kant, and was more pretentious in claiming to have achieved the building of an absolute philosophy, giving an absolutely satisfying and perfect account of the Absolute, he also was more critical than either Fichte or Schelling in his logical demands and their fulfillment. It is a strange paradox that we meet here. But it is just this paradox which characterizes the peculiar greatness and uniqueness of this greatest figure in the development of German idealism.

Decades ago I compared the four main representatives of that development in the following way: Kant was, as it were, the root of the whole tree, its primary origin; Fichte was the trunk, ascending directly to the infinite sky, steep and austere; Schelling was the leaves and blossoms, expanding into the surrounding air in all directions, colorful and pleasant for the spectator, but somehow dispersed and without inner coherence; Hegel was the fruit of the tree in which all its strength was collected and which gathered together the whole development. In order to understand historically this final fruit, one has to study all the various manifestations of the movement that began from Kant, not only the main, but also all the smaller, ones since Hegel was the consummation of the whole epoch. Such a study cannot, of course, be undertaken in this work.

Georg Wilhelm Friedrich Hegel (1770–1831) was the consummation not only of German idealism but also of all modern philosophy and, in a way, even of all speculation since Thales. The scope of his thought and the extension of its contents are enormous. He was perhaps the most universal mind that ever lived; at the same time he was one of the greatest organizers of knowledge. His system seems to comprise the whole range of the intellectually comprehensible world, be it of pure thought or of experience in the widest and most extensive sense. He was the last metaphysician of high rank in the Western world of culture. Ancient, medieval, and modern thought were embraced and fused by him.

But more admirable than the abundance of his knowledge and the riches of the experience envisaged by his mind are the depth of his thought and the penetration of his insight. Even though he appropriated all the systems of the past, he was yet much more original than Schelling. He never imitated anyone. He was always quite himself; even his style differs from that of anyone else so remarkably that one can at once recognize whether a sentence was written by him or not. His German was as peculiar as his whole scheme, but it was not so artificial as that of Heidegger today. It had a classical beauty in spite of its somewhat awkward and strange syntax (noticeably influenced by the ancient classical languages). One always feels that the author was wrestling with the difficulty and obscurity of the matter, and that he sometimes won an intuitive victory, as it were, in shaping his ideas.

He founded a powerful school which reigned in different guises and modifications throughout the nineteenth century and is still alive. As his width of thought was enormous so was his influence upon all the sciences, especially those concerned with history and with the human mind. Since his time to the present day, political ideas were to a great extent determined by an affirmative or opposing attitude, although Hegel's views were rarely interpreted correctly. Religious life in Germany was inspired by his speculation, not only in the field of systematic theology but also in that of preaching. In the beginning his power was, of course, most directly felt in German circles; he has been called the king of the Berlin university. But after his death his doctrine spread to other countries too, and virtually to all of Europe. There were very able Italian Hegelians throughout the nineteenth century and until the present time. There was a very creative and productive English school of Hegelianism at the end of the century, and there are still some minds in England that are formed by this movement. " A European event," Nietzsche exclaimed, grouping him with Goethe, Schopenhauer, and Heinrich Heine.[1]

But in spite of the logical sagacity and ingenuity that prompted Hegel to revolutionize the whole tradition of classical thought it cannot be denied that he also was conspicuously molded by the romantic spirit of his epoch. Although he did violently react against that spirit and although he sometimes speaks like a determined rationalist, he was himself tinged by this spirit, even in his very brand of rationalism. In particular his writings between 1801 and 1807 were strongly modeled by a romantic bias, as was his brilliant early work *The Phenomenology of Mind*. However, the Preface to this work — one of the most inspired and ingenious statements he has written — ferociously attacks speculative romanticism and stresses reason and logic as the necessary implements of all serious philosophy. The essays and manuscripts preceding the *Phenomenology* have a romantic tone, but even here one can notice the future emphasis. Hegel was from the outset a penetrating thinker, subtle and refined in his arguing, eager to give a methodical account of his views and endeavoring to demonstrate logically the truth of his theses. Nevertheless, there is a definite difference between the papers composed before and after the *Phenomenology*. Essays, such as that on *The Difference Between the Systems of Fichte and Schelling,* on *Faith and Knowledge,* on *The Scientific Treatments of Natural Law,* and the manuscripts written in Jena before the *Phenomenology* indicate the romantic temper and manner of think-

[1] Cf. *Götterdämmerung* (Twilight of the Gods).

ing. The mind of Schelling is clearly visible in those papers. It was an aesthetic and intuitive approach which here prevailed.[2]

The *Phenomenology* represents the turning point in Hegel's inner growth. He was still under the spell of romanticism when he wrote it, but the Preface, written after the work had been finished, shows the new emphasis laid upon logic as the basis and organon of his later system. Whereas in the earlier utterances the idea is predominant that reason cannot reach ultimate truth, that the understanding has to abdicate when the Absolute is known, and that insoluble contradictions bar the way to the Highest, the *Phenomenology* culminates in the proclamation of an absolute knowledge which reconciles all contrarieties of thought and life, and which takes the place of religion. Whereas Hegel in the essay on the *Difference* says that " speculation demands in its highest synthesis of the conscious and the unconscious, the destruction of the consciousness itself," [3] in the *Phenomenology* it is the conscious mind which triumphs over all unconscious stages and which establishes absolute knowledge in the end.

UNIVERSAL SIGNIFICANCE [4]

The Hegelian philosophy represents a synthesis of the greatest historical powers in Western civilization: that of antiquity and that of Christianity. These historical forces mutually permeate each other more profoundly than ever before. It was the destiny of Christianity since its beginnings to be allied with Greek philosophy and yet to oppose it. The ancient world could appropriate the new religion only by uniting it with its own spirit and by reinterpreting the new doctrine on the basis of its own speculative thought. Therefore dogma and sacred theology are the children of the marriage between the Greek Logos and the early Christian community. What was unreflected life in the community, feeling and movement of the heart, what was narrative, prayer, sermon, cult, and worship,

[2] Cf. Richard Kroner's Introduction to the translation of *Hegel's Early Theological Writings* (University of Chicago Press, 1948), which sketches Hegel's philosophic development.

[3] *Werke* (Complete edition through an association of friends, 1832 ff.), Vol. I, p. 188.

[4] The following section is taken from my book *Von Kant bis Hegel*, Vol. II, pp. 255–261.

developed into thought, knowledge, science, and system. The history of the medieval spirit is the history of the antagonism and the reconciliation between these tendencies and energies which fought each other, but also supplemented and complemented each other. In the philosophy of Thomas Aquinas both were acknowledged as legitimate; it solved the problem of medieval Christianity and determined the destiny of the Roman Church.

The synthesis of Hellenic thought and Christian revelation which was created in this system implied, however, a belated victory of antiquity over Christ within Christianity. Through Thomism the objective realities of systematic knowledge and of ecclesiastical institution defeated the subjectivity and inwardness of the individual soul (still very strong and dominating in the personality and work of Augustine). Logic triumphed over Conscience, the Logos over the Ethos, cognition over volition — the church, the heir and imitator of the Roman Empire, asserting its imperialistic and universal claim, gained ascendancy over the invisible Kingdom of Heaven and the spiritual glory of love and grace which characterized the bond of the members of the original community.

But as the national states in the long run did not suffer the supremacy of the Roman Church, so the intellectual synthesis accomplished in the field of thought did not satisfy in the long run the Christian conscience and inwardness. The uniting bond between the ancient pagan and the Christian forces burst asunder. The task which the Middle Ages had tried to discharge and which they actually did discharge, in an imposing although one-sided and untenable way, was now renewed. Renaissance and Reformation were at bottom one and the same movement: it was the same basic fact that manifested itself in both events, the fact that the medieval synthesis was destroyed. The powers that had been united separated again and confronted each other in their original purity: in the Renaissance, pre-Christian antiquity, in the Reformation, primitive Christianity revolted against the Scholastic union, each restoring its own peculiarities independent of the other.

However, none of these two retrograde movements, which for centuries had repelled as well as attracted each other, could secure a perfect and exclusive authority over the Western mind. The need for reuniting them began the very moment they were divorced.

The Renaissance could not bring back ancient paganism and lead it to victory over the Christian religion, nor could the Reformation resuscitate the primitive community. Rather, on each side the opposite spirit reappeared again, so that it was necessary to find a new formula for their *rapprochement.*

It is the cardinal theme of modern history to devise a substitute for the lost synthesis, and it was left to philosophic speculation to perform this task. Since the Catholic Church retained the Thomistic solution, it was the peculiar burden of Protestantism to bring about the new reunion of the hostile, but also inseparably associated, historical trends. In the contrast of the Catholic and Protestant creeds the old *concordia discors,* the " coincidence of opposites," continued. Greek speculation and Christian revelation needed each other and yet could not live together. Although Catholicism possessed a majestic and subtle method for reuniting the rivals, the twin events of Renaissance and Reformation had so weakened the authority and creativity of the medieval reconciliation that the modern mind needed a radical revision and required a reunion on a completely new level.

If Protestantism wanted to create a new synthesis adapted to its own particular creed and spirit, it had, as it were, to delegate philosophic speculation to carry out this difficult undertaking. It had to generate a system of thought in which Christianity was no longer overpowered by Greek paganism, by a " natural theology," by a theoretical proof of God, by an ethical intellectualism, and by all those features which are truly Aristotelian in the Thomistic system; this Protestant system was created by Kant. " I had to restrict science, in order to make room for faith " — this famous sentence in the Preface to the second edition of the *Critique of Pure Reason* is fully understood only if it is illuminated by universal history.

The Kantian philosophy opposed the individual self to the institutional realities in every sphere; the individual soul to the visible church, the moral personality to the state, conscience in general to science, faith to dogma. In the Kantian philosophy the *Gemüt,* i.e., the heart, triumphed over the intellect, will over knowledge, action over substance, practical over theoretical reason. For the first time the critical philosophy established in this sense a system of speculation originating from Protestantism. Although in a certain sense the transcendental idealism renewed (as we have seen) Platonism, from the perspective of universal history we must insist that Kant was as adverse to the primacy of contemplation as Luther had been, that he declined Greek wisdom with the same vigor and that he rejected Scholasticism with the same resolution. Kant replaced the superiority of Form and Essence by the spontaneity of the understanding and the activity of judgment; he replaced the superiority of the *theoria,* which Aristotle had called the " sweetest " thing, by the primacy of pure practical reason and by that faith which this reason postulates; not the Good, but the good will was the Highest in his table of values. Fichte even more passionately and almost fanatically defended this basic evaluation. Activity was the supreme virtue in his system.

Schelling opposed this whole trend of thought; he reintroduced the Greek emphasis on the contemplative, theoretical, objective, and intuitive attitude of the mind. In his philosophy of nature, in his aesthetic and romantic idealism, in his system of absolute identity, the spirit of a cosmocentric speculation returned with great power and defeated the ethical *Weltanschauung* of Kant and Fichte. With good reason Schelling chose the figure of the Renaissance poet and cosmological philosopher Giordano Bruno as the hero of a dialogue in which he praised this view. The ancient spirit again came to the fore in him and claimed unrestricted recognition. In his juvenile poem " Epikurisch Glaubensbekenntnis Heinz Widerporstens " (" Epicurean Confession of Faith by Heinz Widerporst ") he expressed his own creed. He frankly admitted here that if he had to choose any religion at all, he would prefer the Catholic religion to Protestantism. It was in an outright anti-Christian mood in which the young Schelling wrote his early works. Therefore, he fought the anti-Hellenic and antipagan ideas of Kant and Fichte, which (though not Christian in any orthodox sense) yet were rooted in the Protestant tradition.

Schelling was a romantic precisely because his religious tendency was aesthetically colored. It was this aesthetic predilection which prompted many romantics to revere the Catholic Middle Ages and to praise them; some of them (such as their spiritual leader Friedrich Schlegel) were even converted to the Roman Church. What drew the romantic mind to that direction was not the authority of the church, but the aesthetic features in medieval culture (as expressed so magnificently in the realm of music, poetry, architecture, painting, and sculpture) in contrast to the puritan tendencies in Protestantism. One cannot understand Hegel's dialectical speculation without considering these universal currents. Out of this background his system rose.

Hegel was from the outset influenced by both the ethical and the aesthetic, the Christian and the Hellenic, the Protestant and the Catholic values and traditions. In a definite way his mind was " catholic," i.e., universal.[5] He was the close friend of the sensitive and speculative poet Hölderlin, whose enthusiasm for everything Greek he fully shared; but he was also profoundly influenced and inspired by Kant's ethics, by Schleiermacher's *Speeches on Religion* (1799), by Fichte's *Wissenschaftslehre*. He wrestled intensely and seriously with the task of reconciling these different streams of thought, as the *Early Theological Writings* and the published and unpublished fragments and papers of the Jena period reveal. He philosophized with the purest zeal about the contrast between thought and faith, between reflection and life, between religion and philosophy. The phenomenon of Greek national and poetic religion deeply occupied his mind. But he also brooded on the idea of love in the Gospels. He was stirred by the Christian message much more than Schelling.

The magnitude of the contrast between these views profoundly influenced his early speculative thinking. The Preface to the *Phenomenology of Mind* discloses the tremendous agitation of both his intellect and his heart. A passionate emotion animates the seemingly logical and rational considerations of those pages. Out of this passion the astounding enthusiasm grew which characterizes this Preface but which is the hidden impulse in all his writings. The " pale cast of thought " is only the surface of his speculative dialectic; below this surface there burns a flame that seems to consume all material things and to transform them into pure spirit. This flame can be observed when he fights the philosophy of nature in that Preface, but also when he defends his dialectical point of view against the philosophers of mere subjectivism, mere faith, or mere intuition; when he argues for absolute idealism against relative or " reflective " idealism.

Hegel was convinced that he had found the key to the problem

[5] See the instructive book by Rudolf Haym, *Hegel and His Time* (1857).

that universal history was posing. Indeed, whatever one might think about the truth of the system, no one who has studied it can overlook its grandiose span, its logical depth and strength, its universal significance. Whether we accept or reject the solution offered by Hegel, in any case we must acknowledge that here at least an attempt was made to reconcile the historical opposites on the ground of Protestantism. Hegel can be compared in this respect with Thomas Aquinas. As Thomism developed the classical speculative synthesis of antiquity and Christianity suggested by the Roman brand of Christianity, so Hegel formulated the same synthesis suggested by the Protestant version. The difference between Thomism and Hegelianism is this: Aquinas used the Aristotelian concepts and tried to Christianize them; Hegel used the Kantian, Fichtean, and Schellingian concepts with the same purpose, but he also continued the Platonic and Aristotelian tradition in a much more genuine way than Kant or Schelling had done.

In a qualified manner Hegel kept the primacy of the ego, of activity, of subjectivity, but he set the divine spirit in the place of the human mind. The primacy of pure practical reason in the Kantian style was abandoned, but it was retained in the primacy of the absolute mind which activates itself. Mind, not nature, is the summit of Hegel's system. Self, not world, is the core of his dialectic. His method is not static as that in Schelling's system of 1801, but dynamic, as in the *Wissenschaftslehre*. Not art but religion was from the beginning the highest form of existence for him, and philosophy he believed was one with religion.

But in spite of this religious emphasis there is another feature in his thought which elevates speculation guided by a dialectical method. Neither of the opposite poles of life is absolute, taken in itself, neither the ethical nor the aesthetic, neither history nor nature, neither the divine nor the human. " The truth is the Whole." If there is any primacy in Hegel's system, it is that of the truth itself. It is the primacy of the dialectical synthesis compared with the notion of single concepts. (I shall say more about this point presently.)

The supreme synthesis is conceived by Hegel as Mind or Spirit.[6]

---

[6] The German language unfortunately does not distinguish between these two terms; it has only one word for both: *Geist*. Much can be explained in Hegel's language and thought by this deficiency.

The absolute mind is the unity of itself and its opposite: nature. It is the synthesis of subject and object, of thinking and being, of notion and intuition. The mind itself accomplishes this synthesis by the energy of its own activity. It enacts itself (as Fichte's absolute ego did) by opposing to itself its counterpart and by reconciling this opposite pole to and with itself. The mind triumphs in the end. " A greater synthesis the world has never seen," the Protestant theologian Ernst Troeltsch exclaims.[7]

Hegel's speculative dialectic is supposed to consummate not only Western philosophy but also the Christian religion. Indeed, both are identical in the last analysis. The dialectic founds the " Third Kingdom " based upon the " Eternal Gospel " of the Spirit, as Joachim of Floris had announced it in the twelfth century and as Lessing and Schelling had again declared it. Time and Eternity, History and Eschatology, the aesthetic and the ethical, are thereby reconciled to each other and united in a higher synthesis. Historians and critics have debated the question whether Hegel was a theist or a pantheist, a rationalist or a mystic, whether his system can be called " panlogism " or whether the Mind is its real principle and not the Logos; they have wondered whether it is objectivistic or subjectivistic, ontological or theological, historical or metaphysical — the " secret " of Hegel's philosophy (as Hutchison Stirling calls it), however, is exactly its claim of comprising these and all other contrasting concepts and views which emerged in the past. Instead of Kierkegaard's Either-Or, Hegel pretended and intended to establish an As-well-as.

One might doubt whether or not this gigantic task was carried out by its author, whether the solution offered is satisfactory or not, but one cannot doubt that Hegel did propose such a solution and that the means employed in expounding it were as gigantic as the purpose itself. Hegel's dialectic, although not without some antecedent in the history of philosophy, was the most daring adventure ever undertaken. The tripartition of his system into Logic, Philosophy of Nature, and Philosophy of Mind was original; although prepared by Kant, Fichte, and Schelling, it was nevertheless an innovation made possible only on the ground of Hegel's dialectical method.

---

[7] *Gesammelte Schriften,* Vol. III, p. 263.

PRINCIPLE AND METHOD

Although the Logic is the most peculiar and most audacious part of Hegel's system, as it is also the basis and the foundation of his dialectical method, it is nevertheless conditioned by the other parts as indeed every step taken in Hegel's movement of thought is both the foundation for all further steps, but also presupposed by the end of the whole movement. The system is an organism in which every organ is conditioned by the life of the whole, as the whole is conditioned by that of the organs. The Logic is therefore something entirely different from what commonly is called logic, whether in the traditional or in the modern sense. Hegel's logic is unique in that it is a system of metaphysical categories which develop according to a logical necessity; however, this logical necessity is again something entirely different from what is commonly understood by it. Hegel reformed logic and logical necessity according to the dialectical principle. Not only Nature and Mind, but thought itself, has to be understood in a speculative manner; in fact, thought in the first place has to be understood that way, since Nature and Mind are to be thought, and since thought is therefore the universal and the indispensable foundation of the whole system.

We must first of all know what thought is, how thought proceeds, what thought can perform, and how it can perform what the philosophical problems demand of it, if they are to be solved. In a way, Hegel went back to Kant's transcendental logic. Kant had distinguished formal and transcendental logic on the grounds that empirical knowledge is not merely formal or analytical, but penetrates something given and is therefore synthetical, permeating the given by means of a priori forms (space, time, and categories). Hegel also insists that speculative thinking is synthetical, although it does not deal with something empirically given. It does deal with something given by intellectual intuition. Fichte had already reduced the contrast between the a priori form and the a posteriori material to that of the absolute ego and the absolute nonego. Hegel resumed the dialectical movement of Fichte's *Wissenschaftslehre*. But he set out from a principle more abstract, more fundamental, more comprehensive than that of the absolute ego, namely, from Being as such. Hegel's logic is an ontological, speculative metaphysics. This reformation of Fichte's supreme principle, the absolute ego, was prepared by Schelling's turning to Nature and to the Absolute. Being as such is the Absolute in its most abstract, most universal, most fundamental form. Everything in some way has the logical character " to be." The category of Being, therefore, is common to everything that can be thought and that has to be thought. Being as such is the supreme principle of Hegel's metaphysical logic. Whatever we may think, it is conditioned by Being and belongs to the realm of Being, whether it is empirical or a priori, finite or infinite, necessary or contingent, Nature or Mind. Being underlies all speculative thought as it underlies all reality and all appearance.

But Being cannot be understood as Indifference, i.e., in a merely negative fashion as Schelling had done. Rather, the opposition of the absolute ego and the absolute nonego which Fichte had placed at the head of his system must be adopted and transformed according to the absolute ontology of Hegel's logic. The supreme contradistinction therefore should be that of Being and Non-Being (or Nothing). This contradistinction sets the dialectic in motion, for Being and Non-Being taken absolutely contradict each other as the given and the a priori, the absolute ego and the absolute nonego; they have to be synthetized so that they can become the basis of speculative knowledge as the synthetical judgments in Kant's transcendental analytic became the basis of empirical knowledge. Only by the unification of the opposites can the store of known truth be enlarged in both cases, i.e., in that of empirical and that of speculative knowledge. All things are the outcome of such a basic synthesis, as Fichte had shown. But now the movement of dialectical thought is no longer leading to an infinitely remote and therefore unattainable end; rather, as Schelling has insisted, the movement ends where all the contradictory concepts are united and reconciled to one another. This happens in an absolute sense only in the Philosophy of Mind when the Absolute is conceived as absolute Mind which is identical with the God of revelation.

However, Hegel's dialectical method should not be compared with Kant's transcendental analytic, but with the transcendental dialectic. Hegel transformed this dialectic into a positive metaphysics by using the dialectical contradictions in order to build up the system of the Absolute. Kant had assumed that the antinomies of dialectical thought can be solved by the distinction of the noumenal and the phenomenal. But the development from Kant through Fichte and Schelling had shown that this distinction itself is not free from contradiction, since the human ego is both noumenal (as the moral agent) and phenomenal (as belonging to the world in space and time) and it is the identity of these two aspects which must be attained. Fichte's metaphysics of the absolute ego had disclosed this deeper contradiction, but his solution was ethically speculative, and therefore could not be applied to the fundamental contradiction of Being and Non-Being.

Fichte's dialectic had to be united with the attempt of Schelling in order to philosophize about the Absolute. Fichte had failed because he had not ascended the highest peak of speculation; Schelling had failed because he had neglected the dialectical movement of Fichte's system. Both must be accepted, but both must be rejected. The dialectical method of Fichte must be applied to Schelling's Absolute. This is Hegel's solution; this is the kernel and the " secret " of his speculative dialectic. Hegel himself declared that this is the right solution in his first publication, *The Difference Between the Systems of Fichte and Schelling,* which gives us the key to the understanding of his own system; although in 1801 this system was not yet written down in its final version, its fundamental principle and its method were already outlined.

In the Preface to the *Phenomenology of Mind,* Hegel voiced the triumph that he felt after he had found the foundation on which he could erect the building of his system. " The truth is the Whole," he exclaims here, intimating the chief principle of his method. No single concept, no single judgment or proposition, no thesis and, indeed, no synthesis can render the truth in its absolute fullness and totality. Only the system itself in its movement from Being to Absolute Mind can perform this end. The truth is not stable as Schelling proposed in his system of 1801; as Fichte had said, it is dynamic. It is dialectical movement that does not permit any rest, any isolated statement. To put it in a paradoxical manner: the principle of Hegel's speculative dialectic is that there is no principle because every statement or thesis is part and parcel of the whole movement and is true only if taken within this movement. Every statement isolated from this whole, understood by itself alone, is false; it is true only if understood as moving, as fluid, as a transition to another statement. Never before (with the possible exception of Heraclitus) and never afterward has the dynamic fluidity and restlessness of thought and reality been so much emphasized and so methodically carried through. Even Bergson's *élan vital* appears as undialectically conceived, if we compare it with Hegel's speculative method.

It is evident that this method makes it almost impossible to indicate any definite principle of Hegel's system. Whatever one could say, even that Mind is the Absolute, is untrue if understood apart from the system in which mind realizes itself through the whole movement from the logic through the philosophy of nature to the philosophy of mind, from abstract Being to concrete Spirit. It would be false to say that Being is the principle, because Being is only the start of the movement, and it is a wrong principle if isolated from Nothing and from all the following categories of the logic; it is wrong also if severed from the philosophy of Nature and Mind. The Whole alone is the truth. One has to go through the whole, in order to know what Hegel regarded as the truth. One has to feel the pulse of the dialectical movement, one has to move with Hegel's thought in order to grasp his mind.

Hegel united intrinsically what Schelling tore asunder as negative and positive philosophy at the evening of his life. Although Hegel did not know this last system of his friend which originated about fifteen years after his death, he had nevertheless anticipated it and refuted it even before it came into being. Indeed, the difference between this last system of Schelling and that of Hegel is not so great as it might seem, if we listen only to Schelling's words. Schelling might have been influenced by Hegel when he excogitated his negative and positive philosophy.[8] Both thinkers wanted to reconcile philosophy and experience, thought and facts, speculation and revelation. Both studied for this purpose the history of philosophic systems and of the religions of the world. Both knew that logic alone is merely negative, that it must penetrate the positively real. Both wished therefore to unite metaphysics and the content of history.[9]

[8] See the Introduction to the translation of Schelling's *The Ages of the World*, by Frederick de Wolfe Bolman, p. 53 footnote.

[9] Cf. Hegel's words: " It must be said that nothing is consciously known which does not fall within experience, or (as it is also expressed) which is not felt to be

However, Hegel alone possessed the method which can possibly carry out this task. He alone was aware that even positive philosophy (his own philosophy of mind) cannot be built without speculative thought. He realized that this task involved a contradiction and can be discharged only by a speculative dialectic. Hegel's logic was dialectical, because he saw that the synthesis of experience and thought, of existence and essence, of history and speculation, can be achieved only on the basis of a logic which acknowledges intrinsic contradictions but surmounts them. This is the reason why he made his logic the cornerstone of the whole building. The categories which unfold in the logic are abstract, but they are at the same time the categories of concrete realities like Kant's categories, but without Kant's restriction which permitted the application of the categories only to the phenomena of nature as the object of the natural sciences. Hegel on the contrary conceived of the categories as the logical and ontological backbone of ultimate reality manifesting itself in Nature and Mind. The separation of the noumena and the phenomena is thereby overcome. In Nature as well as in the realms in which the mind is active the Absolute appears, and we can understand this appearance if we understand the Absolute that appears. Hegel's Absolute takes the place of the " thing-in-itself."

Abstracted from all details, we may state that the Absolute divides itself and reunites itself again. This is the basic intuition of Hegel's system. Schelling was not able to demonstrate how the Absolute divides itself; he simply stated this basic division. Hegel's logic tries to fill this gap in Schelling's system. It shows that the Absolute divides itself because the Absolute can be thought of as the Absolute only if we compose it out of its constituents. If we speak of the Absolute as such, we have already thought of it as being abstracted from the Non-Absolute. But this abstraction contradicts the intention of thinking All in All. The Absolute is the Absolute only if it is not merely abstracted from its opposition but reunited with it; or rather if it is the movement from the opposites to their final synthesis. The abstract Absolute is already its own negation, since the true Absolute is not abstract but concrete. Being abstracted from its concrete content is not Being, but Nothing. Only the synthesis of

true, which is not given as an inwardly revealed eternal verity, as a sacred object of belief." (*The Phenomenology of Mind*, tr. by J. B. Baillie, Vol. II, p. 813. The Macmillan Company, n.d.)

Being and Nothing can be (or rather become) the true Absolute. In this way the movement of the logic is initiated.

Dialectic in Hegel's scheme is the method by which the existing world can be conceived in contrast to pure thought. Pure thought itself is not so pure as formalistic logicians take it to be. On the contrary it is thought only if it is able to comprehend its own contrary existence. Dialectical thinking is dialectical because it is not " mere " thinking, but thinking of what exists. If pure thought is able to cope with the existing world, it must be dialectical. Hegel was in this respect completely in accord with Fichte. In this sense Hegel's dialectic is " existential." Kierkegaard could never have discovered the " existential " thinker, as he understands him, without Hegel's dialectic, although he passionately rejected " the system."

Hegel's logic is an adventurous attempt to make mysticism logical by making the logical dialectical. In a sense Hegel denied the possibility of thinking the Absolute; he denied it, if thinking means the elimination of contradictions, as Aristotle had demanded it in contrast to Heraclitus. The Absolute is self-contradictory if measured by the Aristotelian standard. But this is not at all surprising, since the Absolute is not a tautology or a mere concept, but rather the totality of what exists. If existence is, as Schelling in the last system asserted, the positive in contrast to the merely negative realm of thought, then the logic of the Absolute must contradict itself. Contradiction therefore must not be avoided; on the contrary it must be systematically and methodically acknowledged as Kant acknowledged it in his transcendental dialectic although (like Schelling) in a merely negative fashion, and as Fichte acknowledged it in the dialectic of the *Wissenschaftslehre*. It must be made the very vehicle of the logical movement which is not only the movement of the logic, but the movement of thought as such and therefore also of thought in the philosophy of nature and of mind.

Hegel's logic is the systematic destruction of the prejudice that contradiction has to be avoided at all costs and under all circumstances. If this formal " law of contradiction " is the supreme principle of logical thought, then Hegel's logic is, as he had already proclaimed earlier, the systematic destruction of logical thought itself. " The nature of judgment or the proposition in general which involves the distinction of subject and predicate is subverted and destroyed by the speculative judgment." [10] " Abolishing the form of proposition must not take place merely in an immediate manner, merely through the content of the proposition. On the contrary, we must give explicit expression to this canceling process; it must be not only that internal restraining and confirming of thought within its own substance; this turning of the concept back into itself has to be expressly brought out and stated. This process, which constitutes what formerly had to be accomplished by proof, is the eternal dialectical movement of the proposition itself." [10a] " The proposition ought to express what the truth is: in its essential nature the truth is subject [11]: being so it is merely the dialectical movement, this self-producing course of activity, maintaining its advance by returning back into itself." [12]

I wonder why Hegel is always called a rationalist by those who are themselves much more rationalistic than he because they do not destroy the proposition and the logic of contradiction the way he did. It is quite evident to everyone who has seriously studied Hegel (how many even of those who have written about him have done this?) that Hegel himself meant something entirely different from what commonly is called " reason " when he used this term. He says: " Everything rational is at the same time to be denoted as mystical. This, however, means merely that the rational transcends the understanding, it does not imply that the rational is inaccessible to thinking and thus to be considered as inconceivable." [13] In other words: what Hegel calls the rational is accessible only to his own speculative dialectical thinking which intends to conceive the mystical or which makes the mystical conceivable! The term " understanding " in the passage means, of course, that understanding which obeys the law of contradiction, and which therefore is unable to think speculatively.

The identity of reality and thought which so often is called the principle of Hegel's metaphysics is therefore this principle only if one adds that Hegel knew very well that abstract thought is not identical with reality, and that thought has to undergo its own self-

[10] Baillie, *op. cit.,* Preface, pp. 60 f.
[10a] Baillie, *op. cit.,* Preface, pp. 63 f.
[11] This thesis was taken over by Kierkegaard, but redefined.
[12] Baillie, *op. cit.,* p. 64.
[13] *Werke,* Vol. VI, p. 160.

destruction through contradiction in order to be able to penetrate reality! Hegel's dialectic was "negative" in a much bolder and deeper sense than Schelling's "negative philosophy." Schelling apparently never understood what Hegel meant. Contradiction is the prime mover in Hegel's dialectic. The very first dialectical contrast between Being and Nothing reflects the contrast between thought and reality, between essence and existence, between the logic and the sciences of nature and of mind. Here in a nutshell the whole system is anticipated. To be justified in putting "negative" and "positive" philosophy side by side, Hegel deemed it necessary to show that there is a dialectical relation between Being and Nothing, and that this relation pushes thought on to ever-new positions and ever-new contradictions, until at last the "absolute idea" in the logic resolves and completes the whole movement of thought.

But it is only the movement of the logic, i.e., of the first part of the system which ends in the "absolute idea." The movement then goes on through the philosophy of nature in which the contrast to pure thought is most manifest and the tension between both most intense, so that nature is characterized as the realm in which contingency exists. Out of Nature, Mind finally emerges as the synthesis of thought and nature, or as nature returning to the "absolute idea," which is finally recognized as the result of the inner movement of Mind from Art through Religion to Philosophy. In philosophy thought thinks itself and thereby concludes its movement.[14] I cannot enter here into a discussion of the whole system; I must confine myself to hinting at its general course.

As Hegel combines Fichte and Schelling, so he also combines Heraclitus and Plato (the logic represents Hegel's version of the cosmos of the Ideas), Aristotle and Plotinus, Dionysius and Eckhart, Nicholas of Cusa and Jacob Boehme, Spinoza and Leibniz. In his philosophic history of philosophy he himself points to this solution, judging the various systems according to his own standard and interpretation. Pre-Christian and Christian speculation were thus more reconciled to each other than by any previous school. Fully awake to the greatness of the task, Hegel was convinced that he had achieved its solution and had thereby completed the history of

[14] Hegel quotes therefore at the end of the *Encyclopedia* the famous words of Aristotle describing the nature of the divine mind.

philosophy. There are indications that he was right. After him no one followed him as his successor or surpassed his scheme.

But in spite of the grandeur of Hegel's system, in spite of the profundity of his method (if it can be called a method, since it was Hegel's personal ingenuity which was at work everywhere), in spite of the vast historical scope that his thought embraced, Hegel was nevertheless (as is every thinker) a child of his own epoch. Even his peculiar logic, although it dealt with the perennial problems and gathered together all the concepts of the past, bore the mark of that romanticism which also characterized the systems of Schelling. It is true that Hegel was a severe critic of the romantic trend. But, nevertheless, he did not escape the dominance of that powerful movement.

The very attempt to make the logical mystical and the mystical logical manifests the spirit of romanticism. The work which most evidently indicates the effect of the romantic spirit upon the mind of Hegel was at the same time his most ingenious and most inspired work: *The Phenomenology of Mind.* In his later productions Hegel was more methodically precise, more systematically meticulous, but in this great work of his youth, he was more creative, more subtle, more of a discoverer and adventurer than in any of the later works. One might say that Hegel was in his later period the first Hegelian. In this early masterwork he was not yet his own disciple, not yet a master writing for his students, but he was exalted by his own intuition and overflowing with the joy of the navigator, sailing through unknown seas and toward unknown shores. He himself was aware of the character of this book. He knew that it was not yet quite ripe when he published it. To Schelling he wrote that " the general view of the whole . . . is by its very nature an interplay of thought movements and countermovements so intricately interwoven that it would still require much more time for its perfect clarification." [15] But it is just this lack of logical clarity and methodical accuracy which gives to the work the flavor that distinguishes it from the *Logic* and the *Encyclopedia of the Philosophical Sciences.*

The very idea of reforming thought so that the Absolute can be conceived has a romantic tone. It implies that logic, as we usually

[15] *Hegel, Sämtliche Werke. Neue kritische Ausgabe,* her. v. Joh. Hoffmeister. Hamburg, Felix Meiner, 1952 ff. Bd. XXVII, Brief vom 1. Mai, 1807.

understand it, will be overpowered by vision or imagination, as is true in the *Phenomenology*. It is extremely difficult to comment upon this abundantly rich work.[16] It has many aspects and many levels of thought. It is many things: an introduction to the system (but at least as involved as the system itself); a philosophy of history (but dealing with the facts of history in an unchronological way); a version of the system itself according to a special plan and development of thought; a theory of knowledge comprising all kinds of experience; a philosophy that will lead the reader from his naïve consciousness of outer things to the highest stages of religion, thereby enabling the human mind to unite with the mind of God. Profound insight is mixed with strange construction, illuminating analysis with obscure intuition, ontological perspectives with epistemological, anthropological with theological perspectives, history with metaphysics, experience with theory, speculation with revelation. A more entangled, more mysterious, more baffling and embarrassing book was never written by any philosopher. No one who has read that book will ever again speak of Hegel as a rationalist! I will give a few examples, taken from the Preface.

" Per se the divine life is no doubt undisturbed identity and oneness with itself. . . . But this ' per se ' is abstract generality, where we abstract from its real nature which consists in its being objective to itself, conscious of itself on its own account; and where consequently we neglect altogether the self-movement which is the formal character of its activity." [17] " We misunderstand the nature of reason, if we exclude reflection or mediation from ultimate truth, and do not take it to be a positive moment of the Absolute. It is reflection which constitutes truth the final result. . . . But this result arrived at is itself simple immediacy; for it is self-conscious freedom which is at one with itself and has not set aside the opposition it involves." [18]

The Absolute is Spirit — " the grandest conception of all, and one which is due to modern times and its religion. Spirit is the only reality." [19] It is puzzling that Hegel quotes the Fourth Gospel here and yet insists that the conception of Spirit is modern! " The life of mind

[16] See the very conscientious and instructive account given by Jean Hyppolite in his *Genèse et Structure de la Phenomenology de l'Esprit de Hegel* (Paris, 1946).

[17] Baillie, *op. cit.*, p. 17.

[18] *Ibid.*, pp. 18 f.

[19] *Ibid.*, p. 22.

is not one that shuns death and keeps clear of destruction; it endures its death and in death maintains its being." [20] It is obvious that such a sentence could not have been written by any pre-Christian thinker, since it points to the crucifixion of Jesus Christ. But another passage seems to recall Greek mysteries, when Hegel writes: " Truth is the bacchanalian revel, where not a soul is sober; and because every member no sooner gets detached than it *eo ipso* collapses straight-way, the revel is just as much a state of transparent unbroken calm." [21] Compared with such an utterance Schelling's style is un-romantic, formalistic, and rationalistic!

SPECULATION AND REVELATION

Hegel dared to transform revelation into speculation. The whole philosophy of Hegel culminates in the reconciliation of these two approaches to ultimate truth. As he endeavored to reconcile specula-tion to experience, metaphysics to history, logic to the philosophy of nature and of mind, so he also tried to reconcile the Christian re-ligion to pure thought. Hegel was convinced that he succeeded where so many of his predecessors had stumbled and where most phil-osophical systems were thwarted: in bringing about a perfect har-mony between religious and philosophic insight. This was his high-est ambition from the beginning, as the *Early Theological Writings* show and also the essays in the Jena years and the fragments written there. In his later *Lectures on the Philosophy of Religion,* Hegel spoke from the height of his established system about this subject. He also dealt with the reconciliation between religion and meta-physics in his *Lectures on the Proofs of God.* But the freshest, the most exciting, and the most profound discussion of this relation is to be found in the *Phenomenology.*

Long before Schelling, Hegel gave a survey of the historical re-ligions. He divided them into three groups: the Natural Religions, the Religions of Art, and finally Revealed Religion. The *Phenome-nology* depicts the reality and activity of the mind as it appears in history. Hegel applies the Kantian concept of appearance to the con-sciousness, the understanding, the reason, and the spirit as they mani-fest themselves in the development of mankind in various forms. Mind or Spirit undergoes a significant inner and outer history. Hegel

[20] *Ibid.,* pp. 30 f.   [21] *Ibid.,* p. 44.

arranges the entire content of history in such a way as to illuminate from within the mind and its own experience the stages of this history. From the primitive perception of sensuous things the mind rises up to the most exalted experience of God. Hegel believes that he can show the necessity of this evolution. It is the mind itself that shows this by ascending from stage to stage until at last it reaches its own self-understanding and its unity with the divine Spirit.

The mind is driven not by any external causality, but by its own inner experience. The mind cannot dwell on any of the stages through which it wanders because each stage (until the last is reached) leaves the mind inwardly divided against itself. Since self-identity is the very mark of the mind it follows that thought and reality are likewise prompted to go on until the reconciliation of the mind with itself and within itself is obtained. On the most primitive level we encounter outer things without being aware that they are the objects of our own consciousness. We are therefore driven to realize this truth and to discover that we are ourselves only because we are conscious of ourselves. This self-consciousness is again divided against itself, because it does not yet understand the relation between the individual and the general or universal self. The march toward the remote goal must therefore be continued until finally the knowledge is gained that the individual and the universal self are one and the same. Each stage of the experience of the consciousness has its own truth and reality in history as well as in the system, but each is wrong inasmuch as it does not yet represent the final stage. Hegel describes the journey of the mind to God which had been described before him by Bonaventure.[22]

On the highest stage the mind experiences its unity with the universal and absolute mind in a figurative, imaginative, or pictorial manner. On the lowest level of religious experience these figures are taken from natural phenomena, such as light, plants, or animals; on the next stage the arts, sculpture, music, and poetry present to the mind the images of the divine: in epic, tragedy, and comedy this religious world is consummated. In comedy the religious significance of the human self comes to the fore; the gods are no longer taken seriously. " The individual self is the negative form through which

[22] See Kroner, *Speculation and Revelation in the Age of Christian Philosophy*, pp. 215 f.

and in which the gods . . . pass away and disappear. . . . The religion of art is fulfilled. . . . It is the return of everything universal into certainty of self, a certainty which, in consequence, is this complete loss of fear of everything strange and alien." [23]

The degeneration of aesthetic religion prepares for the coming of revelation. Although comedy manifests the decay of paganism, it also brings to light the truth that the " Self is Absolute Being." [24] But since it is the individual and human self which is exalted on this stage, the religious significance is demolished. The loss of the religious content manifests itself in the fact that the consciousness which creates comedy as its innermost standard is unhappy and finally given over to despair. " Trust in the eternal laws of the gods is silenced, just as the oracles are dumb, whose work it was to know what is right. . . . The statues set up are now corpses in stone whence the animating soul has flown, while the hymns of praise are words from which all belief has gone. The tables of the gods are bereft of spiritual food and drink and from his games and festivals man no more receives the joyful sense of his unity with the divine Being. The works of the muse lack the force and energy of the spirit." [25]

This disintegration of his old faith opens to pagan man the stage on which revelation can attain its persuasive power. Philosophic skepticism contributes to the destruction of the ancient religion, and Stoicism cannot prevent its fall. These spiritual phenomena " compose the periphery of the circle of shapes and forms, which attend, an expectant and eager throng, round the birthplace of spirit as it becomes self-consciousness. Their center is the yearning agony of the unhappy despairing self-consciousness, a pain which permeates all of them, and it is the common birth pang at its production — the simplicity of the Pure Notion, which contains those forms as its moments." [26] In this half-conceptual and half-metaphorical fashion Hegel describes the speculative and religious meaning of the moment in which Christ appears. Destruction and despair furnish to the mind that mood in which the truth can be revealed that the Absolute has to empty itself in order to exhibit its glory; that it has to be annihilated in order to rise again. Such truth can be revealed only

[23] Baillie, *op. cit.*, pp. 757 f.
[24] *Ibid.*, p. 759.
[25] *Ibid.*, pp. 762 f.
[26] *Ibid.*, p. 765.

if the Absolute " is beheld sensuously and immediately as a self, as a real individual being. . . . This incarnation of the divine Being, its having essentially and directly the form of self-consciousness, is the simple content of Absolute Religion. Here the divine Being is known as spirit . . . , for spirit is knowledge of itself in its state of self-relinquishment, the absolute reality which is the process of retaining its harmony and identity with itself in its otherness. . . . In this form of religion the divine Being is . . . revealed." [27]

This revelation of incarnation agrees perfectly with the truth of speculation. " God is here revealed as he is; he actually exists as he is in himself; he is real as Spirit. God is attainable in pure speculative knowledge alone, and only *is* in that knowledge, and is merely that knowledge, for he is spirit; and this speculative knowledge is the knowledge furnished by revealed religion." [28] These words most clearly demonstrate that Hegel was convinced that he had accomplished what all the centuries of Christian philosophy were unable to accomplish: the perfect identification of speculative and revealed knowledge and truth. " The hopes and expectations of preceding ages pressed forward to, and were solely directed toward, this revelation, the vision of what Absolute Being is, and the discovery of themselves therein. This joy, the joy of seeing itself in Absolute Being, becomes realized in self-consciousness, and seizes the whole world. For the Absolute is Spirit, it is the simple movement of those pure abstract moments, which express just this: that Ultimate Reality is *eo ipso* known as Spirit and beheld as immediate self-consciousness." [29]

In order to explain the identity of the speculative and the religious consciousness in spite of the evident disparity of these two forms of knowledge, Hegel declares: " The presentative pictorial thought of the religious communion is not conceptual thinking; it has the content without the necessity; and instead of the form of the Notion it brings into the realm of pure consciousness the natural relations of Father and Son. . . . Absolute Being is indeed revealed to it, but the moments of this Being . . . fall of themselves apart from one another." [30] This external character of revelation hides the true knowledge of its message and tempts the believer to understand it

[27] *Ibid.*, pp. 768 f.
[28] *Ibid.*, pp. 771 f.
[29] *Ibid.*, p. 772.
[30] *Ibid.*, p. 779.

merely as a historical account instead of comprehending its speculative content.

However, Hegel admits that the religious language has a certain truth that is missing in that of philosophic speculation. " The idea of the transition of the divine Being into otherness is in general merely indicated and hinted at when Spirit is interpreted in terms of pure thought; for figurative thinking this idea comes nearer to its realization: the realization is taken to consist in the divine Being ' humbling' itself." [31] Here Hegel seems to realize that revelation is superior to speculation, because the figurative language is better adapted to the truth that is communicated; he seems to admit that the generality of the philosophic Notion is a hindrance to the full understanding of the divine message. But this realization is passing. It is again minimized, when he emphasizes the other side of this seemingly superior nature of revelation, namely, its pictorial or figurative expression which is less adequate to express the truth than conceptual thought. Moreover, revelation is connected with contingent historical events, while pure thought is superhistorical and therefore enabled to comprehend the eternal truth directly and (as he says in the Logic) " without any veil."

Incarnation and resurrection are expounded in speculative terms as negation and as the negation of negation, i.e., the return to the original thesis. The "drama of salvation" is thus rationalized in terms of Hegel's speculative dialectic; it presents in a pictorial manner the movement from Being through Nothing to Becoming which unites Being and Nothing. Creation images the same movement. " Creation is the word which pictorial presentative thought uses to convey the absolute movement which the Notion itself goes through." [32] " Absolute Being would be merely an empty name if in very truth there were an absolute ' fall ' from it. The aspect of self-centeredness, self-absorption, really constitutes the essential moment of the self of Spirit." [33] In other words, creation, fall, and incarnation mean the same basic logical or ontological process from the thesis to the antithesis; only the imaginative form changes. The fall is not the fall of man, it is rather originally the self-negation of the Absolute which appears in the story of Adam and Eve in a religious manner, as " an inconceivable historical fact."

[31] *Ibid.*, p. 785.   [32] *Ibid.*, p. 781.   [33] *Ibid.*, p. 788.

That the fall seen from the speculative point of view really has this metaphysical meaning, Hegel argues, is confirmed by the incarnation which brings together the Absolute and the individual self and demonstrates metaphorically their intrinsic unity. " The inherent and essential nature assumes for figurative thought the form of a bare objective fact external and indifferent to God," says Hegel with respect to the fall. However, he adds, the thought " that those apparently mutually repugnant moments, Absolute Being and self-existent Self, are not separable, comes also before this figurative way of thinking (since it does possess the real content), but that thought appears afterward, in the form that the divine Being empties itself of itself and is made flesh." [34]

Hegel therefore comes to the conclusion that " evil is inherently the same as what goodness is." But such an expression " gives rise to misunderstandings," since good and evil are also not the same but rather contraries.[35] However, speculation knows that the contraries are united in the identity of the Absolute, that it is the Absolute itself which negates itself, contradicts itself, and eventually reconciles itself to itself. The mystery of the fall and of incarnation are thus reduced to the same fundamental principle of speculative dialectic, as are also creation and resurrection. " It must be said that good and evil according to their concepts, i.e., so far as they are not good and evil [*sic!*], are the same, just as certainly it must be said that they are not the same, but absolutely different. . . . Since both [statements] are equally right, they are both equally wrong, and their wrong consists in taking such abstract forms as ' the same ' and ' not the same,' ' identity ' and ' nonidentity,' to be something true, fixed, real, and in resting on them. Neither the one nor the other has truth; their truth is just their movement, the process in which simple sameness is abstraction and thus absolute distinction, while this again, being distinction per se, is distinguished from itself and so is self-identity." [36]

The word of Juvenal comes to mind when one reads such a passage: " *Difficile est saturam non scribere* " (" It is difficult not to

[34] *Ibid.* The translation renders erroneously the word "separable" by "inseparable"!

[35] Baillie, *op. cit.*, p. 789.

[36] *Ibid.*, pp. 789 f.

write a satire "). " There is only one step from the sublime to the ridiculous." Hegel's method and, indeed, his whole speculation seem to defeat themselves if he can write that something taken " according to its concept " is not what is taken, but rather its contrary. If he is right, what sense is there then in speaking conceptually? If the sense is only to show that all concepts are self-contradictory, is this sense then different from non-sense? And if this proves true, truth itself is falseness, and all sayings tumble down. Absolute knowledge and sophistry come dangerously close. The tragedy of speculation is thus emphasized at the end of its history. As medieval speculation finally admitted that all metaphysical knowledge is "learned ignorance," as ancient classical thought turned into skepticism when pagan antiquity approached its conclusion, so modern philosophy ends with a dubious dialectical speculation.

Is the nonspeculative language of revelation which does distinguish between good and evil, creation and fall, fall and incarnation, and between God and man perhaps more to the point than speculative dialectic?

EPILOGUE

THE DISINTEGRATION of the Hegelian school after Hegel's death into a right and a left wing made ostensible the perilous rift in thought within the imposing structure of this speculative edifice, a rift that had been only disguised by the powerful mind and style of the master. The reconciliation of the opposites, which Hegel boasted to having accomplished and which he had certainly succeeded in bringing about personally or existentially, was an illusion. Negation remained an adversary to affirmation and now asserted itself against the very unity and completeness of the proud system. Hegel was persuaded that he had united dialectically the extremes of time and eternity, action and contemplation, freedom and necessity, will and intellect, God and world. Now these extremes again fell asunder. Their union had been only a personal union of the system builder. The old rivalry between these opponents arose again although on a new plane. The strife began anew.

The history of the relation between speculation and revelation in modern times is closed with the gigantic attempt at uniting them through Hegel's dialectical speculation. The Protestant age of philosophy reached its historic apex in the figure of this " mighty thinker " as Karl Marx called Hegel in the Preface of *The Capital*. Although the speculative account of Marxism is void as compared with the system of his teacher, nevertheless, it displayed the danger inherent in the speculative dialectic of being perverted because of the ambiguous way in which it handled the law of contradiction. Moreover, by asserting that there is a final synthesis, the system cut off all further development; in fact, it thwarted the future. It was as a historic vengeance upon this pretension that Marx turned to the political field instead of refuting the logical foundations of the system. He did not refute them, instead he replaced them by a political imperative as pronounced in the *Communist Manifesto;* not a logical, but a revolutionary, step passed by Hegel's conclusion! This step indicated that the period of philosophic speculation had come to an end. Not metaphysics but politics were to inherit the power of thought. A new age was in the making.

It cannot be the task of this book to enter this new era. The nineteenth century after the death of Hegel was not favorable to speculative enterprise. The verdict of Wilhelm Windelband as uttered in his *History of Philosophy* about the philosophic significance of this century is still true and can be expanded to the evaluation of the twentieth century too: "The history of philosophic principles is closed with the development of the German systems at the boundary between the eighteenth and the nineteenth centuries. A survey of the succeeding development in which we are still standing today has far more of literary-historical, than of properly philosophic, interest. For nothing essentially and valuably new has since appeared. The nineteenth century is far from being a philosophic one; it is, in this respect, perhaps to be compared with the third and second centuries B.C." [1]

The main goal of Western culture has shifted from the artistic, religious, and philosophic interests to scientific, technical, and economic aspirations, to problems of social welfare and peace, and to political rivalry on a world scale. Mankind today no longer respects speculation. It does not care for metaphysical truth at all. The works of Friedrich Nietzsche were an alarming symptom of this decay. It is hardly conceivable that in the land of Kant, so soon after the death of this critical thinker, a philosophy arose which did not exhibit the slightest critical self-control, but indulged in impassioned exclamations and violent demands. Nietzsche, as he himself boasted, philosophized "with a hammer." With his philosophy the "love of wisdom" began to turn toward the age of the atomic bomb. Not reasons but wild emotions took the place of argument and thought. In this respect there is but little difference between *Thus Spake Zarathustra* and the *Manifesto* of Karl Marx.

But a word should be added about the other great intellectual and

---

[1] Translated by James H. Tufts (New York, 1901), pp. 623 f.

spiritual figure of the nineteenth century whose writings came to fruition only in our century: Sören Kierkegaard. Like Marx he was a disciple of Hegel; all his speculative concepts were taken from the great dialectician; his own dialectic would have been impossible without that of Hegel. But in substance he was the reverse of the Idealist of Mind. As Marx had done, so Kierkegaard too turned the dialectic upside down, but in a very different way. While Marx had made economics and its history the final synthesis, Kierkegaard made revelation victorious over speculation, as Tertullian had done. The definition of faith which Kierkegaard gives at the end of his treatise *The Sickness Unto Death* could not have been formulated before and without Hegel: " By relating itself to its own self and by willing to be itself, the self is grounded transparently in the Power which constituted it."

Kierkegaard's whole " philosophy " was a reaction to, and a fight against, Hegel's speculative intentions, although utilizing Hegel's dialectic. Kierkegaard, as he openly admits, admired Hegel, but his enmity against the system was deep-rooted. He hated it because he rightly felt that it strangled faith and offended revelation. In him revelation found an enthusiastic and eloquent defender. If everything and anything can be conceived as a step in the universal dialectical movement of the Notion, not only the freedom of the individual is abolished (as Hegel in his Introduction to the *Philosophy of History* frankly admitted), but also the Will as such, be it that of man or that of God. If freedom is impossible, then sin also is deprived of its meaning, and if sin is no longer a valid conception, then the whole Biblical message of the Old and the New Covenants is annulled.

Kierkegaard realized that the " category of the individual " can never be truly appreciated, if the individual is nothing but a link in the chain of the dialectical process. " Sin is a characteristic of the individual; it is frivolity and a new sin to act as if it were nothing to be an individual sinner. Here Christianity is superior. It marks a cross before speculation." [2] " Christianity begins by making every man an individual — an individual sinner." [3] Kierkegaard mocked

[2] Sören Kierkegaard, *The Sickness Unto Death*, tr. by Walter Lowrie (Princeton University Press, 1941), pp. 196 f.

[3] *Ibid.*, p. 200.

at " the system " in a thousand ways. " A thinker erects an immense building, a system which embraces the Whole of existence and world history, etc. — and if we contemplate his personal life, we discover to our astonishment this terrible and ludicrous fact, that he himself personally does not live in this immense high-vaulted palace, but in a barn alongside of it, or in a dog kennel, or at the most in the porter's lodge." [4] " Hegel vanquished idealistic skepticism by means of pure thought which is merely a hypothesis, . . . a fantastic hypothesis. The triumphant victory of pure thought . . . is something both to laugh at and to weep over." [5] " A philosophy of pure thought is for an existing individual a chimera." [6] The individual sinner cannot find his salvation in an impersonal speculative dialectic.

Kierkegaard was most indignant about Hegel's attempt to understand Christianity from the point of view of his metaphysical system. " Since man is a synthesis of the temporal and the eternal, the happiness that the speculative philosopher may enjoy will be an illusion in that he desires in time to be merely eternal. Herein lies the error of the speculative philosophy." [7] " The speculative philosopher is perhaps at the farthest possible remove from Christianity, and it is perhaps far preferable to be an offended individual who nevertheless sustains a relation to Christianity than a speculative philosopher who assumes to understand it." [8] Kierkegaard fought Hegel's system so passionately because he realized that the Gnostic heresies had arisen again in its claim to surpass religion by means of knowledge; indeed, Hegel presumed that speculation can do what revelation alone is able to do — that it can achieve man's salvation. As Irenaeus had bitterly criticized and condemned the Gnostics of his time, so Kierkegaard accomplished the same for his own period when he opposed impetuously the Gnosticism of Hegel's system.

Against the pretense of speculation to know by pure thought the divine mystery better than revelation does and thereby to annul the chasm between man and God, Kierkegaard renewed the insight that Christianity is a redemptive religion precisely because it is not merely

[4] *Ibid.*, p. 68.
[5] *Concluding Unscientific Postscript to the Philosophical Fragments,* tr. by David F. Swenson (Princeton University Press, 1942), p. 292.
[6] *Ibid.*, p. 275.
[7] *Ibid.*, p. 54.
[8] *Ibid.*, p. 193.

a speculative system built by the effort and energy of an individual thinker, but is based upon an ecstatic experience. "Christianity is not a doctrine but an existential communication expressing an existential contradiction. . . . Existence and existing constitute precisely the opposite of speculation . . . , there is a tremendous difference between knowing what Christianity is and being a Christian." [9] Unfortunately the existentialists of our own century have forgotten that the word "existence" in the pregnant sense of Kierkegaard has an apologetic origin and a Christian meaning, so that it cannot be used in order to cement non-Christian speculative systems. They have done exactly what Kierkegaard wanted to prohibit by his emphasis upon the word "existence." [10]

Kierkegaard's attack upon the Titanism of Hegel's speculative interpretation of the Christian dogma was entirely to the point. Hegel had frivolously challenged the religious consciousness of the Christian believer (as later on Schelling also did in his "positive" philosophy, which disgusted Kierkegaard, who was a listener in Schelling's lectures). The idea that God develops in history was really a recapitulation of Gnostic idolatry, although philosophically much more refined and logically much more tempting. But both ancient Gnosticism and Hegel's philosophy of Christianity neglected the basic foundation of Biblical revelation, its roots in historical events. According to Hegel's speculation the truth of the Christian religion could have been brought into the world without the sufferings of Jesus and without the ecstatic experience of the disciples and the apostles. And the individual Christian believer would be able to receive forgiveness and redemption without being united with Christ in his innermost repenting soul, without surrendering his total self to his Lord, without any self-humiliating confession, and without feeling in his heart what the crucifixion means. His thinking mind could instead take the place of all religious acts. This is the grave and portentous implication of Kierkegaard's word "existence."

Kierkegaard pointed to all these religious facts. He was abundantly right when he insisted that it is not the same to know what Christianity is and what Creation and incarnation mean from a specula-

[9] *Ibid.,* p. 339.

[10] Cf. Richard Kroner's essay "Existentialism and Christianity" in *Encounter,* 1956, Vol. 17, No. 3, p. 219. See also Hermann Diem, *Kierkegaard's Dialectic of Existence,* tr. by Harold Knight (Oliver & Boyd, Ltd., Edinburgh and London, 1959).

tive perspective, and to be a Christian. If we confront the alternative whether we shall adhere to Hegel or to Kierkegaard, there cannot be the slightest doubt: as believers we must admit that Hegel miserably failed to understand the essence of faith, and that Kierkegaard's censure was absolutely justified.[11] But it is another question whether Kierkegaard's own quasi-philosophic thought is acceptable, and whether as a thinker he really understood the adventure of Hegel's speculative dialectic. Although Kierkegaard (like Clement of Alexandria) stressed that faith is not scholarly knowledge, but common to all Christians who understand the divine message and have a devout heart, he nevertheless promoted a kind of learned knowledge of God. He was not merely the critic of Hegel; in attacking Hegel's metaphysics he could not help asserting that he knew better than Hegel the nature of God, not only as a believer, but also as a thinker. As he admits that speculation was the strongest element in his mind, and that he practiced it throughout his life, so he defended a definite doctrine concerning the essence of God although in a less elaborate and more occasional form than Hegel.

The term "knowledge of God" is ambiguous from the start. It may simply mean that kind of knowledge which is inherent in faith — a religious or spiritual knowledge — but it may also presume that revealed knowledge is not enough but requires a theological or philosophic interpretation and explication, stating what is the nature and reality of God in conceptual and quasi-rational terms. Such statements would claim an unexistential and objective knowledge like that of metaphysical systems. The religious thinker (a strange expression in itself) is always tempted to transgress against the limits of knowledge drawn up by revelation itself. If he yields to that temptation, he ceases to be "existential" and enters the arena of pure thought or of speculation. Kierkegaard did not entirely withstand this temptation. It is a historical irony that the same man who saw so clearly the danger of speculative romanticism, nevertheless, was himself a thorough romantic who not only sympathized with many traits in romanticism but indulged himself in romantic fantasy and subjectivism. He was therefore throughout his life divided against himself.

There was one Kierkegaard, who would have liked to be (and in-

[11] Cf. Richard Kroner's essay "Kierkegaard or Hegel?" in the *Revue Internationale de Philosophie*, No. 19, 1952.

deed was to a great extent) a poet, a writer inclined to romantic irony and disguise, an essayist who romanticized everything about which he wrote; and there was a quite different Kierkegaard, who censured himself for being a romantic on the basis of a most serious religious devotion, a man who had indeed a strong tendency toward sainthood although he never quite obtained it. Kierkegaard never achieved the reconciliation of the two persons who lived in him.[12] This was the reason why he impersonated the figures whom he chose as the alleged authors of his philosophic books. Only in his edifying addresses was he the religious preacher, which he longed to be entirely. His most romantic work *Either/Or* was published under the name of Victor Eremita; but Kierkegaard was not yet satisfied with this camouflage. He chose another device in order to make his disguise more complete by relating in the Preface of his work that it is composed of papers which the " editor," Victor Eremita, found in a secretary, which fascinated him a long time after he had discovered it at a merchant's shop. " My daily path took me by this shop and I never failed a single day to pause and feast my eyes upon it. I gradually made up a history about it; it became a daily necessity for me to see it." This is not only a poetical, but also a spiritual, contrivance in order to conceal himself behind a fanciful screen. He hesitated to identify himself with the author of his own work because he was both a romantic poet and a moralistic saint.

Only in his *Edifying Discourses* did he disclose his identity. The purpose of these philosophic sermons (as one might call them) is illuminated by a sentence he spoke at the age of twenty-two: " What I really want is clearness with respect to what I ought to do, not what I ought to know, except in so far as knowledge must precede every action. . . . I must find the truth which is a truth for me. . . . I want to find the Idea for which I can live and die." [13] The author of the *Discourses* was a man who passionately and assiduously aspired to become a true Christian, but also knew that it was extremely difficult for him, if not outright impossible, to reach that goal.

The romantic, speculative, philosophizing and the preaching, pray-

[12] Cf. Arland Ussher, *Journey Through Dread* (The Devin-Adair Company, 1955).

[13] Cf. *Edifying Discourses*, Vol. I, tr. by David E. and Lillian M. Swenson (Augsburg Publishing House, 1943), Introduction, p. v.

ing, and confessing Kierkegaard never completely joined each other. The disciple of Christ would not have agreed with the speculations of the pseudonymous authors. Only the first was a consistent existential writer; the second philosophized about existence. The speculative philosopher infringed upon the territory of metaphysics which the existential writer warned himself not to enter. The speculative philosopher uttered thoughts about the nature of God, his relation to thinking, and the thinker's relation to him of which the existential believer would have disapproved. The tragic antagonism between faith and thought, between revelation and speculation, found its most pointed and most excruciating expression in the duality of Kierkegaard's personality and authorship. In this respect the whole history of philosophy was epitomized in him. Perhaps Kierkegaard never fully understood himself and the twofold motives which conditioned his plight. But he did occasionally remark that it would be disgraceful in him to disrespect speculation.[14]

The way he treated the gigantic labor of thousands of years dedicated to the solution of the ultimate metaphysical problems seems to indicate that he was not fully aware of the real tension which tore his own mind. He did not appear to have ever realized that metaphysics, even if its problems can never be satisfactorily settled, is an extremely grave and unavoidable task incumbent upon man as a thinking being, a task that can never be discharged by revelation alone. Man is like Kierkegaard himself, both a thinker and a believer, and it is his inexorable obligation to find some sort of reconciliation between these two antagonistic, and yet also cognate, personalities. Philosophy and religion are consequently companions in him that cannot part from each other, although they must always quarrel with each other.

Kierkegaard mostly speaks in a cavalier manner of the prodigious work done by Hegel without ever seriously examining Hegel's argument and without ever penetrating the issues at stake; he treated too lightly the reasons which determined the speculative dialectic. He did not acknowledge the formidable gravity of the problems which Hegel tried to solve. The result was that he himself offered solutions of the very same problems which must be called superficial and even amateurish. Hegel's thesis that the Notion moves was the conclu-

[14] Cf. Swenson, *Concluding Unscientific Postscript,* Book I, ch. II, p. 54.

sion of the efforts of human thought beginning with Thales. By ignoring the deep motives behind this doctrine, Kierkegaard simply fell back to earlier and more primitive stages of thought. He asserted that in God, Being and Thinking are immediately one, as Parmenides had taught in his identity thesis.[15] How could the existential believer know this?

Hegel had not only logical, but also religious, reasons for his idea of the movement of thought. Whereas Greek speculation always had a tendency to think of God as immutable and as exalted above the realm of change, and the Aristotelian god represents such a timeless and immovable deity, the living God of Scripture does undergo a certain change because he lives in close contact with changing man and is resolved to guide him and to redeem him. The Creator acts; the Lord appears to Moses and speaks to the prophets; the Father sends his son into the world to reconcile it to himself. The Biblical God does not dwell in heaven alone, he interferes with the historical development of his people on earth; the Eternal does not live isolated from temporal events, but brings them about. God as he reveals himself is the Ruler of history and the Provider of his devotees.

The Hegelian movement of Being and of Thought does agree with revelation better than the Kierkegaardian God who is as immutable and eternal as the Platonic Ideas. He is conceived in the manner of pagan speculative thinkers, in so far as he is conceived at all.[16]

Kierkegaard's thesis that the Christian truth is "absurd" also points to a principal defect originating from his clandestine speculation in contrast to his existential faith. The individual believer may feel the abysmal mystery when he contemplates and worships the Crucified, but as an existential believer he would never think that he worships an "absurdity," precisely because he is not a speculative thinker! Only because he is a speculative thinker against his will, did Kierkegaard come to teach that the Christian truth is absurd. Such a half-speculative, half-existential statement is certainly less satisfying than is speculation taken for itself or faith taken for itself.

The problem with which this work was concerned — the relation between speculation and revelation — rests here. No later contribu-

[15] Cf. Kroner, *Speculation in Pre-Christian Philosophy*, pp. 109 ff.
[16] Cf. Richard Kroner's essay "Kierkegaard's Hegelverständnis" in *Kantstudien*, Vol. 46, 1954–1955, pp. 19 ff., esp. pp. 25 f.

tion clarified the obscurities left. They seem to veil the truth so tightly that no thinker can dissipate them. Would it therefore not be the most reasonable solution to admit that there is a hard core of difficulties which cannot be settled by way of speculation because of inherent contradictions as Kant already pointed out? But today we would have to avoid Kant's own solution based upon his contradistinction of phenomena and noumena. We would rather have to agree with Hegel that this contradistinction leads to a new contradiction and that all concepts whatsoever, if applied to the solution of the ultimate problem, are at bottom dialectical. But we would not share with Hegel his assertion that an allegedly absolute dialectical knowledge can save speculation. Instead, we would have to insist that the appeal to revelation is justified because thought can never find any final solution within itself on the basis of its own resources. In this sense and in this way the word of Kant, " I had to deny knowledge, in order to make room for faith," would be confirmed, but not as Kant taught, by means of substituting for religious faith a rational faith that is illusionary; rather, by pointing out that for intrinsic and imperative reasons revelation must ultimately take the place of speculation where the relation to the Absolute is at stake. However, such a program can only be intimated here.

INDEX